# CHARLESTON'S
# GERMANS

## AN ENDURING LEGACY

## ROBERT ALSTON JONES

Design and distribution by Bublish, Inc.
ISBN: 978-1-647044-46-6 (eBook)
ISBN: 978-1-647044-45-9 (paperback)

# TABLE OF CONTENTS

# ACKNOWLEDGMENTS

Over the years devoted to this effort to document Charleston's *German* history, I have benefitted from the knowledge and assistance of a number of individuals to whom I owe my sincere thanks. Their assistance has not been taken for granted, nor has their generosity in responding to my requests been forgotten.

Much of my research was done in the South Carolina Room at the Charleston County Public Library. Over the years, each of the librarians there graciously offered assistance. I am especially grateful to Marianne Cawley for suggesting that a study such as this *needed* to be undertaken, and for Dorothy Glover's consistent willingness to dig out information I had, or would have, missed and to set me straight when often I veered off track. At the University of Wisconsin-Milwaukee's Golda Meir Library, I benefitted from the sleuth-work of the dedicated librarians in Interlibrary Loan, who never lost patience with my persistent requests for hard-to-come-by materials. My thanks also to Jovanka Ristic, on whom I regularly depended in exploring the extensive resources of the American Geographical Society's collection housed at UW-Milwaukee. Early stages of my research were conducted in the archives of Charleston's St. Matthew's Lutheran Church, where archivist Nancy Kruger helped focus my inquiries. Most recently, it was my pleasure to work with Karen Emmons at the Historic Charleston Foundation. Her assistance in locating and digitizing most of the images included in *Charleston's Germans* is much appreciated.

# ACKNOWLEDGMENTS

Special thanks are due to my UW-Milwaukee colleague Beth Weckmueller for the time and effort she dedicated to reading and commenting on earlier drafts of the book. Her excellent sense of authorial style and good eye for typographical and grammatical errors saved me repeatedly from embarrassment, her sage advice more substantive than I deserved from a reader. Both Ehren Foley at the University of South Carolina Press and Christopher Johnson at Francis Marion University were dutiful readers as well, both offering critical commentary and insight that helped immensely.

To each and all, my heartfelt thanks.

September, 2021

# PREFACE

On any Sunday morning during the 1950s when the congregants in any of Charleston's several Lutheran Churches might have had the opportunity to sing the often-sung hymn, *Glorious Things of Thee Are Spoken,* it is likely that none of them noticed that the tune was designated "Austrian Hymn"—the melody written by Joseph Haydn in 1797 that for years had served as the musical setting of the national anthem of the Austro-Hungarian Empire. Nor did it occur to anyone that the tune was the same as that of the *Deutschlandlied*—the words written by Hoffmann von Fallersleben in 1841—with the third stanza's well-known line, "Deutschland, Deutschland, über alles, über alles in der Welt," permanently associated with Nazi Germany. Nor that the hymn tune had become the musical setting of West Germany's national anthem since 1952.

To those Lutheran congregants in this historic southern city, none of this mattered any more than the English words they were mouthing to the joyful Haydn melody. It was already a century ago that a number of these congregations had been founded by members of Charleston's nineteenth-century German ethnic community. By the 1950s, these congregations were heavily populated by third- and fourth-generation descendants of those German immigrants, and now, after almost a decade since the end of WWII, it was evident that their ethnic heritage had been relegated to the historical past, the awareness of that heritage effectively suppressed to the point that it no longer existed.

On a personal level, the author can attest to the fact that at mid-twentieth century one could grow to adulthood in a Charleston family of pure German heritage without being cognizant of such a lineage; that one could regularly attend services at the Lutheran church where the family belonged and be catechized after a brief study of Martin Luther's tenets without ever being apprised of the denomination's or the catechism's historical German background; that one could have friends and acquaintances whose surnames were never acknowledged as *German* names; that one could interact with family friends, among whom the older generation might speak with a distinct accent, but not realize that the accent and the friendship denoted a mutual ethnic heritage; that when in college, the student could enroll in German-language classes without being aware that the language had any relevance to his ethnic roots; that, whatever the occasion, one could visit the city's "Lutheran" cemetery and hardly notice that many of the headstones were inscribed in German, never wondering what story those headstones told of Charleston's dead. It would take dedicated research to learn that there had once been a vibrant German community in Charleston, and that that ethnic community had played a significant role in determining the character of the city. Did Charlestonians in general know that German was the only language other than English that had been widely spoken in Charleston?

This book is an examination of how it came about that by the middle of the twentieth century Charleston's German heritage had been swept under the proverbial rug; how descendants of German immigrants lost an appreciation of their ethnic and cultural identity; how, when, and why they were capable of denying their forebears' contribution to the cultural heritage of Charleston; how it was that everyone, despite the frequency in the community of German-sounding names, had become so completely acculturated that Wittschen, Rugheimer, Zerbst, Zobel or Heins was as Charlestonian a surname as Jones, Riley, Symthe, DeSaussaure or Legare; how Charleston natives could be born of German heritage yet become adults completely innocent of their ethnic lineage, blithely ignorant of a cultural identity that was consistently less acknowledged than that of the city's Irish, Scots, Huguenots, Italians, or Jews.

Even if a Charlestonian were fortunate enough to have a clear understanding of his or her family's descent from Charleston's nineteenth-century German immigrants, by the 1950s that awareness would have little, if any, significance. The Lutheran singing the Austrian hymn would not have sensed any musical or emotional connection to those of his/her ancestors who in times past had been called *German*-Americans. There would have been no inclination to think of him/herself as a *German*-Charlestonian, since by now the city's Lutherans had become one with the Lowcountry society by virtue of the national phenomenon that historian John Higham described as the "most spectacular case of collective assimilation."[1]

I initially intended to describe what had been experienced in Charleston by the descendants of nineteenth-century German immigrants after the sinking of the *Lusitania* in 1915, an event that brought to bear a pervasive bias against anything or anyone associated with pre-WWI Germany. By the time the United States entered the war in 1917, there had developed a palpable anti-German sentiment throughout the United States. I was interested in describing what had transpired locally in that regard, and my research confirmed that the topic had not been investigated or analyzed. Whatever had happened nationally and locally had inexorably brought about a kind of amnesia with regard to Charleston's German heritage.

On reflection, however, my undertaking seemed too much like an impetuous jump *in medias res* that lacked context. In order to explicate the causes and symptoms of the post-*Lusitania* amnesia, it seemed appropriate, indeed necessary, to explore in detail the nature of what had been forgotten by those Charlestonians with a German background and, for that matter, by everyone else in the Charleston community. Thus the scope of this study was expanded, resulting in my effort here to portray the essential character of Charleston's earlier German community, how it had begun, the nature of its development, what it had meant to the antebellum city. I wanted to understand how and why its character over the years had been diluted, how and why the legacy of the ethnic community had been steadily pushed into the background, forgotten and no longer honored. How was it that by mid-twentieth century almost no one knew of Charleston's "German" history?

In chapters that follow, I outline the life-stories of several immigrant families from the mid- and late nineteenth-century community and suggest that their stories, each unique in its own way, are typical of the biographies of many who crossed the Atlantic to seek their future in lowcountry Charleston. Those

---

1.  In Russell A. Kazal, *Becoming Old Stock: the Paradox of German-American Identity* (Princeton: Princeton University Press, 2004), 4.

biographical outlines have for the most part been constructed from "externals," i.e. from details found in municipal and census records, newspaper accounts, and various other sources that reveal the footprint of the families' existence in the city. None of the individuals whose stories are told here left personal records such as a diary, journal, or memoir, nor is there a cache of letters or other materials that would provide insight into the immigrant's personal, subjective, perspective on what his/her life in Charleston was like. While we can assume that the majority of Charleston's nineteenth-century immigrants were literate, it is understandable that they would not have considered their personal stories of interest to anyone other than possibly the friends and relatives they had left behind. There was certainly written communication crossing the Atlantic in both directions, but letters sent from Charleston to the homeland—those that might have articulated the "inner state" of the immigrant to Charleston—are unfortunately not part of any preserved record.[2] It was probably the case, as well, that the individual immigrant had little time to reflect and write about his/her life in the new country: it would have taken the individual's entire effort to manage the myriad aspects of survival within the new cultural framework. While on occasion I cite letters written by or for a Charleston immigrant, for example, several found in the records of the Charleston Orphan House or in the archives of the South Carolina Historical Society, these are letters written for a specific purpose and are not reflections on the individual's experiences as an immigrant.

These life accounts thus constructed are intended to demonstrate how varied the individual immigrant experience was. No less significantly, these stories articulate how the cultural context of the host community affected the immigrant's course of acculturation and assimilation. The several families'

---

2. There is an archive of immigrant letters, the Nordamerika-Briefsammlung (NABS) maintained by the Forschungsbibliothek Gotha in Erfurt that contains over 11,000 letters written to immigrants by family members or friends who did not emigrate, as well as letters received from those who did. The collection was first established by Wolfgang Helbich at the Ruhr-Universität Bochum in the 1980s (the Bochum Emigrant Letter Collection) that is now part of the archive in Gotha. Given the relatively small number of immigrants going to the South, and the small number comprising the Charleston community, it is not surprising that the collection does not hold letters either originating, or received, in Charleston.

stories are intended to reveal the character of what was predominantly a community of North Germans transported to a unique southern city. Their stories background my effort to show how the German ethnic community evolved to reach its zenith prior to the onset of World War I. Both Charleston and its German immigrants would play a role in the region's transition from the antebellum nineteenth-century "Old" South to the twentieth-century's "New South," the city suffering a kind of demise into a backwater after its heyday, the Germans, a marginalization that would ultimately obscure the legacy of the nineteenth-century German community in the city's historical record.

In later chapters I examine how the ethnic community would have its substance denied, confronted as it was by nativistic tendencies inherent in American society that emerged aggressively in the period marked by two world wars. I maintain, nonetheless, that the legacy of Charleston's once-vibrant nineteenth-century ethnic community, while currently overlooked by residents and visitors alike, lingers yet in the city's cultural atmosphere. This study is an endeavor to bring that legacy to light for those who seek a more comprehensive history of "America's most historic city."

The lengthy process of assimilation and acculturation that transformed numerous generations of nineteenth-century immigrants and their descendants into native Charlestonians is relevant to both the historical and the contemporary nature of our pluralistic society: the complex issues under discussion in the present with regard to acceptance and assimilation of immigrants to the United States are resonant of the same processes at work in the not-so-distant past. The story of Charleston's Germans is but one narrative that illustrates that cultural merger is affected as much by the nature and collective character of those newly arriving, as by the character and ideologies of the host community that the immigrant hopes to join.

# CHAPTER 1:

# CHARLESTON'S "GERMAN" HISTORY

The German population in Charleston was never of much concern to anyone living outside the South Carolina Lowcountry, much less beyond the state's borders. While people of German descent represent the largest ethnic group in the United States, their forebears who lived in Charleston—whether they were seventeenth-, eighteenth-, or nineteenth-century immigrants—did not figure significantly in considerations of the country's multicultural settlement patterns. If Benjamin Franklin and others in the eighteenth century were worried that "German migration and propagation would overwhelm English America,"[1] they were doubtless thinking about the recently arrived immigrants in Pennsylvania, not those in South Carolina, who were distinctly fewer in number. Somewhat later, early nativist groups felt threatened by the ethnic presence, but their concerns did not emanate from fear that Germans were overtaking the South Carolina coastal enclave in Charleston. And later still, during the height of German immigration in the nineteenth century, little notice was given to the outliers who went

---

1. Randall M. Miller, *Germans in America: Retrospect and Prospect. Tricentennial Lectures delivered at the German Society of Pennsylvania in 1983* (Philadelphia: The German Society of Pennsylvania, 1984), 1.

to the South, in contrast to widespread awareness of the significant numbers of German immigrants who settled in the Northeast or who found their way to states in the Midwest.[2]

That so little attention was paid to the Germans in South Carolina can be explained by the fact that they never comprised more than a small fraction of the population. In his study of German immigrants in Charleston, James Strickland points out that in 1860 "German immigrants comprised 5 percent of the total population and 9 percent of the white population in Charleston...The German immigrant community was a distinct minority, outnumbered by both black and white southerners."[3] According to the Twelfth (1900) U.S. Census, the German population in the United States was close to 2.7 million, of whom fewer than 3,500 could be counted in South Carolina.[4] In his atlas of nineteenth- and early twentieth-century German-American settlements in the United States, Heinz Kloss records that in 1910, of cities with a population greater than ten thousand, Charleston had 2,154 "foreign white stock from Germany," equaling 7.7 percent of the city's total population.[5] In addition to these indications of minority status, the case has been made that, at the time, the South was markedly different from the rest of the country by virtue of its large slave and free-persons-of-color population, as well as its agricultural, non-industrialized economy that did not need the cheap labor that drew so many immigrants to cities in other parts of the country. These

---

2. "Germans were fairly concentrated in the cities of the Northeast between New York and Baltimore and above all in the urban and rural Middle West...The 'German belt' stretched from Ohio in the east to Nebraska in the west, from Missouri in the south to Wisconsin in the north. This region offered climatic conditions that were most nearly familiar to Central Europeans." *News from the Land of Freedom: German Immigrants Write Home,* Walter D. Kamphoefner, Wolfgang Helbich, and Ulrike Sommer, eds. (Ithaca: Cornell University Press, 1991), 12.

3. "How the Germans Became White Southerners: German Immigrants and African Americans in Charleston, South Carolina, 1860-1880," *Journal of American Ethnic History* 28, no. 1 (2008): 53.

4. Don H. Tolzmann, *The German-American Experience* (Amherst, NY: Humanity Books, 2000), 452.

5. Heinz Kloss, *Atlas of 19th and Early 20th century German-American Settlements* (Marburg: Elwert, 1974).

indicators are particularly relevant to Charleston's nineteenth-century German community in explaining why at its zenith the city's German population was of little notice other than to its host community. The disappearance of that German community's cultural legacy during the early years of the twentieth century has likewise escaped notice, since until very recently its origins, development, and substance were rarely, if ever, analyzed by historians of local and/or ethnic culture.

Records indicate that small groups of German-speaking Swiss had settled in South Carolina as early as the seventeenth century, and that a noticeable number of Germans had congregated in Charleston by the middle of the eighteenth century. The city's St. John's Lutheran Church was established already in 1743, and by 1766, those Colonial immigrants had founded the German Friendly Society in support of what were already German "interests" in the city. These early German immigrants found their place as factors in the mercantile life of the city, participated in the Revolutionary War, and established the first German militia in the country—the German Fusiliers. A number of them could be counted among the city's leaders. By the middle of the nineteenth century, when a second wave of immigrants would immigrate to Charleston, the Colonial-era German immigrants had become acculturated and integrated into "old Charleston" society. Insofar as this earlier group had never established a separate, homogeneous, residential community, by the early decades of the nineteenth century they would have thought of themselves as Charlestonians and not separate from the established native population as a distinct ethnic group.

The later post-Colonial immigrants settling in Charleston would find themselves in a southern city of a particular character. There was no "little Germany" into which they might transplant themselves. There was little continuity between the earlier and later group, and the experiences of the one had little to do with those of the other. Most of the earlier group, for example, had originated in central and southern German states and had found their cause in religious freedom. The later group originated from a different area and came for different reasons. Beyond that, there was no concept of a common "German" ethnicity through which either group might identify with the other. The German Friendly Society's acculturated Charlestonian-German members were indeed somewhat reluctant at first to receiving the newcomers landing on their doorstep, despite the Society's professed support of "German interests."

The relatively few German immigrants coming to Charleston in the nineteenth century are to be distinguished from the significant numbers of immigrants who left Europe to settle in the northeastern and midwestern states during the pre-Civil War period between 1830 and 1865. Those immigrating to Charleston are also not to be numbered among the second wave of heavy immigration during the post-Civil War period into the eighteen-nineties. Nonetheless, in speaking of a nineteenth-century German "community" in Charleston, one cannot ignore what was the common background of those who left Europe in waves of emigration due to the European population explosion in the nineteenth-century. That it was a predominantly rural population moving because of a general decline in the standard of living was indisputably a factor in the migration that lured so many to the less populated and opportunity-rich young United States. The "leaven of democracy" had taken effect in every state in Western Europe and worked to awaken hopes in the general population for personal freedoms that could only be imagined in a different society: "What poor people wanted was freedom from laws and customs that curbed individual economic enterprise. In the cities they wished to escape the regulations of guilds and trade unions; in the country they sought exemption from traditional restrictions upon the transfer of land, the working at a trade, or the conduct of agriculture... Republicanism and monarchism were only shadowy backgrounds to something more personal and vital."[6]

Specific to the great migration of German immigrants to the United States, "[t]he routes of transportation and the available economic opportunities tended to dictate the cities where they would locate: some remained at the principal ports of entry, mainly Baltimore, New York, New Orleans and Philadelphia; others followed the main routes of travel inland, first to such river cities as St. Louis, Cincinnati and Louisville, and a little later to the newer cities of the Great Lakes region, such as Milwaukee, Chicago and Cleveland."[7] Invariably, one could find in nearly every large American city a "German district," as James Berquist puts it, a "visible and tangible reminder to the presence of the

---

6. Marcus Hansen, *The Immigrant in American History* (New York: Harper & Row, 1940), 81-82.

7. James Berquist, "German Communities in American Cities: An Interpretation of the Nineteenth Century Experience," *Journal of American Ethnic History* 4, no. 1 (Fall 1984): 11-12.

country's largest foreign-speaking element." These German communities were for the most part well established by mid-century and represented in many ways a collective effort to resist full acculturation and assimilation with the host society. Most of them would harbor a number of those who left German lands during the European revolutionary period, the so-called Forty-Eighters, who likely would have advocated maintaining their "district" as a separate and more authentic German community. These relatively large German communities in major cities were characterized by a heterogeneous mixture of individuals from the numerous small German states and were able to support a diverse number of social and cultural organizations attuned to the needs of a diverse population.

The characteristics of these "little Germanies" in the major urban communities in the North and Midwest, however, were not evident in the German community that was established in Charleston. In her research compendium, *The Germans of Charleston, Richmond, and New Orleans during the Civil War Period*,[8] Andrea Mehrländer confirms that a relatively small percentage of emigrants chose as their destination the states of what would later become the Confederacy, in contrast to the large number who migrated to the northern states. Thus while German immigrants settled in other cities in the South, such as New Orleans, Savannah, Mobile, and Richmond, their smaller numbers encouraged their dispersal among the host population and less inclination to form separate ethnic enclaves protecting the interests of foreigners. Those who came to Charleston, moreover, would put down roots in a city that was different from any of the other southern cities that were attracting and accepting an immigrant population.

While Charleston had once been among the five largest cities in young America, it was not quite what it had been earlier by the time German immigrant families began to arrive in the early decades of the nineteenth century. It was a city with a long history and one that was not exactly like any other in the South. It had always been South Carolina's principal city and had served as the state's capital before the legislature was transferred to Columbia in 1790. Despite the government's move to Columbia, Charleston enjoyed enormous prosperity during the plantation-dominated economy of the post-Revolutionary years. The invention of the cotton gin had enabled the

---

8.  Berlin/New York: De Gruyter, 2011.

production of this crop to the point that it had become the state's number one export. Cotton production depended on slave labor, and from early on, the black population was equal to, or larger than, the white: In 1761, there had been 4,000 white persons and 4,000 slaves in the city. By 1790, slaves and free blacks were a majority, as they were in 1820, as well as in 1850, when the white population was forty-six percent of the total.[9]

Those Europeans who immigrated to Charleston thus stepped into a patriarchal planter society that ruled over an economy based to a unique degree on an enormous slave population. It was a financially top-heavy society with a broad base of the poor and enslaved supporting an aristocracy of the wealthy:

> The strength of the patriarchy rested ultimately not just on the quantity but on the nature of the estate: land and slaves. The Charleston planters were among the nation's largest landowners; their mean real estate value of $27,300 easily put them among the top 1 percent of landowners in the nation. Even the planters' $13,000 median real estate value was more than that owned by the top 2 percent of American men. In fact, a full 60 percent of the Charleston planters owned more real estate (in dollar value) than 97 percent of their countrymen. Slightly less than 7 percent of the planters were grandees with more than $100,000 worth of real property, a level attained by just under five American men in ten thousand—a disproportion in favor of the Charleston planters by a factor of 137.[10]

Beyond this chasm between the wealthy and the less affluent, Charleston early on presented a tense environment. In the prevailing social structure of a majority ruled by a minority, the Denmark Vesey slave insurrection in 1822 had transformed the city into something like a police state, with the white community convinced that the blacks threatened their very existence. The populace convulsed with alarm followed by trials, public hangings, and new

---

9. George Rogers Jr., *Charleston in the Age of the Pinckneys* (Norman: University of Oklahoma Press, 1969), 141.

10. Michael P. Johnson, "Planters and Patriarchy: Charleston, 1800-1860," *The Journal of Southern History* 46, no. 1 (1980): 53.

ordinances meant to protect the city's whites from further revolution by those it held in subjugation. The police force was strengthened, a guardhouse erected in the center of town, and the slave population monitored ever more vigilantly. Charleston would never let down its guard.[11]

In his 1996 University of South Carolina dissertation, *"Hurrah für dies süsse, dies sonnige Leben": The Anomaly of Charleston, South Carolina's Antebellum German-America*, Michael Everette Bell was the first to examine comprehensively the nineteenth-century German community in Charleston. Thus not until 1996 was there a clear picture of how that ethnic community had been formed, or how German immigrants experienced life among the antebellum society of the South Carolina Lowcountry. The title of his work begs the question of just how sweet and sunny the immigrant's life actually was, and the "anomaly" suggests that the Charleston context was different than what was to be found elsewhere.

The fact that Bell chose as his dissertation topic an analysis and description of the Charleston German community indicates that he was working in unchartered territory, indeed, that his work would present—primarily for the academic community—something that was still unknown just a few years before the turn of the twenty-first century. Bell's comprehensive analysis, now almost a quarter-century old, confirms the earlier assertion that the nature of Charleston's German ethnic community has been something of a closely held secret. Had the dissertation not been an academic exercise, it would have been a revelation to local history buffs, as well as to present-day Charlestonians who can—should they be interested—trace their origins back to those who emigrated from German lands to come to Charleston.

In his dissertation (published in book form in 1999) Bell distinguished the nineteenth-century group, the *Neudeutsch* (new Germans), from the earlier, colonial-era, fully-acculturated, group of German Charlestonians, the *Altdeutsch* (old Germans).[12] He has determined that the influx of immigrants

---

11. John P. Radford, "Race, Residence and Ideology: Charleston, South Carolina in the Mid-Nineteenth Century," *Journal of Historical Geography* 2, no. 4 (1976): 331.

12. Book published under the same title, *"Hurrah für dies süsse, dies sonnige Leben": The Anomaly of Charleston, South Carolina's Antebellum German-America,* I frequently use the German terms and, when appropriate to the context, use the plural forms *Altdeutsche* and *Neudeutsche*.

to Charleston that started in the early 1830s met with little resistance from the native population which had already accepted Germans into their midst, albeit fewer in number. The number of *Neudeutsche* immigrating during the thirty years from 1830 up to the Civil War was, while noticeable, never so large as to appear threatening. Immigrants settling in other areas of the United States not infrequently met with resistance from nativist groups, but a similar anti-immigrant bias was not in evidence in Charleston. The resident population existing with its enormous slave population had little reason to worry about additional white Europeans arriving, who, with usable skills, would contribute in positive ways to the local economy. This relatively homogeneous group of immigrants seemed more than willing to adopt the ways of the southern, coastal society taking them in. They appeared ready to join with the native population rather than set themselves apart in their own enclave to pursue their foreign ways. According to Bell, some two-thirds of them were from the state of Hanover, and many of them came from the same local area in a corner of northwest Germany. If the German Friendly Society had been established in 1766 to address "German interests" in the city, the *Freundschaftsbund* was founded in 1832 to assist in melding similar German "interests" with those of the host society. Understandably, more than half the number of single immigrant German males (according to Bell, 56 percent) sought German wives among the immigrant community, marrying in Charleston to establish families with native-born children. German couples might immigrate together with their first-born, with subsequent issue born once the family was settled, however tenuously, in Charleston. Bell's data indicate that no more than 30 percent would own their own home, the others living in shared quarters or renting, Not every immigrant family would count among the financially successful.

A significant factor in the apparent ease with which the predominantly North German immigrant group undertook to transition into the host culture was the fact that they were speakers of "Plattdeutsch," the Low German dialect that was closer to English than standard, or "High" German. The pronunciation of cognates would have facilitated the immigrant's efforts to interact with the local English-speaking population. Insofar as the ethnic group's settlement pattern indicated a strong desire to live among the English speakers, rather than separate from them, Charleston's German immigrants had from early on seemed intent to accommodate and use the English language. The eighteenth-century-founded German Friendly Society kept its minutes in

English and had to have its constitution translated into German. There were services in English as early as 1800 at St. John's Lutheran Church, founded in 1743. The nineteenth-century immigrant Neudeutsche appreciated that if they were going to practice their trades and crafts, or enter the mercantile sphere between the enslaved and wealthy planter class, they would be interacting with, and dependent on, an English-speaking clientele.

By 1850, Charleston's ethnic German community would constitute 11.56 percent of the free white population.[13] Bell suggests that by mid-century, the Neudeutsch community had come of age, enjoying "acceptance and approbation in the eyes of their fellow Charlestonians" and "able to participate in the life of the city at all levels, including the 'peculiar institution'." He proposes that the ethnic community developed as it did largely under the leadership of a select group of influential individuals, primary among them, the triumvirate of John Andreas Wagener, Franz Melchers, and Heinrich Wieting.

In Charleston by 1833, the young and energetic John Andreas Wagener was an inveterate organizer. He founded a German Fire Engine Company; by 1839, he was instrumental in establishing a "German" Lutheran church (St. Matthew's) and in 1843 started the *Teutonenbund,* "a society for 'the encouragement of German literature, song, culture, and the improvement of German thought and character.'"[14] Bell suggests that Wagener's influence in the Neudeutsch community was "almost overwhelming. By his thirty-second birthday he had helped start three German ethnic organizations, a weekly newspaper, served as an officer in two different military companies, and become a notary in Charleston—all within the span of fourteen years."[15] Only a few years later, Wagener was instrumental in creating the *Deutsche Ansiedlungs Gesellschaft von Charleston,* the "German Colonization Society of Charleston." Under his primary leadership, the organization bought a large tract of land in the northwest corner of South Carolina, where immigrant families ultimately established the town of Walhalla, South Carolina.[16]

---

13. Bell, *"Hurrah…* , 106.

14. Ibid., 92.

15. Ibid., 92-93.

16. There had been other German colonization/emigration societies. Walter Kamphoefner cites three: the small groups from Giessen and Solingen going to eastern Missouri, and the larger Adelsverein, a group of some seven thousand "led by a

It was John Andreas Wagener, as Bell explains, who, as he became ever more prominent in the German community, changed what had become the "established route to social and economic acceptance" for Charleston's immigrants. The ladder to success, if one followed the Altdeutsch protocol, was to join St. John's Lutheran Church, then, through congregational connections, establish a viable business operation, become naturalized, join the country's first German militia, the German Fusiliers, and ultimately become a member of the German Friendly Society. Under Wagener's leadership and within the framework of the numerous ethnic organizations he founded, the Neudeutsche found it possible to by-pass the Altdeutsch sequence of steps to find their own, more expedited, way to acceptance in Charleston's social order. [17] Wagener would later hold the rank of Colonel in the Confederate Army and would be elected as Charleston's forty-third mayor from 1871 to 1873. He died in Walhalla, the Lutheran town in upstate South Carolina he had founded, in 1876, aged sixty.

As the editor of the *Deutsche Zeitung*, the news source of the German community, published from 1853 until December of 1917, Franz Adolph Melchers had come to Charleston in 1843. Bell argues that Melchers "worked diligently to convey the attitudes of antebellum Charleston to the German community, and to transmit the attitudes of Charleston's Germans to others in the city and to other German communities in the United States."[18] Melchers's *Deutsche Zeitung* served effectively as a bridge between the immigrant community and the host society. As its editor and publisher, Melchers spoke *for* and *to* his fellow Germans, exercising considerable influence on the attitudes of the Neudeutsche, as well the Altdeutsche and their fellow native Charlestonians, while facilitating the ethnic community's on-going process of acculturation.

---

group of German nobles to colonize Texas in the mid-1840s." None of them were successful. "Immigrant Epistolary and Epistemology: On the Motivators and Mentality of Nineteenth-Century German Immigrants," *Journal of American Ethnic History* 28, no. 3 (Spring 2009): 40-41. Wagener's success in organizing the *Deutsche Ansiedlungs Gesellschaft von Charleston* was unique in that it was founded to encourage individual immigrants and immigrant families already in Charleston to establish a separate settlement in another area of the state.

17. Bell, *"Hurrah . . .* , 94.

18. Ibid., 170.

The success of the Germans who had come to Charleston in the early 1830s helped set the stage for the wave of immigrants that would follow in their footsteps. But for those arriving after 1830, the several factors weighing heavily on the decision to emigrate—whether published "propaganda" and/or misinformation promising unlimited opportunity and unfettered freedom to do as one chose, or persistent recruiting "agents" extolling the opportunities to be had in the young republic, or the enticing idea of cheap land to be owned and farmed unencumbered by laws and rules—were likely overruled by the pull of the long-standing connections that Charleston had with the North German communities in the vicinity of Bremen. The result was a chain migration pattern that set up in the early 1840s, and which operated independent of propagandistic travel accounts, recruiting agents, or letters to relatives and friends back home encouraging them to join those already in place.

Charleston had long had a significant trade relationship with Bremen, with ships crossing the Atlantic taking Charleston exports of cotton and tobacco to northern Europe through one of its major ports. The German port of Bremen had developed in competition with neighboring Hamburg and other European trading centers, and by the early decades of the nineteenth century had undertaken to enlarge its role and to secure its existence as a port. By 1827, the Hanseatic city had signed a treaty with the government in Hanover to purchase land on the Weser estuary to develop a more navigable harbor. The acquisition of an area of land between the river Geeste and the estuary of the Weser in the vicinity of Lehe led to the creation of the city of Bremerhaven. The founding of Bremerhaven coincided with the significant increase in the rates of emigration during the late 1820s-early 1830s, and the Bremen authorities sought out the emigrant "trade" in support of the city's new port capacities. As Hamburg focused on trade with Britain, Bremen exchanged emigrants for goods from America. By 1843, steamships plied the Weser, and before long, "emigrant" trains arrived at Bremerhaven every two weeks during the season from marshaling point elsewhere in Germany.[19]

The city of Bremen and its port of Bremerhaven almost immediately passed legislation aimed at protecting the emigrants who waited there to board ships to take them to their U.S. destinations. In 1832 and 1834, laws were passed

---

19. Mack Walker, *Germany and the Emigration 1816-1885* (Cambridge: Harvard University Press, 1964,) 88.

that regulated inns and other accommodations providing temporary shelter, and requiring ships leaving port to provide adequate space for passengers and to carry sufficient food supplies for a crossing that could take up to three months. Shipping companies were required to carry insurance in the event of shipwreck on European shores. In the mid-forties, the authorities in Bremen undertook to comply with new American regulations stipulating an increase in the amount of space per passenger and "forbidding the embarkation of a criminal or a deserter on pain of a hundred-thaler fine imposed upon the captain." By 1849, an emigrant hostel, the *Auswanderungshaus* had been built, a facility able to feed 3500 emigrants and to sleep 2000 at a time. In 1853, almost sixty-five percent of the 58,000-plus emigrants passing through Bremen and Bremerhaven made use of the *Auswanderungshaus*.[20] Bremerhaven would become the most popular embarkation point for the majority of nineteenth-century emigrants from northern and central Europe. For the emigrant families living in the northwest corner of Hanover, Bremerhaven lay literally on their doorstep.

The third member of the triumvirate who was instrumental in establishing the Charleston German immigrant community was Captain Heinrich Wieting. In the employ of the Bremen shipping company of N. Gloystein Söhne (N. Gloystein & Sons), Wieting commanded three ships, the *Johann Friedrich*, the *Gauss*, and the *Copernicus* from the 1840s to the late 1860s, usually twice a year bringing on average some 200 emigrants to Charleston each trip. The record of Wieting's departures from Bremerhaven and arrivals in Charleston and New York is shown in the list of Wieting's sailings: [21]

| SHIP | DEPARTED | DESTINATION | ARRIVED | # PASS | #DAYS |
|------|----------|-------------|---------|--------|-------|
| JFriedrich | 4 Nov 1843 | Charleston | - | 6 | - |
| JFriedrich | 29 Apr 1844 | Charleston | 14 Jun 1844 | 23 | 46 |
| JFriedrich | 6 May 1845 | New York | 19 Jun 1845 | 140 | 49 |
| JFriedrich | 7 Oct 1845 | Charleston | 25 Nov 1845 | 131 | 49 |

---

20. Ibid., 89.

21. Taken from "Was fernern vorkömmt werde ich prompt berichten": *Der Auswanderer-Kapitän Heinrich Wieting* Briefe *1847 bis 1856,* Jörn Bullerdiek and Daniel Tilgner, eds. (Bremen: Temmen, 2008), 285.

| | | | | | |
|---|---|---|---|---|---|
| JFriedrich | 5 Oct 1846 | Charleston | - | 116 | - |
| JFriedrich | 19 Mar 1847 | New York | 1 May 1847 | 140 | 43 |
| JFriedrich | 8 Oct 1847 | Charleston | 15 Nov 1847 | 135 | 38 |
| JFriedrich | 19 Mar 1848 | New York | 30 Apr 1848 | 1265 | 42 |
| JFriedrich | 10 Nov 1848 | Charleston | - | 122 | - |
| JFriedrich | 19 Apr 1850 | New York | 16 May 1850 | 126 | 27 |
| JF/Leontine | 20 Oct 1850 | Charleston | - | 125 | - |
| Copernicus | 6 May 1851 | New York | 19 Jun 1851 | 217 | 44 |
| Copernicus | 7 Nov 1851 | Charleston | - | 135 | - |
| Copernicus | 6 May 1852 | New York | 10 Jun 1852 | 249 | 35 |
| Copernicus | 12 Oct 1852 | Charleston | 28 Nov 1852 | 190 | 47 |
| Copernicus | 21 Apr 1853 | New York | 30 May 1853 | 229 | 39 |
| Copernicus | 6 Oct 1853 | Charleston | 21 Nov 1853 | 242 | 46 |
| Copernicus | 5 Apr 1854 | New York | 18 May 1854 | 238 | 43 |
| Copernicus | 8 Oct 1854 | Charleston | 24 Nov 1854 | 258 | 47 |
| Copernicus | 9 Oct 1855 | Charleston | - | 176 | - |
| Copernicus | 6 Mar 1856 | Charleston | 27 Apr 1856 | 14 | 52 |
| Copernicus | 7 Oct 1856 | Charleston | 24 Nov 1856 | 223 | 48 |
| Gauss | 12 Oct 1857 | Charleston | 23 Nov 1857 | 233 | 42 |
| Gauss | 9 Apr 1858 | Charleston | 16 May 1858 | 36 | 37 |
| Gauss | 10 Oct 1858 | Charleston | 18 Nov 1858 | 197 | 39 |
| Gauss | 7 Mar 1859 | Charleston | 4 May 1859 | 18 | 56 |
| Gauss | 8 Oct 1859 | Charleston | 19 Nov 1859 | 161 | 42 |
| Gauss | 11 Feb 1860 | Charleston | 20 Mar 1860 | 7 | 37 |
| Gauss | 14 Oct 1860 | Charleston | 4 Dec 1860 | 227 | 51 |
| Gauss | 14 Mar 1861 | Charleston | = | 11 | - |
| Gauss | 6 Oct 1867 | Charleston | - | 158 | - |
| Gauss | 6 Oct 1868 | Charleston | 29 Nov 1868 | 278 | 54 |

An analysis of the record provides a good sense of the traffic across the Atlantic during those years, and particularly the role that Charleston played on the receiving end. While Wieting sailed on occasion to other ports, his transatlantic passages with immigrants and goods were only between New York or Charleston and Bremerhaven. Some of his passengers were undoubtedly immigrants returning from visits back to the homeland, but the majority disembarking in New York or Charleston would have been immigrants following those relatives or friends who had preceded them, not travelers. Wieting's eight trips to New York carried a total of 1465 passengers, while the twenty-five trips to Charleston brought 3,350 passengers to their southern destination. The average length of the trip was more than a month, sometimes almost two months, under conditions that were trying, in spite of everything Wieting and the Bremen authorities did to make the passage tolerable.

Although other ships traveled regularly between Charleston and Bremerhaven (it was relatively inexpensive—a third-class ticket was less than forty dollars), it was Wieting's caring and personalized concern for the well-being of his passengers, as well as his regular schedule, that helped to anchor the chain of migration from Bremerhaven to Charleston. Those whom he had brought were a magnet for friends and relatives in the communities close to Bremen still contemplating emigration. Moreover, Wieting was a "local": born 1815 in the village of Rönnebeck, about 30 km from Bremen, by the time he was working for the Gloysteins his name would have been familiar to the households in the small communities around Bremen and Bremerhaven. In Charleston, while waiting for his ship to be readied for the return voyage, he participated in the life of the Charleston German community as if he were a Charleston resident. His veneration by the Germans he had been instrumental in bringing to the city was known on both sides of the Atlantic. On his last trip from Bremerhaven to Charleston, Wieting contracted typhus and died in Charleston in December 1868. His death was a heartfelt loss to the Charleston community. A notice of his death was reported in the *Wochenzeitschrift für Vegesack und Umgebung* (*Weekly for Vegesack and Surrounding Area*) and stated that "…only rarely was there a captain who enjoyed as much popularity among those who knew him, here as well as on the other side of the ocean." ("…denn wohl selten gab es einen Capitain, der im Kreise aller derer, die ihn kannten, hier sowohl wie jenseits des Oceans sich einer größeren Popularität erfreute.") A large monument in Charleston's Bethany Cemetery attests to the significant role Wieting played in establishing the city's nineteenth-century German community.

*The prominent gravesite in Charleston's Bethany Cemetery of Heinrich Wieting, the beloved ship's captain who brought most of the North German immigrants from Bremerhaven to Charleston.*

That Wieting's sailings would serve to encourage so many emigrants from the area is attested in the lists of passengers who traveled with him. The list of passengers embarking in Bremerhaven was published regularly in the local German newspaper, the *Deutsche Zeitung*, approximately two weeks before the expected arrival date, furnishing the names of the passengers as well as the towns they came from. While in any given list there are many citations of localities in other German states, the majority of the names and places of origin consistently indicate that Wieting's passengers were from towns and villages close to Bremen and Bremerhaven. Andrea Mehrländer claims that "more than 73% of the Germans in Charleston were Protestants who came from the northwestern German states of Hannover, Oldenburg, and Holstein," and that Wieting transported "more than three-quarters of all Charleston Germans across the Atlantic."[22] For many of the Germans who immigrated to Charleston during the 1840s and 1850s, it was Wieting who brought them to a place where they would benefit from the financial and social infrastructure that Wagener had helped to create, and where they would be tutored by the *Deutsche Zeitung*'s editor, Franz Melchers, as he "translated Charleston and America to the new immigrants, interpreting the city's institutions in the immigrants' own language."[23]

By 1860, Charleston's German ethnic community was well established. During the decade prior to the Civil War, it had successfully transitioned to become remarkably one with the Charleston community. The German immigrants had let themselves in, had uncharacteristically settled throughout the city rather than forming a distinct ethnic enclave, and had set about to quietly find their place in their newly adopted home. Their successes were in spite of the fact that they had entered a host society that was perpetually on edge; that continually felt threatened by a minority population that was difficult to control; that was accosted by political issues such as nullification, states' rights, and political-party squabbles more and more oriented to regional differences; that struggled against a developing and increasingly viral abolitionist movement that hemmed in and interfered with the status quo. By mid-century, the 1,817 Germans in Charleston represented 39 percent of Charleston's foreign-born and 9.1 percent of the free white population. The free whites themselves, 20,012 in number, were 46.6 percent of the city's total population. 19,532 enslaved blacks represented 45.4 percent of the total, free blacks, 8.0 percent.[24]

For the most part, the few analyses of the Charleston German community portray the Germans as unconditionally loyal to the South. In her study of the German communities in Charleston, Richmond, and New Orleans,

---

22. "'With more Freedom and Independence than the Yankees': The Germans of Richmond, Charleston, and New Orleans during the American Civil War," in *Civil War Citizens: Race, Ethnicity, and Identity in America's Bloodiest Conflict*, Susannah J. Ural, ed. (New York: New York University Press, 2010), 65.

23. *"Hurrah . . .* , 254.

24. Mehrländer, *The Germans of Charleston, Richmond and New Orleans during the Civil War Period* (Berlin/New York: DeGruyter, 2011), 397.

Mehrländer sees clear distinctions among them and asserts that Charleston's Germans were possibly the most loyal to southern causes of them all. She emphasizes the fact that during the years leading up to secession and the subsequent war, Charleston's Germans rallied to the cause by fielding numerous militia companies: by 1860 "Charleston's German minority not only had the oldest German militia unit in the United States—the Charleston German Fusiliers of 1775—but also could support six active militia companies of which five were formed between 1842 and 1859, including the only ethnic German cavalry militia of the South." She states that "because ethnic militias did not belong to the regular militia, but rather to the voluntary militia of a state, and were founded on the private initiative of individual persons, their founding alone was a statement of the desire to participate in the military and political culture of the adopted country."[25] Here, the implication is that, by organizing militias, a close-knit group of military-minded leaders demonstrated their "loyalty" to the Southern cause and that, by extension, their demonstration of loyalty could be ascribed to the entire group of their fellow Germans. The question of whether the ethnic community was "loyal" to the host society would haunt Charleston's German immigrants during the years after the turn of the century. We will see in later chapters how the matter of "loyalty" played out.

Both Bell and Mehrländer propose that because of their publicly declared acceptance of the Southern way of life, there existed a symbiosis based on mutual respect between the natives and the German immigrants. Bell had earlier suggested that what made Charleston's German-America unique was that it appeared so homogeneous: it was the external uniformity "that prevented embarrassing situations from breaking out between the native-born whites and the Germans. There were no German radical socialists in the city, personal liberty

---

25. To the degree that the ethnic community cohered, recognized itself and was recognized by others, acknowledged and listened to its mentors, the individuals who comprised these militia units, according to Mehrländer, held considerable sway. The minority German community's social life was "almost completely in the hands of … twenty-four militia officers who, through a complex network of clubs, nepotistic connections, and their business contacts as merchants, had created a watertight structure of mutual interests that allowed them to reach nearly every aspect of community life." Mehrländer, *With more freedom,* 66-67.

was guaranteed by the constitution, and the Germans bought-in to the political and social structures of the old south. Everything was as it should be."[26]

There is no reason to doubt that such a symbiosis indeed existed between Charleston's native community and that of the immigrants. But it is certain that there were cracks in the structure. The city's nineteenth-century Lutheran community's efforts to establish a separate settlement in up-state South Carolina suggest that that "mission" community acted as a "safety valve" for those who did not entirely buy into the Charleston native/immigrant relationship. Mehrländer's suggestion that the Germans were "loyal adoptive citizens" based on the fact that some of them were slaveholders conflicts with the evidence that, at the same time, some not infrequently co-habited with blacks, in some cases flaunting local custom by marrying them. Such behavior flew in the face of white citizens' customary attitude and suggests what must have been the equivocal nature of German immigrants' interactions with a culture grounded in slavery. To judge German immigrants' "loyalty" to a Southern way of life that always fought against "outside" interference in defense of its system of slavery, and to see in the immigrants' social behavior a consensus with a Southern morality based on the inferiority of a laboring class serving a propertied elite to which the immigrant would never belong, is to ignore a number of factors that would argue against the solidarity that some commentators find *distinctive*. No matter how loud the message coming from the *Deutsche Zeitung*, no matter how congenial the brotherhood in any of the numerous social and cultural associations, the immigrant knew in his heart that he was a guest in his new community, and that his conduct was under constant scrutiny. It was the case that with or without instruction, Charleston's Germans appeared to be so well-behaved because they were so anxious to please. They consistently demonstrated the propriety that would keep them in the good graces of their hosts. The Neudeutsche had not only to prove themselves to the Altdeutsche, but also to the wealthy planter society in which they would seek a *modus vivendi*. To all appearances, the Charleston ethnic community of predominantly non-radical North Germans appeared to agree that it was better to be "agreeable" than to cause any trouble; to lend support—outward support at least—when the corporate society appeared in trouble; that it would be politic to do as Charlestonians did and to adopt the ways of those who held the reins.

---

26. Bell, *"Hurrah . . .* , 261-62.

As long as one stayed on the side of the most-of-the-time comprehensible majority, there were advantages to lying low and getting on with the business at hand—that is, becoming a productive member of the local community and carving out a sustainable existence for oneself and one's family. That they vied for acceptance by the community at large led them to accept many of the ways of that community, for to openly dissent would carry risk, and to attempt to swim against the current would invoke unnecessary hardship when things were already hard enough.

It is nonetheless questionable whether the relationship between the community of German immigrants and the host society can be wrapped and tied in such a relatively uncomplicated package. It would be erroneous to think of the general ethnic community as one comprised of docile sheep being managed and controlled by a few shepherds. We need not assume that because this group of predominantly North German Protestants came, more than likely, from families of small farmers based in a rural area of Hanover, that they were somehow less intelligent or less "enlightened" than the urbanized, radical intelligentsia who emigrated after the failure of the revolution of 1848. In their volume about the various attitudes revealed in letters written by Germans fighting in the Civil War, Walter Kamphoefner and Wolfgang Helbich claim that collective stereotypes and prejudices were operative among both native and foreign (German) soldiers. They cite evidence that for American soldiers fighting along with German enlistees, the war exacerbated already-extant nativist prejudices, leading them to label their German comrades as unheroic, demoralized, and too often likely to run from the battle scene. The Germans, on the other hand, could readily describe Americans as "uncultivated, hypocritical, money-grubbing swindlers." "The unpopular Germans insisted on believing they were the better soldiers and could thus win the respect of the Americans, and many Americans were eagerly waiting for a chance to prove that these incompetent foreigners were inferior to *real* Yankees. The mutual demand for recognition seems to have been so strong that both sides were blind to the irony of the situation."[27]

It will be shown in later chapters that a self-assured attitude of superiority, similar in many respects to that displayed by some German soldiers fighting in

---

27. Walter D. Kamphoefner and Wolfgang Helbich, eds., *Germans in the Civil War: The Letters They Wrote Home* (Chapel Hill: The University of North Carolina Press, 2006), 25.

the Civil War, would manifest itself in the defensive stance taken by German immigrants or German-American immigrant descendants in the years leading up to WWI. Here, we can acknowledge the existence of such an attitude as a cultural trait derived from a European background that had much to be proud of, a trait that inevitably would be brought along by those abandoning their older culture in exchange for a new life in a much younger one. Indeed, the German immigrants arriving in Charleston, despite their non-radical background, had little reason to feel inferior to the natives who greeted or ignored them. I suggest that Charleston's Neudeutsche might better be described as *smart*, rather than as exceptionally amenable, in their efforts to please and assimilate with the native community. Even from rural north Hanover, there would have been no reason to suffer from an inferiority complex, no reason to approach the new cultural context obsequiously. It is certain that John Andreas Wagener did not bumble into Charleston without a sense of how he would work within the conditions he found or had already assessed. As he and others found themselves in leadership positions, they were focused on "German" interests and consciously undertook to accomplish their objectives in ways that would accommodate local cultural parameters. From such a perspective, Mehrländer's assertion that the German community's readiness to establish six German militias "proved" their loyalty to the South might better be interpreted as a small group of military-minded men determining that it would be preferable for them to have their own military units in which they could satisfy their "German" militaristic instincts, while at the same time signaling their readiness to offer the assistance of their well-trained cadres if needed by the local, native, authorities.

Similarly, the *Deutsche Zeitung* under Melchers's leadership always placed German interests front and center before the local public. The newspaper proudly proclaimed on its masthead, *Wöchentliche Zeitung zur Wahrung deutscher Interessen* (Weekly for Safeguarding German Interests), that it was the most read and widely distributed newspaper in North and South Carolina, Georgia, and Florida dedicated to German interests. While it was principally oriented to its German readership, it covered other areas of interest to the wider public and acknowledged that its advertisements addressed both its German and its English-speaking readers. It offered political opinion and took stances on issues of the day, whether or not the "German" perspective might run counter to the prevailing sentiments of the host community. As the ethnic community's principal channel of communication, the *Zeitung* never sought to stand on the sidelines: at the same time, it never sought to offend.

In essence, then, what has been acknowledged as a "declared" acceptance by the ostensibly homogeneous German community of Charleston's cultural "ways" can be viewed as the ethnic community's considered method of managing the relationship between the parallel cultures. The method rested on what might be termed "reverse nativism," a subjective pride and self-assurance whereby the managed ethnic community could acknowledge its minority status, yet not accept subservience to the host society, in effect "managing" the native culture itself and enabling the latter's acceptance of the ethnic community in its midst.

Regardless which "attitude" formed the basis of the German immigrants' approach to the foreign culture—a conscious intention to display an agreeability that would not rock the local boat, or an assured conviction that they were of stock that could handle whatever they might encounter—they would find that Charleston presented a unique set of social, economic, and personal challenges. In those challenges, nonetheless, lay opportunity. It was opportunity and a freedom to act in their own interests, after all, that they had come for. If within Charleston society's pyramid there was somehow space between the high and the low to accommodate those vying to create a middle, it was principally the Germans who persevered to make that happen. The individual stories that follow reveal a lot about the North Germans who crossed the Atlantic to seek a future in lowcountry Charleston.

# CHAPTER 2:

## MID-CENTURY PIONEERS

Johann Heinrich Rosenbohm was listed as a 19-year-old passenger on the *Constitution*[1] that arrived in New York from Bremen on June 21, 1824. Exactly when he made his way south to Charleston is not known, but he was naturalized as a U.S. citizen in Charleston in October 1830. His story is important in that he represents an early link in the chain stretching between Charleston and the villages in northwestern Germany in the vicinity of Bremen.

---

1.    The Bremen brig *Constitution* was built at Vegesack-Grohn by the shipwright Johann Lange, for the Bremen-New York packet service of the Bremen firm of H. H. Meier & Co, and was launched on 21 October 1820. Masters, in turn, were Gerd Klockgeter, Jürgen Meyer, Johann Wächter, and J. F. Volckmann. The *Constitution* was wrecked sometime in 1833; she was replaced by a 3-masted, square-rigged bark of the same name, launched by the same shipwright for the same owners in November 1833. See Peter-Michael Pawlik, *Von der Weser in die Welt; Die Geschichte der Segelschiffe von Weser und Lesum und ihrer Bauwerften 1770 bis 1893*, Schriften des Deutschen Schifffahrtsmuseums, Bd. 33 (Hamburg: Kabel, c1993), pp. 164-165. Gerd Klockgeter was indeed the Master who signed the Manifest of Passengers that included Johann Rosenbohm, one of the ten passengers, all ranging in age between 18 and 26.

By the time he became a citizen, twenty-six-year-old Rosenbohm had sufficient means to invest in real estate—a rental property that he would sell two
years later. Either he had been successful in establishing himself as a grocer
(the Charleston City Directory for 1835-36 shows him operating a grocery at
a prime location in then-"downtown" Charleston, where in all likelihood he
lived in quarters above the store) or he had emigrated with monetary assets
already in hand. He was granted a U.S. passport in 1836 and traveled back
to Germany that year to be married. Upon his return, he purchased another
dwelling in a neighborhood not far from his store. In 1839, however, the naturalized German-American grocer abandoned Charleston, leaving his grocery
store and its stock worth $2,849.35 to be disposed of by a fellow German
immigrant, who would retain half of the sale monies. Rosenbohm resettled
his family in New York City. The family had sufficient means to make a return visit to Germany in 1841. Passenger-ship records show a party of four
Rosenbohms arriving in New York from Bremen on the *Charlotte* on June 1,
1841: John Henry, 37; Caroline Louise, 22; Catherine, 2 ½; and Auguste, a
one-year-old infant. They travelled as cabin passengers—not in steerage—and
arrived with "seven boxes and beds." The same ship would return in November
to bring Johann's widowed father, Caspar Rosenbohm, to the United States
where he would take up residence in the house in Charleston that his son still
owned. John Henry made another voyage to his hometown of Geestendorf
a few months later: the *New York City Lutheran Church Records, 1834-1854*
indicate that he was a witness to a marriage (likely of a relative) in November
1841 in Wurffleth, a village near Geestendorf and the birthplace of his sister,
Anna Maria Rosenbohm. John Henry Rosenbohm died in New York in May
of 1843. His will left the Charleston property to his widow, but after her
husband's death, Caroline Rosenbohm remarried and thus relinquished her
inheritance. John Henry's father, Caspar, would live in the house in Charleston
until his death in 1872.[2]

It is impossible to know with any certainty why young Rosenbohm decided
to emigrate. Conditions in German lands were not inordinately stressful in the
1820s: there was no unusual shortage of food, the Napoleonic wars were in the

---

2. The house was put up for auction in 1845 to satisfy the debt ($1119.82) John
Henry owed to his executor, Luder Rust. It was purchased by John Henry's brother-in-
law, Herman Knee, married to Catherina, née Rosenbohm.

past, and emigration as a factor of population density was not yet the driving force it would become in some of the German principalities. The number of German emigrants did not exceed 10,000 until 1832.[3] Nor can we explain how, having landed in New York, he ultimately ended up in Charleston, other than to suggest that a North German contemplating emigration would, at the very least, have known of the city because of the long-standing connection between Charleston and the North German port of Bremen. Whether Rosenbohm had a personal connection, a friend or acquaintance already re-located in the city who might have encouraged the mature teen-ager to come south, we cannot know. It is easiest to propose that he left the family on his own to seek his fortune, or, alternatively, was sent by the family in Germany to determine whether—and where—it would make sense for other family members to follow. It would turn out that, with the exception of his mother, who died in 1836, the entire family would come to Charleston.

That Johann Rosenbohm undertook to make his fortune as a grocer is indicative of a pattern that would become characteristic of German immigrants to Charleston. The nature of the Lowcountry economy, and Charleston's in particular, was noted previously: a wealthy, planter/plantation elite to whom manual labor was anathema, an enslaved majority that served the white population in almost every capacity, and a small class of free laborers and artisans who practiced the service functions that the composite society relied on. Ira Berlin and Herbert Gutman's analysis of the relationship between native, slave, and immigrant workingmen, confirms that "[t]he black and white competition in craftsmen's occupations was looked upon with justified suspicion; in competition with blacks, white laborers were seen as inferior persons. Indeed, the slave-holding elite of Charleston feared for social peace in their city; free white laborers were unreliable, and were met with deep suspicion."[4] According to Mehrländer, "Charleston was one of the few southern cities that prevented the displacement by immigrants of free blacks from their typical workplaces, because Charleston employers refused to give up their preference for free black employees. Instead a radical racial division continued in specific occupations."[5]

---

3. Walter D. Kamphoefner, "Immigrant Epistolary and Epistemology," 38.

4. "Natives and Immigrants, Free Men and Slaves: Urban Workingmen in the Antebellum South," *American Historical Review* 88 (1983): 1175-2000.

5. Mehrländer "*With more freedom ...* '," 41.

Berlin and Gutman argue that immigrants astutely undertook to find niches in the social order where they could operate without displacing and antagonizing those who were already in place. "As a group, immigrants entered Southern society at the bottom of the free social hierarchy and made up a large part of the lower ranks of urban society." In the thirty years after J. H. Rosenbohm became a grocer, "native-born white men composed better than two-thirds of the male merchants, political officials, and professionals in Mobile, Charleston, and other Southern cities, while foreign-born men equaled a similar proportion of petty proprietors— grocers, restauranteurs, stable keepers, and the like."[6] Rosenbohm's early attempt to find an occupation in his new-found home was not the choice of a "trade" for which he had been trained in his native land, but rather an effort to establish a business to retail provisions he could expect his fellow immigrants would need: he would serve an existing neighborhood of both native- and foreign-born and would not appear arrogantly competitive—something the newcomer would want to avoid. While the grocer Rosenbohm did not establish a "trend," he was an early representative: "By 1870, Germans still owned almost 80% of all Charleston groceries."[7]

We might wonder why Rosenbohm would leave Charleston in 1839, abandoning the city and his store in what seems a somewhat hasty fashion, willing to close down his business in absentia. As was the case in considering the reasons that led to his decision to emigrate fifteen years earlier, there is only conjecture. That he would abandon the Southern city for the one in the North where he had first landed may have had to do with the Charleston context. Already during the years before he was naturalized (a three-year residency requirement), the immigrant Charleston resident would have realized that his adopted state of South Carolina was becoming politically and economically embroiled in the "nullification crisis": South Carolina's 1832 Ordinance of Nullification resulted in a stand-off with the federal government.[8] That crisis dominated South Carolina and Charleston politics

---

6. Berlin and Gutman, 1178.

7. Mehrländer, *"With more freedom… ',"* 40.

8. "Nominally, the Nullification Crisis concerned the tariffs of 1828 and 1832, both of which the state's cotton and especially rice planters found onerous. At its base, however, the South Carolina Nullification Convention's decision to declare the two tariffs unconstitutional and unenforceable in the state after February 1, 1833, was an attempt to check federal power that might eventually be aimed directly at slavery." Ethan J. Kytle and Blain

for many years, ultimately putting the state of South Carolina in a category by itself. Nullification brought forth the volatile career of John C. Calhoun, and the issue was precedent to South Carolina's secession from the Union thirty years later. The state's—and Charleston's—population was almost evenly divided: the individual could not count on a neighbor of any ilk to hold the same opinion on these political matters. In such a context, the mood in Charleston would likely have been significantly disconcerting for the immigrant: to know which side to take, to know how it all might impact one's future—a future which was supposed to be free of the political discord and instability that was rampant in Europe. The immigrant would have wanted to think that he had exchanged the unsettled European past for a new, more peaceful and stable existence in a land that had put its revolution to rest. For the prescient German immigrant, the handwriting on the wall likely suggested that the state's adamant insistence on its right to oppose laws designed for the good of the united country was a cover-up for an increasingly divisive sectionalism dependent on the "peculiar" institution of slavery. Rather than fall in with the nullifiers and risk offending the other half of the community over a policy which he could hardly have fully understood, discretion might have helped Rosenbohm decide to abandon the complicated tensions in Charleston and seek refuge in the North.

On the other hand, perhaps Johann Rosenbohm's efforts as a grocer were economically disappointing. The German immigrants who were there at the time would not yet have had a chance to benefit from the influence that John Andreas Wagener would have on Charleston's German community with his dynamic personality beginning about 1836. Or Rosenbohm could have been spooked by the sequence of devastating fires that ravaged large sections of the city, barely missing the neighborhood where he ran his store. Or he might never have forgotten that in his first year of residence Charleston had experienced its first epidemic of Asiatic cholera.[9]

---

Roberts, *Denmark Vesey's Garden: Slavery and Memory in the Cradle of the Confederacy* (New York: The New Press, 2019), 23.

9. In 1833, a widely-read travel author had written: "The people of Charleston pass their lives in endeavoring to escape from … the … fever. This continual dodging with death strikes me as very disagreeable." Walter J. Fraser, Jr., *Charleston! Charleston! The History of a Southern City* (Columbia: University of South Carolina Press, 1991), 211.

Whatever the immediate reasons that caused Rosenbohm to pull up stakes in Charleston and move his family to New York, his example suggests what it was like to be a German immigrant trying to settle in Charleston prior to the 1840s—testimony that the Neudeutsche faced numerous challenges, physical and psychological, in establishing a new footing for themselves in Charleston. It was debatable whether those who followed during the next decade would experience anything much different.

## —THE FEHRENBACHS

Johann Rosenbohm unquestionably initiated the chain that would draw his three sisters to Charleston. Each of his sisters' stories represents a telling chapter in the development of the immigrant German community in Charleston prior to the Civil War. Johann's sister Anna Maria came to Charleston married to a watchmaker from the Black Forest, Nicholas Fehrenbach. The native of Baden and the young woman from the environs of Bremen were married in 1830, and the baptism of their first child, Wilhelm Eduard, is recorded in the Geestendorf church record in May 1831. Probably in 1832, the couple immigrated to Charleston with their young son. A second son, Nicholas Jr., was born in Charleston in 1833. The Fehrenbach family grew exponentially with the birth of six more children between 1835 and 1846. An additional son would be born in 1851, when the family had left Charleston and moved to the village of Sheboygan, Wisconsin. Nicholas Fehrenbach Sr. was naturalized in 1840.

If the senior Fehrenbach had left his native Baden because of chronic economic hardship (emigration from the Grand Duchy of Baden due to population density was heavy even before the 1840s) and come to Charleston— where his wife had a brother who had become a U.S. citizen and established himself as a grocer—hoping for opportunity to practice his artisanal talents as a clockmaker, he would be sorely disappointed. The Fehrenbach name would later become a well-known one in the Charleston German community, but the family's renown—if it ever amounted to that—rested on the shoulders of the second son, Nicholas Jr., who became a successful restauranteur and in whose home the well-known Captain Wieting, the "Father of Immigrants," would draw his final breath in 1868. The immigrant parents, Nicholas Sr. and his wife, Anna Maria née Rosenbohm, struggled mightily. Nicholas Sr. was unsuccessful in establishing himself as a clock- or watchmaker in Charleston. As the family was increasing in size during the decade after their immigration to Charleston, the family revenues decreased to the point that the Fehrenbachs would have numbered among Charleston's neediest residents.

In her book, *Benevolence Among Slaveholders: Assisting the Poor in Charleston 1670-1860,*[10] Barbara Bellows cites the case of Anna Maria Fehrenbach as an example of the Charleston community's demonstrable concern for the indigent among its citizenry, including its efforts at educating the children of the lesser classes. The founding of the Charleston Orphan House already in 1790 emanated from that sense of civic benevolence, and the immigrant Fehrenbachs would number among those who had little choice but to throw themselves on the mercy of that institution.

*Founded in 1790, the Orphan House building was the temporary home of Nicholas and Johann Hinrich Richard (Frederick) Fehrenbach, as well as Charles (Georg Karl) Weber and his niece Wilhelmina Plath.*

The dire straits in which the Fehrenbach family found itself in the early 1840s caused Anna Maria Fehrenbach to make application in August of 1844 for her eleven-year-old Nicholas to be admitted to the orphanage. An undated

---

10. Baton Rouge: Louisiana State University, 1993.

letter signed by John Phillips and W. Heemsoth, "pastor of the German Lutheran congregation in Hasell Street," accompanied the mother's application and read as follows [unedited]:

> Nicolaus Fehrenbach the father of the good boy came from the Grandduchy of Baden (Germany) and has resided in Charleston S.C. till last spring, when he left for New orleans; since when his wife never heard from him. Shortly before the time of his leaving the whole property was sold for the benefit of creditors; but by the assistance of some friends, the wife opened again a small retail dry goods store, by which she tries, although with great difficulty to support a large family of six children, the smallest of whom is an infant of three weeks: Unable therefore to superintend and educate the children, the aforesaid boy Nicolaus is at present in great danger to become a bad member of the society. For this reason the Committee of the Orphan House is respectfully solicited to receive the said boy under their protection.

The signatories then recommended " ... the boy Nicolaus Fehrenbach as one peculiarly and particularly a subject for the charity of the Orphan House of Charleston. His parents are very poor and his Father has deserted his Family. His Mother is unable to afford him support or educate him properly. The boy if now taken may become a good and useful citizen." Accordingly, on September 5, 1844, Nicholas Fehrenbach Jr. was legally transferred to the Charleston Orphan House for a ten-year indenture until September 5, 1854.

With Nicolaus successfully placed in the orphanage, several weeks later Anna Maria wrote a second letter [quoted verbatim]:

> To the Chairman of the Commissioners of the Charleston Orphan House / Gentlemen / You will allow to express the grateful feelings of my heart for that kind sympathy you partook in my bereaved circumstances and that benevolence you bestowed upon my second son Nicolaus in giving to his youth an asylum in the Charleston Orphan House. But alas! though my heart in somewhat is raised, that now one of my children is

under the care and guidance of faithful tutors, it nevertheless gets depressed when I look on the other children, bereaved of the parental care and the means for their support, for their [*sic*] are left to me five more. I therefore, encouraged by your kindness, take once more my refuge to you, gentlemen, trusting and fully assured you will exert all means which a benevolent community bestowed upon you to save poor children from want and destruction against me and my children, and confer upon one of them: Johann Hinrich Richard born in Charleston S.C. 8th of July 1838 the great favour which now so richly enjoyes [*sic*] the above named in giving him too an asylum in the Charleston Orphan House. I remain / with sincere gratitude / Gentlemen / your obedient servant / Mary Ann Fehrenbach / corner Tradd and Church Street.

Mary Ann Fehrenbach's application to admit her son John Henry Richard Fehrenbach, aged 6 years, was denied. But she persisted. Orphan House records contain an undated, two-page letter from A. M. Fehrenbach. The perfect penmanship makes it obvious that it was a German who was the scribe: at every instance of s "ss," the writer uses the orthographical convention of German script and writes "ß." The letter is the poignant plea of an abandoned immigrant mother:

> To the Honorable the Commissioners of the Orphan House / Gentlemen /I have heard with deep regret the decision you have recently made in refusing to admit John H. F.[11] Fehrenbach my son to the benefit of the Orphans Charity. I do not wish to vex your attention with complaining. The complaints of the poor and friendless are too important to excite attention, and I would be untrue to my feelings if I entertained other than the kindest regard for those who are sheltering and properly educating an older child who I was

---

11. The initial "F" suggests that "Frederick" had replaced "Richard." In the supporting letter from John Philips that follows, the young Fehrenbach is referred to as "John Henry Frederick."

unable to support and over whom I was losing all control. If
you shall do no more for me and mine you have my gratitude,
the gratitude of a heart stricken by misery and misfortune,
and the mother's prayers that neither you nor yours shall ever
require that public charity over which you preside. My object Gentlemen is to entreat that you would reconsider your
determination-a determination which must have resulted from
a mistaken apprehension of the facts. At least hear my story
and then decide whether the boy is not entitled to this charity.
My husband Mr. Fehrenbach was unfortunate and about the
beginning of this year the Sheriff seized and sold out everything he possessed for debt leaving us destitute. To save his
family from begging or starvation he consented that I should
by the assistance of my brother in law Mr. Herman Knee open
a small dry goods shop. Discontented however at being unable
to obtain work he suddenly left the State about eight months
ago leaving his wife and six children in want and wretched-
ness to [illegible] for themselves. I believe he went to New
Orleans. I have heard so to my knowledge he has never been
back since, and if has made any enquiries respecting his family I have never heard of them. I had and have no credit. Mr.
Knee buys goods in his name and I repay him from the sales
I make one half of the premises which I rent and let out and
thus by a rigid economy and ceaseless industry I have scarcely
been able to shelter and feed my children. I have never received
nor will I as long as I can work receive charity for myself. It
has however never been offered, unless the suggestion made I
presume in kindness by Mr. Loundes that I could apply to the
poorhouse for bread may be considered an offer of Charity. I
do not know that my feelings are more sensitive than others.
I do believe the remark was meant not to offend but if I have
prayed to you to take my boy to aid a deserted wife in living
honestly, to assist a mother in saving her child from the ruin
of a neglected education, to relieve her from a burden she felt
she could not bear. Oh do not think that it was for the purpose
of enabling her to seek charity for herself. It was to escape this

mortification. It was to avoid this shame that I have solicited your charity towards my children. In my native land I was taught that poverty was not crime that to beg when one could work was dishonest and that the bread of charity was very bitter. I am now too old and too unwilling to unlearn this lesson. My children are yours. They are natives, they are southerners: and though their Father had forgot himself and deserted them this is their country. And though poor and friendless shall my son not be heard because a mothers tongue alone urges his claims. If poverty if destitution if perfect friendlessness avail my childs rights are they not great. Oh save him from being a curse to the soil that gave him birth and spare the mother from the anguish which the mother must endure at the moral debasement of her child. Be not offended at my language I am filled with anxiety: Again reject him and to whom shall he go. It has been said I have been supported by the contribution of German friends. No one ever loaned or offered to loan much less gave me a dollar since Mr. Fehrenbach left. Take my boy let him go with his brother and although I have myself and three children to support this relief will be encouragement to live in the fear of God.

Gentlemen excuse what has here been written which may be considered boldness and be assured / I am with consideration / of profound respect your / Petitioner / A. M. Fehrenbach

Even without punctuation, the letter reveals the desperation of an immigrant mother trying her level best to enable the survival of her family, beset as it was by hostile conditions she would never have thought to encounter. She is gracious in allowing that the recommendation by Mr. Loundes that she ask for food from the "poorhouse" emanated from the good, if somewhat cold, heart of a Charlestonian; she acknowledges her embarrassment in again seeking the charity of the community—something that goes against everything she was taught in her German home; and she testifies that, with the exception of her brother-in-law, her fellow German immigrants have not offered a helping hand.

Her plight is confirmed by another letter on record. A second recommendation from John Phillips (who, we learn, was the property manager of the quarters the Fehrenbachs rented) is dated November 5, 1844, and reads:

To the Commissioners of the Orphan House / Gentlemen /

Having been requested by Mrs. A Fehrenbach to state for your information all that I know respecting her family and circumstances, I very cheerfully comply. My acquaintance with the Fehrenbachs commenced some six or eight years ago, Fehrenbach becoming the tenant of a house which was under my control as Agent for Mrs. Mills. He was in the habit of frequently consulting me respecting his affairs. During the last eighteen months he complained of the great difficulty he found in supporting his family and I thought he was often tipsy. In the early part of the year after he had been sold out by the sheriff, I urged him to leave the house as I appreciated he was not able to pay the rent. He refused to go, declaring he had no place on earth to which he could carry his family and his credit would not enable him to own a room. Soon after he called and told me he was going to run away. That he was miserably poor, that he could get no work and he could not endure the misery of seeing his children starve. He wept very bitterly and said as I was his only friend he trusted I would be kind to his family. He did not exactly know where he was going. He however spoke of going on the guard in New Orleans and of working at his trade, that being the watch making. I have never seen him since. I am confident that if he had ever returned he would have called on me. Mrs. Fehrenbach still continues to occupy the house, the rent having been greatly reduced from the fall of rents and at her earnest solicitation. I see her often and I take great pleasure in expressing the high opinion which I entertain of her integrity and industry, and intelligence. She has six children, the eldest boy is bound an apprentice to Mr. Stein the watch maker, her second is in the Orphan House and she had four living with her. She hires or underleases the greater part of the premises and with the proceeds of her little shop and Mr. Knee's assistance she is enabled to exist. She is miserably poor and with the exception of Mr. Knee friendless. If her son John Henry Frederick Fehrenbach was admitted into the Orphan Asylum it would be a great relief. It would certainly enable her to support herself and her other children with less slaving than what she is now compelled to undergo. It would however in a moral point of view be of still greater consequence. The boy is getting above her control and he will soon be selecting his associates and taking amusements where neither a mother's influence is felt or will be acknowledged. It is now that education is to establish his principles or if neglected he is to incur the fearful consequences resulting from allowing his pleasure to be ["the only" stricken out] law for his government. I have felt and still feel an interest in this family. I have always found Mrs. Fehrenbach a worthy woman: and her boys if not neglected will become useful citizens.

This time, Anna Maria was successful: Johann Hinrich Richard/Frederick ("John") Fehrenbach was admitted November 14, 1844. Her success, however, was short-lived. A year later, the Fehrenbachs' situation changed dramatically. In a letter dated October 30, 1845, Anna Maria wrote:

To the Hon. Commissioners of the Orphan House / Your Hon. Body had the kindness about a year ago to admit into the Orphan House two of my sons Nicholas and Richard[12], at a time when I was unfortunately reduced to needy circumstances. These circumstances having been greatly improved by the return of my husband, and feeling myself perfectly able to support my children, I would now respectfully request your permission for them to return home again, at the same time rendering to you my sincerest thanks for the timely aid

---

12. "Frederick" changed back to "Richard."

afforded to my family./ I remain with feelings of the highest respect / Your obedient servant / Ann Fehrenbach.

Her petition was granted, and the two Fehrenbach sons were delivered up to her on October 30, 1845.

Thus the two boys were in Charleston's orphanage only briefly. The letters Anna Maria Fehrenbach wrote make clear that the father of a growing family was unable to find steady employment as a watchmaker. Even though the eldest son was apprenticed in the same occupation, he was doubtless working for an already-established competitor. The family's poverty became all too real, and the desperate husband had little choice but to leave the family in search of some means of income. At the time, it made sense for him to seek his fortune in New Orleans, another Southern city with a significant German immigrant population. Apparently no more successful there than in Charleston, he returned after a year, somewhat restored, but not entirely economically stabilized. In his absence, the wife had survived by availing herself of the city's benevolence by giving two of her sons over to municipal authorities. In her efforts to gain entry for her children into the Orphan House, Anna Maria acknowledges her strong resistance to accepting the charity of her hosts—a mark of her immigrant background. The landlord's letter arguing the abandoned wife's case tells of the family's threatened eviction, the father's alcoholism, the way the mother struggled to keep a roof over her children's heads. The supporting letter by Mr. Phillips also suggests that there were Charlestonians with genuine compassion for the foreigners in their midst and who regarded the German immigrant as more than a stranger.

Anna Maria Fehrenbach's last request to the civic institution to return her children to her shows her still capable of hope that the family's situation might be salvaged and that better times lay ahead. With her two sons back in her household, she apparently had faith in her husband Nicholas's plans for the future. But whatever brighter future was promised by Nicholas on his return from New Orleans, shortly thereafter the decision was made to leave Charleston and move to Sheboygan, Wisconsin, a small town north of Milwaukee, on the shore of Lake Michigan—a distant shore indeed. Why? We can only postulate that opportunity of some sort beckoned, sufficient to warrant what would have been an arduous trip from the South Carolina Lowcountry, likely west, possibly back to New Orleans, then up the Mississippi, then east from some point to the western shore of Lake Michigan. In 1846, the town of Sheboygan was a small village compared to Charleston, with only about four hundred residents, and as one brief sketch put it, "no churches, newspapers or passable roads." But Wisconsin was a magnet for German immigrants, and Milwaukee, fifty miles to the south, would soon develop into a "German Athens" in the Midwest. Of all the states, Wisconsin would harbor the largest number of German immigrants in the latter part of the nineteenth century. Perhaps this large tide of Germans to the less settled environment in Wisconsin—one of whom may have been a relative who settled in Sheboygan—was what swept Nicholas Fehrenbach along. He purchased property in the "village" of Sheboygan in 1848, and the 1850 Census lists the entire family, comprised of Nicholas, 44, watchmaker, with personal property worth $1,000; Anna, 44; Edward, 19, sailor (inaccurately claiming birth in the United States); Nicholas, 17; Premos, 15; Richard, 12; Caroline, 8.[13] How successful the watchmaker was in Sheboygan is questionable. The couple had yet one more child, Wilhelm, born in Sheboygan in March 1851, but during the ensuing decade the family broke apart. The 1860 census shows Nicholas Sr. alone in Sheboygan and listed as a "convict." The nature of his crime and whether or not he was incarcerated is unknown. In 1857, he had given power of attorney to Edward Gaertner (from the name, a fellow German immigrant) to sell part of a property he had purchased in 1848, and in 1873 he sold another property in Sheboygan for one dollar. There is no record of his death and burial either in Sheboygan or Charleston. It is likely that he died a pauper in Wisconsin, having abandoned, or been abandoned by, his family many years earlier.

Records suggest that after the birth of the last child, Anna Maria gave up on both her unsuccessful husband and the struggle for a stable existence and returned to Charleston with her family in tow. In 1856, twenty-three-year-old Nicholas Jr. married a young widow, Antoinette Mehrtens, née Frank, at St. Matthew's German Lutheran Church in Charleston. He is listed in the church records as a local restauranteur. Seeing opportunity in the temperance movement, young Nicholas Fehrenbach opened his *Teetotal Restaurant* in 1859 in the building adjacent to

---

13. There is no mention in this census record of the daughter Adelheid (b. 1840), nor of Hermann Heinrich (b. 1844) or Adeline Catherina Mariana (b. 1846). It is likely that Adelheid died an infant in Charleston. The absence of the other siblings is likely the fault of the census-taker or the possibility that they were not living in Sheboygan at the time. Hermann Heinrich died 1905, Adeline Catherina in 1917.

Charleston's Institute Hall where the Ordinance of Secession was signed a year later in December 1860. An advertisement in the *Charleston Courier* of December 14, 1859, announced that no expense had been spared in outfitting the saloon as handsomely as any "first class restaurant": meals were available from 7 a.m. until noon; he would cater dinner or supper for parties, societies, organizations, etc., "at the shortest notice, and upon the most reasonable terms." After Charleston suffered the major fire of 1861 that destroyed a large section of the city, including Institute Hall and the adjacent buildings, Fehrenbach opened a "bar room" in 1866 on the corner of one of the city's most-frequented intersections.[14]

*Restauranteur Nicholas Fehrenbach Jr.'s "Teetotal" establishment next to the South Carolina Institute Hall, where the Ordinance of Secession was signed in December, 1860. Both were lost in the fire of 1861 that destroyed more than five hundred acres of the city.*

---

14. The *Charleston Daily News* of April 17, 1866 congratulated him on re-establishing his business: "... we are satisfied he will furnish to his friends and the public refreshments of all kinds, in his own peculiar and elegant style."

Nicholas Fehrenbach Jr. and his wife had four children: Ida Juliana (b. 1857), Clarence Nicholas (b. 1859), Edwin Nicholas (b. 1860), and after almost a decade, another daughter, Linda (b. 1869). We will learn more about Nicholas Fehrenbach in a later chapter in connection with another immigrant's story. At this point, it can be acknowledged that the Fehrenbach family had achieved some notice in the Charleston German immigrant community. As noted earlier, it was in the Fehrenbach home that the well-known ship captain, Heinrich Wieting, died in 1868. It was not entirely coincidental that the man who brought so many Germans to Charleston was "hospitalized" in the home of a fellow Geestendorfer in the ethnic community.

The 1870 census shows the household of Nicholas, aged 36, owner of a bar-room; Johanna A., aged 38, keeping house; Ida, aged 12; Linda, aged 6; William, Nicholas Jr.'s brother born in Wisconsin, aged 19, a clerk in a store; and Anna, aged 67, "at home." [15] The household at that time included three others, two of whom are listed as domestic servants, one black, the other a native of Bremen. The family lived in Charleston's Ward 1, where they were neighbors of the Danish Consul, C. Wunderlich. Nicholas was sufficiently established that he could buy pew No. 49 (Nos. 1-84 were sold either as a whole or half) in the new St. Matthew's German Lutheran Church in 1872, and church records indicate that his mother, Mrs. M. Fehrenbach, gifted the church a brass baptismal bowl.[16] Nicholas Jr. survived his friend Wieting's death by twenty-three years, dying in Charleston in 1891, aged fifty-eight. His occupation at that time was given as "Planter," the rather generic census designation for a household head of some means. The couple's daughter, Ida, was married in Wisconsin—where her grandparents and father had lived—in 1877. The younger daughter, Linda, would marry a New Yorker and live in Hartford, Connecticut, where in the 1900 census the household included both Linda's mother and her elder sister, Ida. Nicholas's widow outlived him by twelve years. She died in Hartford in 1903 but is buried in the family plot in Charleston's Bethany Cemetery along with her husband, Nicholas, their daughter Ida, and the couple's two young sons. At some point after the death

15. The two sons born in 1859 and 1860 died before the age of two.

16. Winnie J.M. Butt, *100 Years of Christian Life and Service, St. Matthew's Lutheran Church, 1840-1940* (Charleston, SC: St. Matthew's Evangelical Lutheran Church, 1940).

of her mother, Linda and her husband moved to Jacksonville, Florida, where Linda died in 1925.

It is clear that the second and third generations of Fehrenbachs moved far beyond the family's immigrant beginnings in Charleston in the early 1830s. Nicholas Jr.'s parents' experience articulates the hardships experienced by an immigrant family that was able to establish a degree of success only in the second generation. The senior Fehrenbachs would not have been inclined to encourage others to come and enjoy the good life in Charleston. Their American existence was a struggle from beginning to end, their story similar to those of other first-generation immigrants who managed to eke out an existence in Charleston that fell far short of the expectations they brought with them.

## —HERMANN KNEE AND FAMILY

Other members of the Rosenbohm family had more luck, or managed to make their mark by different means. Johann's sister Catharina had married Hermann Knie,[17] a native of the small Lower Saxony town of Bockel, in 1834. The couple immigrated to Charleston shortly thereafter, and their children were all born in Charleston: Johann in 1836, Julia in 1841, Hermann Carsten in 1844, Nicolaus Heinrich in 1846, Friederich Eduard in 1847, and finally, Clarence Andreas in 1851. The three youngest boys died in infancy, so that by 1850 the census shows the household consisting of Hermann, aged 47, Catherina, aged 34, with children John, aged 14, Julia, aged 9, and Hermann, aged 7. By the time the census was taken, Hermann Knee Sr. was head of a large household domiciled in the house he had acquired at auction in 1845 from his brother-in-law, Johann Rosenbohm. In addition to his wife and children, the household included Catharina's father, Caspar, aged 75, Catherina's widowed sister, Adelheid Bequest, aged 40, as well as Adelheid's sixteen-year-old daughter, Adeline, plus the man she would marry, Frederick Schroeder, aged 27. Hermann is listed as a "shop keeper" with real estate valued at $3,000.

Hermann Knee demonstrably managed the transition to his adopted community better than his brother-in-law Nicholas Fehrenbach. There are seventeen

---

17. Once in Charleston, the spelling of the surname was changed to *Knee*, although likely still pronounced as '*kni*.

transactions under his name recorded in the Register of Mesne Conveyance in Charleston between the years 1845 and 1878, indicating that little grass grew under his feet from the time he arrived until he died. An active player in the German community, he was accepted into the German Friendly Society in 1836. He was a contemporary of the dynamic John Andreas Wagener and worked with him as a founding member of the German Evangelical St. Matthew's Church in 1840. Knee was apparently a stabilizing force for his extended family, providing, for example, the means for his sister-in-law Anna Maria Fehrenbach to support her family while her husband was seeking his fortune in New Orleans. He was a vital member of the Lutheran church community and a key advocate for establishing a German community in Walhalla, South Carolina, which Wagener and the St. Matthew's congregation organized for settlement by the increasing numbers of German immigrants to Charleston. Knee was one of four committee members sent in 1849 to examine the lands of Colonel Joseph Grisham in up-state Pickens District that the German Colonization Society had negotiated to purchase. He was sufficiently sold on the idea of Walhalla that he left Charleston and was one of the first to purchase land in the new town and establish a business there. In 1856 he was elected as a warden for the town after its incorporation by the South Carolina Legislature the previous year. Benefitting from advantageous connections to other immigrant leaders, Herman and Catharina Knee were able to make a life for themselves that justified their earlier decision to emigrate. Their emigration to Charleston and subsequent involvement in establishing the up-state Lutheran community—true "pioneers" as it were—can rightfully be described as a success story.

## —FREDERICK and ADELINE SCHROEDER

As noted above, the 1850 Census showed Hermann Knee housing his wife's elder sister, Adelheid Bequest née Rosenbohm, her daughter, Adeline, and the latter's fiancé, Frederick Eduard Schroeder. The young couple were married at St. Matthew's German Lutheran Church in 1852. Five children were born to them in the decade between 1853 and 1863. Only one of the children, their son Julius—born in the first year of the Civil War—would survive to adulthood. Frederick was a native of the village of Ovelgönne bei Brake, not far from

Geestendorf, where Adeline was born. The couple had undoubtedly met and planned their future prior to their emigration: the bachelor Frederick followed Adeline and her mother to Charleston, where the Bequest mother and daughter had family connections.

The Schroeders' story is not particularly remarkable, and in that sense it can be viewed as an example of an immigrant's success in establishing a business and sustaining it in the face of the vicissitudes that Charleston offered. After their marriage, Frederick set himself up as a merchant selling imported cigars and other tobacco products. As a family, the couple would lose four of their five children, all during the turbulent decade leading up to the Civil War when Charleston was a hotbed of political unrest. The circumstances they would face were distinctly not what they had anticipated a decade earlier when they left their North German villages to come to America.

The couple made their start at a time when there was already anti-immigrant sentiment in the air. As previously noted, many nativist Charlestonians were dubious about working-class immigrants, suspecting them of inciting unrest by virtue of their alleged abolitionist sentiments, somehow "disturbers of the peace." White workers, both male and female, created competition with hired-out slaves, and threatened the city's economic foundations.[18] As the owner of a cigar business, however, Frederick Schroeder would not have been considered a "working-class" immigrant, nor someone who would likely disturb the peace. His choice of occupation would not have put him in competition with any of the city's free blacks, but represented instead, the immigrant's effort to find a niche position in a uniquely constrained labor market.

Nonetheless, there were other cultural and social challenges that confronted the immigrant couple. Even before they were married, the United States declared war on Mexico, and the ensuing arguments about permitting or banning slavery in the territories acquired during the war swept the matter of slavery from under the rug into the political arena. The prevailing edginess among the white population with regard to the enslaved among them was in evidence in 1849, when a number of black inmates escaped from the workhouse. Although most were caught and then hanged, a few escaped, with the result that "hysteria swept the city. A mob gathered before Calvary Church, a nearly completed Afro-American church ... that white Episcopalians in the

---

18. Fraser, *Charleston! Charleston!*, 227.

city were assisting in building. Some among the mob called it the "nigger church" and wanted to destroy it. Urging on "the rabble of the city" were prominent citizens who sought, one observer noted, "to arouse the fears of a community which had not forgotten the events of 1822."[19] Charleston's white citizens lived in fear of any place where free blacks and slaves could or would meet, such as the yet-to-be completed Calvary Church, concerned that such meetings would threaten the "public peace and order." Frederick Schroeder and Adeline Bequest and the city's other German immigrants counted as "white citizens," but were neither Charleston's "rabble" nor its "prominent citizens." Nonetheless, the immigrant would have had ample cause to wonder and worry about the "public peace and order" in racially divided Charleston.

While living in the Knee household in 1850, the soon-to-be-married couple likely witnessed the ceremonial funeral in Charleston of South Carolina's John C. Calhoun on April 25-26, what Fraser calls "perhaps the most elaborate ceremony of its kind the city ever witnessed." Calhoun had been the state's most vocal advocate of nullification, an issue and a cause that would re-ignite the coals of secession before the end of the decade. His funeral involved almost everyone in the city, either as spectator or participant, including members of both the older and the more-recently-formed German fraternal or civic organizations. The cultural context that Charleston offered at this time could be described as "complicated," and it would likely have been unsettling to any recently-arrived German immigrant trying to get a footing in the city. Only those in the ethnic community who were completely acculturated could participate enthusiastically in civic ceremonies such as the one arranged for Calhoun's funeral. The more recent immigrant would be challenged to figure out what these frequent crowd-scenes really meant.

From another perspective, this was a time when some of Charleston's residents appeared to be oblivious of internal dissention. The elite classes were visibly enjoying themselves, with parties in grand houses and strolls along the waterfront, while the northern extent of the peninsula—the recently incorporated "Neck"—was occupied by the less fortunate, among them, many of the German immigrants. It was nonetheless during this period prior to the outbreak of the Civil War that two books were published that commanded the attention of the public in both the North and the South: Harriet Beecher

---

19. Fraser, 228. The "events of 1822" is a reference to the Denmark Vesey uprising.

Stowe's *Uncle Tom's Cabin* and the *The Pro-Slavery Argument*. The former was the classic attack on slavery, the latter, its classic defense. *The Pro-Slavery Argument* contained essays by prominent Southerners quoting Aristotle, the Bible, and purported scientific evidence proving that blacks were inherently inferior. *The Pro-Slavery Argument* was published in Charleston. [20]

As if the political turmoil in the air were not sufficiently stressful, "in the summer of 1854 a hurricane lashed through the city, flooding the streets, and yellow-fever-carrying mosquitoes returned bringing a virulent epidemic. While the disease raged in the city during the late summer, the Charleston press advised that 'no real dangers exist' ... but from mid-August to mid-November 627 persons died."[21] The Schroeder newlyweds might well have thought they would have experienced fewer traumas had they stayed in their Hanoverian homeland, where hurricanes and yellow fever would not have threatened to destroy them or their young daughter.

After the mid-1850s, just when the Schroeder couple was beginning married life as immigrant residents, Charleston began to suffer an economic downturn. According to Fraser, the number of inmates in Charleston's Poor House doubled, where the ratio of foreign-born to native was seven to one. "Class divisions became as obvious as racial divisions. Economically most whites living in the city had more in common with blacks than with the white elite."[22]

By the late 1850s, Charleston's leaders were making a concerted effort to clean up the city. A significant amount of money was spent in beautifying certain sections, although nothing seemed to cure the city of the yellow fever pestilence. That little-understood fever was likely responsible for the death of some of the Schroeder children. Frederick Law Olmstead claimed in 1860 that Charleston had "the worst climate for unacculturated whites of any town in the United States."[23] And by the time the war was imminent, Charleston had come to resemble a military garrison—a state of defensiveness to which the uniform-prone German immigrants had possibly contributed: Frederick Law

---

20. *The Pro-slavery argument, as maintained by the most distinguished writers of the Southern States /containing the several essays on the subject of Chancellor Harper, Governor Hammond, Dr. Simms, and Professor Dew* (Charleston: Walker, Richards & Co, 1852).

21. Fraser, 233-34.

22. Fraser, 235.

23. Quoted in Fraser, 240.

Olmstead observed that "the cannon in position on the parade ground, the citadel … with its martial ceremonies, the frequent parades of militia … the numerous armed police, might lead one to imagine that the town was in a state of siege or revolution."[24]

It was during these times that Captain Wieting was unloading literally *boatloads* of German immigrants onto the wharves in Charleston, the large numbers of newcomers causing some degree of tension with the native whites and their slave labor force. For the most part, however, the Schroeders and their German neighbors living in the unsettled and ever-changing Charleston scene kept their heads down and minded their business. Frederick and Adeline possibly witnessed the first action in the Civil War—the bombardment of Fort Sumter in Charleston harbor—although that famous first shot would likely have been more worrisome for the immigrant than celebratory, as it was for the native-born. The couple had buried three children by 1860, and Adeline would have been pregnant with their fourth child during the critical months leading up the action in April of 1861. Julius Nicholas was born just two months later. Adeline herself would die in 1864 before the war was over.

On December 11, 1861, less than a year after the Ordinance of Secession had been signed, one of Charleston's worst fires swept through the city, destroying a substantial portion of the lower city. The fire spread from Charleston's eastern to its western edge consuming the Circular Congregational Church, St. Andrews Hall on Broad Street, where secession had been debated and enacted, and Institute Hall on Meeting Street, where the Ordinance of Secession had been signed. More than five hundred homes (mostly wooden) were lost to the flames.

At the time of the great fire, Frederick Schroeder's cigar importing business was located in the section of the city devastated by the fire. Having to relocate the business during the early years of the Civil War would have seemed like yet another blow to the family's personal and business life, just another test of the Schroeder couple's immigrant fortitude. The fire had similarly tested Nicholas Fehrenbach, Jr. and his family.

Ever since their marriage in 1852, the Schroeder couple belonged to the St. Matthew's Lutheran congregation. Frederick served early on as financial secretary to the Church. He, like Nicholas Fehrenbach Jr., was among the

---

24. Fraser, 241.

original pew holders when the newly built church's pews were sold to members of the congregation in 1872. The 1900 census shows him heading a household consisting of his son Julius and his wife and their four children between the ages of five and ten. The census record confirmed that Frederick Schroeder had immigrated to Charleston in 1849 and had lived in the city for fifty-one years, by which point he would have been considered a seasoned German-Charlestonian. When he died a widower in 1901, he was living at the same address where he had lived for many years with his mother-in-law, Adelheid, who had died six years earlier in 1895. The entire family is buried in Bethany Cemetery in a prominent plot close to the cemetery's entrance gate and not too far distant from the grave site of Captain Heinrich Wieting, who likely brought them to Charleston. A laurel crown sits atop a broken obelisk marking the grave of Adeline.

## —THE WEBERS

Two Neudeutsch immigrant brothers by the name of Weber came to Charleston in the 1840s, but not from the environs of Bremen like the majority of the city's other recent immigrants. Both Johann (and wife, Friederike) and Peter (and wife, Susanne) Weber, belonged to the congregation of St. Matthew's German Lutheran Church. Church records indicate the two men were from the town of Billigheim in the southern German state of Bavaria. Although the south was a predominantly Catholic area, the brothers were both Protestants. Like everyone in that region, they would have been subject to the emigration stimuli of overpopulation, land partibility and unemployment that characterized the *push* for emigration in the southern German states in the early decades of the nineteenth century.

The outline of the life led by the immigrant Johann and his wife is delineated in the St. Matthew's records and in Charleston city directories. The church record indicates that Friederike was indeed a North German from the small village of Wulsdorf, in the vicinity of Geestendorf. She and Johann were married at St. Matthew's in 1844, shortly after their immigration to Charleston. Coming from two widely separated regions in Germany, it is doubtful that they were acquainted prior to emigration, rather that they were singles who met after arriving in Charleston. Friederike, like many from the closely connected region in northwestern Hanover, was doubtless following a pre-established chain of acquaintances or relatives. Johann was following his brother Peter. The younger Peter Weber and his wife had their first child in Charleston before Johann and Friederike became parents: the latter couple's daughter, Susanna Elisabeth, was born March 1, 1845, and baptized at St. Matthew's with Peter and Susanne Weber as godparents, already resident in the community.

Johann Weber worked in Charleston as a boot- and shoemaker. St. Matthew's records indicate that a daughter born in 1845 died in July 1846, just a little over 16 months old, and that a son, Johann Heinrich, born at the end of March 1846, had lived only five days. The 1850 census shows the household consisting only of John Weber, aged 38, Friederika, aged 26, and twenty-five year-old C. Muller Weber, another shoemaker from Germany.[25] The 1860 census lists a bootmaker John Webber [*sic*], aged 49, and his wife, aged 35, with two children, John, 4, and Virginia, a 3-month-old infant—both parents born in Germany, the children in South Carolina.

The couple had a second son, Louis Conrad, born in 1869 when Johann was in his late fifties. Johann Weber died in 1872. The Charleston city directory for 1874-75 indicates that Friederike was managing by selling "fruits," with her elder son John employed as a clerk. Four years later, "Mrs. Frederica Weber" was still dealing in "fruits" and John still employed as a clerk and boarding with his mother. By 1881, Frederica had expanded her business somewhat and was selling "varieties." The following year, she was operating a "variety store." John was still a clerk and living at home with his mother and younger brother.

This family's story sounds typically unremarkable: an eked-out existence, acculturation during Charleston's sometimes glorious, sometimes troubled, antebellum times, survival during the years of the Civil War, a husband and wife with two sons (the daughter Virginia died shortly after the war), muddling through the years of Reconstruction before disappearing from the scene in the fog of Charleston's postbellum period. Coincidentally, the Johann Webers had begun their Charleston life in the same year that Anna Maria Fehrenbach, deserted by her husband, had pleaded for assistance from the Charleston Orphan

---

25. Margaret Motes, *Migration to South Carolina. 1850 Census: from England, Scotland, Germany, Italy, France, Spain, Russia, Denmark, Sweden, and Switzerland* (Baltimore: Clearfield Press, 2005), 136-37.

House, and the Weber couple's first daughter was born into the St. Matthew's congregation in the same year Hermann Knee acquired the Rosenbohm house on Church Street. Both Weber families were doubtless acquainted with those other members of the German community, but each family was dealing with life in Charleston in its own way.

Peter Weber's story is no more or less dynamic than his brother's. The St. Matthew's record for Peter shows six children born to him and Susanne. Unlike Friederike, Susanne was from a town within five miles from her husband's Billigheim, and unlike Johann and Friederike, Peter and Susanne—from neighboring villages—emigrated as a married couple. Their six children were baptized at St. Matthew's: Anna Maria (b. 1843), Martin (b. 1845), Elisabetha Susanna (b. 1848), Heinrich Wilhelm (b. 1850), Georg Karl (b. 1852) and August (b. 1855). The Charleston record for this family is otherwise rather sparse: the city directory for 1849 lists a Peter Webber [sic] at an address on Charleston's Queen Street. The city directories for 1852 and 1855 show Peter Weber employed as a tavern keeper at a different, but not-far-distant, address on the same street, residing there as well.

With whatever capital it took to open a tavern, the immigrant couple must have decided that there was a market among the increasing numbers of their fellow European newcomers who would need to quench the stresses of immigration in such a public house. There was something entrepreneurial in Peter's decision to open a tavern: in 1850 there were only some twenty-odd immigrants running taverns in Charleston; in contrast, his bootmaker brother, Johann, was one of about eighty such craftsmen shoeing the feet of the city's inhabitants.[26] Neither's occupation would lead to riches or social advancement.

Of the six children born to Peter and Susanne Weber between 1843 and 1855, only two survived to adulthood. The daughter Anna Maria would marry another German immigrant, Charles Plath, a year after the Civil War ended, and her younger brother Charles (Georg Karl) would follow the Fehrenbach boys into the Charleston Orphan House. Peter Weber was dead by 1856 and his wife by 1859. We can ponder how modestly they had survived economically by keeping a tavern, and how minimally successful they might have felt for seeing two of their six children through infancy. It would be up to the second generation to carry the Weber legacy forward.

---

26. Motes, *Migration to South Carolina*, 176-81.

The Charleston record indicates that Peter and Johann Weber never assumed any leadership role in the Charleston German community other than Peter's involvement in a number of ethnic associations. Their names are not listed among the pew holders at St. Matthew's, nor were they invited to join the German Friendly Society. They did not move to Walhalla, but held out in the Lowcountry until their respective ends—the one, fortunate in a way, to miss the imminent hostilities, the other, surviving through the war and halfway through the new order of Reconstruction. Both Webers' stories can be viewed as unremarkable, but not atypical of the German immigrant family in Charleston before the onset of the Civil War.

Those immigrants prone to dull their suffering with drink in taverns such as Peter Weber's—as was indeed the case with the senior Nicholas Fehrenbach— would soon draw the attention of participants in the national Know-Nothing movement, a nativist reaction to the increasing number of foreigners populating American cities. The movement disturbed the 1850s and was characterized by agitation for temperance, an intolerance of Catholics, and an ethic of extreme Puritanism. Michael Bell claims, however, that the Know-Nothings had little success in Charleston: "In the city election of November 1855, their candidates for mayor and city council seats were soundly defeated by candidates of the South States Rights Party. Their failure to secure even a single alderman's seat on the city council signaled the virtual end of the American party in Charleston." Additionally, Bell argues that Charleston's Germans were somewhat immune to what was happening within the larger American context: the city's citizens "were too tolerant of both Catholics and foreigners to be swayed into the nativist camp." As stated earlier, by the mid 1850s, the members of the German community were well on their way to being integrated with the native population that permitted them to exist as their ethnic selves as long as they behaved in a manner deemed appropriate.[27] They would deal with the demographics and rules that prevailed in the city that had taken them in.

---

27. Bell, "Hurrah . . . , 225.

# CHAPTER 3:

# THE PECULIAR INSTITUTION

T he *institution* of slavery that could have been considered *peculiar*[1] ever since the nation was founded had divided the United States into two opposing factions already in the 1820s. In the decades following the passage of the Missouri Compromise of 1820, the institution of slavery that existed in both the South and the North was never absent from the national political scene. Arguments about the institution's legal and moral legitimacy—its spread and acceptance into new territories as the country expanded westward, its critical role in the economy of the Southern states—all hung infectiously in the very air the nation's citizens breathed, until the opposing sides undertook to settle the matter by fighting the Civil War. Institutionalized slavery had roiled the surface of life in Charleston less during the colonial period than it would decades later, so that the Altdeutsch immigrant had been able to accommodate himself to it with fewer qualms. The nineteenth-century Neudeutsch

---

1. The term "peculiar institution" in reference to Southern slavery only came into vogue around 1830. In 1828, Calhoun had spoken of the "peculiar labor" of the South and in 1830, referred to slavery as the South's "peculiar domestick institution." (https://encyclopedia.com/history/dictionaries-thesauruses-pictures-and-press-releases/peculiar-institution)

immigrant in Charleston, however, would have to meet it head-on. As the South marched to secession in defense of slavery with South Carolina leading the way, Charleston became the wellspring of the dispute over slavery.

The few historians who have written on the German immigrants to Charleston suggest that the newcomers approved of slavery and were enthusiastic supporters of secession and the war effort of the Confederacy. Andrea Mehrländer writes: "The Germans of Charleston approved and supported the institution of slavery and swore absolute loyalty to their adopted home." She cites the fact that although by 1860 the number of slaveholders in the city had declined, 8.9% of the Germans in the city owned a total of 325 slaves, and that "in the case of secession, this clearly meant a decision in favor of leaving the Union."[2] Michael Bell sees "acceptance of the practice" in the fact that while "fewer of Charleston's German heads of household than Richmond's owned slaves (about 5 percent in 1860, down from 9 percent in 1850), they owned more of them (an average of 4.75 each)."[3]

Statistics such as these, however, are generalizations and warrant further investigation. Other historians have cautioned that "immigrant workers in the urban South cannot simply be incorporated into the extant understanding of the nature of Southern society, the evolution of slavery, or the character of antebellum politics. Instead they demand reconsideration of all."[4] Jeffery Strickland writes that "[w]hite southerners fought the Civil War to preserve slavery. The German Charlestonians' response to the Civil War was mixed, and most of the Germans who fought for the Confederate Army were not committed to a slave society."[5]

In evaluating the attitude and stance of the typical German immigrant in Charleston with regard to slavery prior to the Civil War, it is important to consider the basic quandary of the immigrant: he was *forced*, as it were, to navigate between the overweening racial prejudice of a society that sanctioned bondage and his own personal quest for independence, the latter an endeavor

---

2.  Mehrländer, *"With more freedom … ',"* 66.

3.  Bell, "Regional Identity in the Antebellum South: How German Immigrants became 'Good' Charlestonians," *The South Carolina Historical Magazine* 100, no. 1 (January 1999), 16.

4.  Berlin and Gutman, "Natives and Immigrants," 1200.

5.  "How the Germans Became White Southerners," 61.

that required, and was dependent on, individual freedom. In their study of the inherent tension between natives and immigrants, between free workingmen and slaves, historians Ira Berlin and Herbert Gutman capture the essence of that dilemma: "Men and women who had fled the landlord-dominated societies of Western Europe were hardly predisposed to sympathize with the planter class. Slavery remained the linchpin of the southern order, and the relationship of free workers to that institution continued to be ambiguous at best. Many were too newly arrived to understand it, and some found good reason to oppose it."[6]

As was proposed earlier, the situation in Charleston presented the nineteenth-century German immigrant with a context different than almost anywhere else. In her study of the Germans in Charleston, Richmond, and New Orleans during the Civil War period, Mehrländer argues that immigrants in these three southern cities exhibited different behaviors, such that the different metropolitan areas had in common only their location in the South. While much of the difference stemmed from the geographical location, economy, and character of the host city, just as much stemmed from the nature of the ethnic communities that settled in the respective locations. There is little doubt that the factors of location, economy, and civic character impacted the Germans in Charleston and to a large degree determined their behavior.

The concept of an ethnic German community's concentrated leadership guiding a homogeneous group of constituent followers leading a "settled and comfortable life" requires clarification. While generalizations might apply within a broad perspective, a more nuanced view will show that not all individuals fit the mold into which the general community is frequently poured. Within institutions founded for their benefit and welfare, with instructions from their own higher-ups, and daily reminders that they were guests in town, individual German immigrants to Charleston still had to deal with the inherent dichotomy between the fact of slavery and the ideal of freedom. Understanding this fundamental tension in the German immigrant's experience in Charleston goes a long way in explaining the ethnic conscience as frequently a troubled one. It explains how many of Charleston's German immigrants—while their group seemed to the outside world to behave somewhat differently than German immigrant groups elsewhere—might well have shared

---

6. Berlin and Gutman, "Natives and Immigrants," 1197.

the sentiments of those Germans who settled in the hill country of Texas and who were loath to subscribe to the idea of slavery, or those in the Midwestern and Middle-Atlantic states who were strong supporters of what was clearly a widespread and vocal antislavery campaign.

In 1859, abolitionist Frederick Douglass pronounced that "a German has only to be a German to be utterly opposed to slavery. In feeling, as well as in conviction and principle, they are antislavery." It can be argued, however, that Douglass ignored the fact that his estimation of the Germans was often contradicted by the actions of many German-Americans. A uniform German "antislavery conviction" was hardly ever evident in the politics of most of the German-American press; it was not often manifested in the subcultures within German ethnic communities; it was not obvious in the responses of many Germans to the conflicts that played out on the national stage, such as "Bleeding Kansas" and Harpers Ferry. "The substantial diversity of opinion manifested with the German-American population," Bruce Levine writes, "makes clear that, as Frederick Douglass knew, one actually needed to be more than simply 'a German' to be 'utterly opposed to slavery.'" It was primarily the "radical democrats" who had impressed Douglas and who were the strongest antislavery German-Americans—those who "traced their ideological ancestry back to the European Enlightenment by way of the eighteenth and nineteenth-century Age of Revolution." Such liberally radical democrats "opposed all forms of political privilege and inequality, championing instead the recognition and protection of universal human rights." Their aspirations were the result of what had been brewing in Europe for much of modern times and which emanated from those conditions that compelled so many to emigrate—conditions that were specific to Germany, as well as "ideological influences that were international in origin and circulation."

The kind of Germans that Douglass believed to have antislavery convictions and whom Levine describes as "radical" were in short supply in Charleston. As stated earlier, there were virtually no such *radical* democrats escaping the European "Age of Revolution" who settled in Charleston. As a consequence, hardly any of the Germans in the city would have assumed anything like a *radical* stance on any issue. If any one of them had harbored or overtly demonstrated *radical* thoughts regarding the South's peculiar institution, s/he would have been vulnerable as a lone voice in the wilderness. The Charleston immigrant from the more rural North German village, would nonetheless have similarly "aspired to a more stable and humane society governed by and in the interests of all actual producers." Like those elsewhere who were *radical* and/or *enlightened*, he would have aspired to be a member of a society "whose carefully monitored and regulated economy would safeguard ... the 'social freedom and independent existence' of each and a just and amicable coexistence among all."[7] No matter: in Charleston, the pressure of the native white culture would keep the ethnic community in line as it sought the approbation of the larger community. Therein lay the symbiotic relationship between the ethnic and the host community that appeared healthy and immune to disruption. We can easily understand, however, that while the ethnic group seemed in general to be aligned with the local cultural tradition of slavery, individual responses would have been varied: not just a few would have been bothered by the idea of humans as property and nagged by a heaping measure of doubt.

Among the individual immigrants examined in the previous chapter, Nicholas Fehrenbach Jr. owned slaves. The 1860 census slave schedule shows him in possession of five—a 58-year-old mulatto woman and a 45-year-old black male (possibly a couple) and three mulatto children, aged 8, 6, and 3. At this point in time, the two adults owned by a Charleston businessman would have been considered domestic servants, a class whose bondage as "house slave" seemed less offensive than that imposed on those who belonged to the plantation labor force. Nicholas Jr. was of true immigrant stock, but by 1860 he had become a German-Charlestonian in every sense of the hyphenated label. As a restauranteur/bar- and tavern-operator and well-known figure in the ethnic community, Fehrenbach appears to have had as few moral qualms about employing/owning domestic slaves as did any other Charlestonian who had means sufficient to do so. He did not inherit his slaves: these servants had been purchased. As the son of a struggling German immigrant family that had had to place two of its children in the Charleston Orphan House, he had used his proverbial bootstraps to pull himself up into the ranks of independent businessmen and was acculturating himself in the city's ways. That Nicholas Fehrenbach, Jr., of obvious immigrant background, had means to own and

---

7. Bruce Levine, "'Against All Slavery. Whether White or Black': German-Americans and the Irrepressible Conflict," in David McBride, Leroy Hopkins and C. Aisha Blackshire-Belay (eds.), *Crosscurrents, African Americans, Africa, and Germany in the Modern World* (Columbia: Camden House, 1998), 56-59.

employ servants from the existing labor pool—primarily slaves—in his home and/or in his business would have been considered a testament of his success. Fehrenbach Jr.'s uncle (by marriage), Hermann Knee, was also a slave owner— of a 45-year-old female, according to the 1860 slave schedule. His ownership of a domestic servant would have seemed entirely appropriate to his status in the Walhalla community, and her labor an expected and acceptable contribution to daily life in the pioneering household. Lastly, Frederick Schroeder, as another Charleston businessman, had at one point five slaves in his possession—doubtless justified through his proprietorship of the cigar store/import business and his membership in the merchant community.

But the overwhelming majority of Germans in Charleston did not own slaves, a fact that suggests that either their means were insufficient, or that they had an inherent distaste for holding bondsmen. In any case, an outside observer would conclude that, whether slave owner or not, most of antebellum Charleston's Germans were content to operate within their own, relatively small, backyards and not take issue with a host society dependent on slavery. A majority of them simply struggled to build and hold onto a life for their immediate family, to survive the odds that Charleston challenged them with. They understood themselves to be part of a minority community trying hard to align with the dominant population: most were inclined to acceptance because they had little choice; relatively few stepped conspicuously into the mainstream for what were obvious economic reasons. It was doubtless more than individual circumstances that distinguished the German slaveholder from the German who could not, or would not, participate in the peculiar institution.

The ambiguity with regard to slavery that was observable in the nationwide population of German immigrants seems to have manifested itself less in Charleston than in other urban—or rural—settings. There can be little doubt, nonetheless, that Charleston's immigrants were not so of one mind that the peculiar institution supporting the host community was accepted unconditionally and without qualm. The immigrant to the Lowcountry's pugnacious city was undeniably in a most peculiar predicament: the cards he had been dealt required demonstrated loyalty to a way of life that was foreign to the foreigner, and which commanded allegiance without dissent to principles that countermanded those that lay deep within him. When the Civil War became a reality in defense of the peculiar institution, the German, not-quite-yet-Charlestonian, would have further reason to search his soul.

# CHAPTER 4:

## IMMIGRANT FAMILIES DURING THE CIVIL WAR

t can be—and has been—argued that the *peculiar institution* lay at the heart of the composite social, political, and cultural construct of everyday life for most antebellum Southerners, but especially for South Carolinians, and most particularly for Charlestonians, both native and immigrant. The reality of the relationship between whites and blacks was admittedly different in South Carolina compared to any other Southern state, and there is no lack of opinion to explain how, in its defense of slavery, the state was moved to lead the efforts toward disunion, and why it was considered by the nation to be the hotbed of rebellion. For almost a decade, South Carolina's leading citizens and its legislators had waved the banner of secession and, unsatisfied with any mediating compromises, had moved inexorably toward independence and resumption of the state's "position among the nations of the world as a separate and independent State": it was to have "full power to levy war, conclude peace, contract alliances, establish commerce, and to do all other acts and things which independent States may of right do." As of December 20, 1860, the ordinance signed in Institute Hall made it official: "We, the People of the State of South Carolina, in Convention assembled, do declare and ordain ... that the union now subsisting between South Carolina and other States, under the name of 'The United States of America,' is hereby dissolved."[1]

As suggested earlier, the immigrant's attitude on the matter of slavery was an equivocal one. Led, pushed, and pulled by contending but influential forces, the non-native antebellum Charleston immigrant labored under the stress of a personal tension caused by his inheritance of different and less synonymous cultural values. In facing the "radical" idea of secession in defense of slavery, how easily could the immigrant accept the notion that what had been the beckoning, *United-through-revolution*-States—a *unified-by-trial* nation offering new hope, opportunity, freedom, and independence—should now be dismissed, broken up, by a host community persistently arguing a separatist and unproven ideology? Even if the immigrant mind could comprehend the superficial arguments, they would have been impossible to refute. The populace had been whipped into a kind of frenzy celebrating separation, ready to condemn anyone who might appear to disagree with the state's position. Ever since the immigrants had arrived during the earlier years of the century, what might have seemed like white noise in the background when the issue of nullification was first being discussed and disputed, had, by the time Lincoln was elected in 1860, been turned up to a deafening decibel level that no one could disregard. Indisputably *not* in control of what was happening, the immigrant might well have felt that the 1860 ordinance was a penultimate step that would surely bring darker times. While most South Carolinians had talked themselves into thinking that their defection from the Union would somehow be peacefully accommodated, most European immigrants would have thought it folly not to expect serious repercussions. They would have been sympathetic to the sentiment expressed by the elderly South Carolina statesman, Judge James Petrigru, who declared South Carolina "too small for a republic, and too large for a lunatic-asylum."[2] Over the months that followed, German immigrants would be condemned to sit by and watch how their newly adopted world would change.

---

1. *Declaration of the Immediate Causes which Induce and Justify the Secession of South Carolina from the Federal Union; and the Ordinance of Secession* (Charleston: Evans and Cogswell, 1860), 10.

2. Adam Goodheart, *1861: The Civil War Awakening*, (New York: Alfred A. Knopf, 2011), 12.

So many questions beg for answers. Did the Germans who were slave-holders believe, like John Andreas Wagener, that "the Negro must be ruled by force" and, if necessary, "with the help of the whip"?[3] Did they subscribe to the oligarchs' program to separate the state from the Union in order to maintain their *right* to own slaves? Did the Germans sense the heavy hand of the newly formed Confederate government when, through the Banishment Act of August 1861, it forced them to declare their loyalty to the Confederacy in order to remain in their new country—the *country* that overnight had rejected the one to which they had immigrated? What did they all feel when hostilities seemed to be on their very doorstep? The 1862 Battle of Secessionville on James Island was only ten miles away; by July of 1863, Union troops had taken Morris Island, and Rear Admiral John B. A. Dahlgren had demolished Fort Sumter; in August General Quincy A. Gillmore, "reinforced by 3,000 fresh troops, had begun installation of the famous 'Swamp Angel,' a powerful eight-inch cannon capable of hurling 200-pound shells into the heart of Charleston itself."[4] How strong was the sense of loyalty to a political and cultural entity that had been

---

3.   In a letter Wagener wrote to his former teacher in 1840, he expressed his personal stance with regard to slavery: "Dear teacher, concerning the blacks you are mistaken. You keep thinking the term Negro slave is an excuse for all poor and cruel treatment. This is not the case. The Negroes at the plantations live in neat, pleasant houses within families. They are treated well, as they deserve it. They are also nourished well, and they do not work half the time a worker does in Germany. During bad times the master is in charge; during good times they have plenty of everything. During sickness there is medical and good nursing. They do not worry about tomorrow. Old and ailing, they are still better off than the elderly in Germany. Looking at the blacks in New York or the northern states in general where they are free, everyone would agree that the slave in the South is much better off, happier, and morally a better human being than he is elsewhere. Man in general but especially the Negro can only be governed by force ... What else but force is it, if God or Nature gifted a person with the nobility of the soul that now dictates his actions, while others need to be forced by the use of the whip?" "'Turning My Joy Into Bitterness'; A Letter From John A. Wagener. Edited and translated by Gertha Reinert," *South Carolina Historical Magazine* 100, no. 1 (1999): 49-69.

4.   W. Stanley Hoole, "Charleston's Theatricals during the Tragic Decade, 1860-1869," *The Journal of Southern History* 11, no. 4 (1945): 540-41.

cultivated by the native whites and forced on the less acculturated newcomers? Did one question it, or accede to its demands?

Within a broader perspective, and as acknowledged previously, the trajectory of the individual immigrant's life was determined by the cultural forces that were in play on the municipal, regional, and national stages. On a personal level, the Charleston immigrant family would experience in its own way the political upheaval leading to secession and the subsequent military engagement between a confederacy of rebellious states and a federal government defending the constituency of the Union. How did these families manage the war years, how much of their immigrant selves came into play during the time that, quite literally, changed everything, and after which nothing would ever be the same? Where were immigrant family members in their lives when their adopted state decided to sever its relationship with the Union? How did they react to what became the new *law of the land*? How did they individually respond to being a resident of a *rebellious* state? What did they go through during Charleston's prolonged bombardment?[5]

The German immigrants whose stories have been examined in the preceding chapters had little choice but to weather the Civil War that began in the city where they had put down roots. Absent any surviving record that would give us their perspective on how their lives were shaped and affected during the war years, we must rely on a bare scaffolding of their biographies for any insight as to what the war meant for the typical German immigrant who had come to Charleston. Some stories are but meagre accounts; others have sufficient detail to make them significantly telling.

In the years immediately leading up to the war, the Peter Weber family was in the picture only through the couple's son Charles (Georg Karl) and daughter Anna Maria: both parents had died by 1859. In the Charleston Orphan House as of early 1862, Charles was evacuated from Charleston along with the other children to safer quarters in a small town to the northwest of the city (Orangeburg) for most of the war. He was under the protection of the orphanage when the fighting ceased and was released to his sister and brother-in-law in 1867. Charles's sister, Anna Maria, was a mature sixteen-year-old when

---

5. The bombardment has been described as "an instrument of terror to carry out the wanton destruction of private property and the persecution of a civilian population." Chris Phelps, *The Bombardment of Charleston 1863-1865*, (Gretna, LA: Pelican, 2002), 10.

her mother died in 1859. She experienced Charleston's turmoil all by herself, while her immigrant husband-to-be, Charles Plath, fought as a Confederate soldier. He survived the war, and he and Anna Maria Weber were married in 1866, the marriage recorded in the records of Charleston's St. Matthew's German Lutheran Church. The couple experienced the post-war decade of Reconstruction and the re-alignment of the threads of the social fabric. The 1880 census shows them with three children. In 1883, three years after the death of Anna Maria, the youngest daughter, Wihelmina, was placed in the Charleston Orphan House. She was released five years later to her uncle, Charles Weber—he who had earlier been released from the orphanage to Wilhelmina's parents. Practicing as a carpenter, Plath likely faced tough competition in the rebuilding of devastated Charleston in view of a reconstructed labor force and new rules. The three Plath children survived to adulthood; the widowed father disappeared from the civic record after 1885.

The shoemaker Johann Weber, like many fellow German-Charlestonians of his age, was too old to be called into Confederate service. He had taken his nephew Charles into his household after the death of the child's father, but had subsequently entered him into the Charleston Orphan House, likely because of the family's straitened circumstances. As was noted previously, the couple's daughter Virginia, born shortly before the war, died shortly after the war ended. The immigrant Johann survived the war on the home front, dying in 1872 at the height of post-war Reconstruction. After his death, his widow, together with the couple's young sons, eked out a tenuous existence. Despite their parents' hardscrabble lives, the couple's two sons carried the Johann Weber family well beyond the turn of the century: John Jr. lived until 1902, Louis, until 1940.

As would have been expected, each of the life stories of Johann Rosenbohm's three sisters who followed him to Charleston followed its own course during the war period. At home in the settlement in Walhalla, Catharina, married to Hermann Knee, was somewhat removed from the war-time unrest and conflict in Charleston. Successful as a grocer and respected in the German community, her husband had played an instrumental role in the creation and settlement of the up-state Lutheran community. After the colony's founding in 1850, the Knees had left Charleston to live among the newly-established community's founding families. As residents in Walhalla, the couple and their children were not among the crowds celebrating the signing of the Ordinance of Secession, nor among those watching the fireworks at Fort Sumter a few months later. While the senior Knees spent the war years in Walhalla, their two sons were in Confederate service. A pillar of that Lutheran community, Hermann died before the end of the decade. Catherina Knee was one of fourteen "widows of former members" to receive a $60.00 pension from Charleston's German Friendly Society. She survived the war by twenty years: her death was reported in Melchers's *Deutsche Zeitung* of June 29, 1885.

As early as September of 1861, Catharina Knee would have to worry about her two sons going off to war: John, aged 24, enrolled in Confederate service in August 1861, and his younger brother Hermann, only sixteen, was in by the middle of that December. Service records indicate that John signed up at Camp Pickens and belonged to one of ten companies of the First Regiment, South Carolina Rifles (Orr's Rifles). Those companies were organized in July of 1861 for three years or for the duration of war and comprised mostly recruits from the up-state counties of Abbeville, Anderson, Marion and Pickens. John's unit was initially stationed on Sullivan's Island and purportedly called "The Pound Cake Regiment" by the other troops because of its light duty. Then in April 1862, the regiment moved to Virginia with 1,000 men. Assigned to General Gregg's and McGowan's Brigade, the regiment fought with the army from the Seven Days' Battles to Cold Harbor. Later, it endured the hardships of the Petersburg trenches and the Appomattox operations.[6]

This eldest Knee son apparently had sufficient musical talent to serve as a *musician,* and was transferred in late 1861 "not from the company, but ... to the roll of the band which is kept by the adjutant and on which he is to be paid." Some musicians served as drummers, fifers, or buglers—performing such critical military functions as providing and keeping the cadence during a march, or communicating musically coded orders above the din of battle—but they were usually chosen from the youngest among the group. John's age and the unspecified nature of his assignment suggests that he was not one of the above, but performed his duty as an instrumentalist in the regimental band. In *The Life of Johnny Reb*, Bell Wiley notes that instrumental music served as an "important source of diversion" for the soldiers, providing "marching airs for drills" and occasionally giving concerts. General Robert E. Lee is reported

---

6. See http://sciway3.net/proctor/marion/military/wbts/OrrReg.html.

to have remarked, "I don't believe we can have an army without music."[7] If a regiment or company had an organized group of musicians, they were likely a somewhat protected entity, not soldiers who performed only when they could lay down their weapons: their function in relieving the stresses of battle was considered too important to the unit to allow them to be found among the wounded, dead, or missing.

To whatever degree his assignment in the band provided protection from the hail of musket fire and/or hand-to-hand combat, the musician John Knee survived in his lengthy service until the very end of the war. His service records indicate that he was on the list of prisoners of war "belonging to the Army of Northern Virginia, who have been this day surrendered by General Robert E. Lee, C.S.A. commanding such army, to Lieut. Genl. U. S. Grant, commanding armies of the United States. Paroled at Appomattox Court House, April 9, 1865." Some seven months before that momentous day, he had been admitted to Jackson Hospital in Richmond suffering from hepatitis, but was later released to go back to his brigade. His service records do not indicate that he was otherwise wounded. The 1880 census lists him married to a woman from Tennessee eleven years his junior with no issue. He applied for a pension from the Confederacy in Sevier, Tennessee, suggesting that the couple lived in her home state after their marriage—not all that far from his home in Walhalla.

John's younger brother Hermann apparently did not possess comparable musical ability, and his service to the Confederacy took a different course. He enlisted four months after his older brother in Captain Wagener's Company, Co. A German Artillery, SC Light Artillery.[8] Wagener's Co. A was one of those engaged in the battle of Port Royal in November 1861. Hermann's unit was involved subsequently in the defense of Charleston harbor in August and September 1863, and was active during the bombardment of the city. Knee's rank varied from Private, to 1st Sergeant, to 2nd Sergeant, to 5th Sergeant: the first notation of his promotion to sergeant is dated February 1862.

---

7.   Bell Irvin Wiley, *The Life of Johnny Reb: The Common Soldier of the Confederacy* (Garden City, NY: Doubleday, 1971), 156-57.

8.   This was the same company in which Anna Maria Weber's fiancé, Charles Plath, had enlisted. It was under the command of Friedrich Wilhelm Wagener, John Andreas Wagener's brother.

Hermann Knee's records do not indicate exactly where he was at any point during the siege of Charleston harbor—whether on Sullivan's Island, or on Morris, at which battery, or the nature of the skirmishes in which he undoubtedly participated. The records nonetheless show him as "present" from the time of his enlistment to the last week in December 1863. In the November-December 1863 record, however, he is "absent; absent without leave since December 24, 1863," and the January-February 1864 record indicates that he was "last paid" October 31, 1863, with the additional notation: "Deserted December 25, 1863." His final service record reads: "Oath of Allegiance to US, subscribed and sworn to at Chattanooga, Tenn, March 14, 1864. Place of residence: Pickens Co, SC; Complexion: dark; hair, brown; Eyes, blue; height, 5 ft. 9 in."

In her seminal work on the topic of desertion by soldiers on both sides of the Civil War, Ella Lonn cautions that "there can be no cause so just or beloved that war in its behalf will not be attended by desertion among its defenders ... The fires of patriotism burn more brightly at the outbreak of war than towards its close. Men at the beginning of the struggle are more oblivious of personal discomfort, less selfish than they become as the struggle progresses, and more willing to contribute in all ways to the expected victory."[9] The reason for Hermann Knee's desertion on Christmas Day, 1863, remains a matter of conjecture. It is entirely possible that after two years of service—particularly at a point when the *cause* held anything but a bright future—this son of German immigrants felt that there was little point in his suffering further for the "burning" American question of states' rights. While he had not been conscripted, he was a sufficiently *foreign* enlistee to wonder just why and for what purpose he was a participant "at the gate of Hell," fighting for reasons he had barely lived long enough to comprehend. Among the many factors that contributed to desertion in the Confederacy, Lonn writes of one that may have held particular relevance for Knee: "Men sincerely believed that they had a kind of right to serve in certain localities—usually near their homes, and were averse to being transferred to other points. Numerous desertions followed the transfer of some troops to the Army of Virginia in 1863."[10] Knee's record for the period September-October 1863, three months prior to his desertion, indicates

---

9. Ella Lonn, *Desertion during the Civil War* (New York: The Century Co., 1928), 5-6.
10. Ibid., 16.

"transferred from Co. A, 20 Reg SC V[olunteers], October 10, 1863." This would have been shortly after the end point of the fifty-eight-day battle over Charleston harbor, when "the war—along with public attention—moved on to the more dynamic campaigns in Virginia, Tennessee, and Georgia."[11] At this point, Knee could have despaired of continuing on in the war farther removed from his home in South Carolina and his parents in Walhalla. Additionally, as Lonn explains, "speculation and extortion … were rampant throughout the Confederacy in the months of 1863 and were resented as the cause of military disasters on the ground." The situation in which the army was not adequately supplied nor the camps provided with requisite stores was loudly condemned in the press and by public officials and private citizens. The corruption and confusion provoked a kind of mutiny among the troops, who held it intolerable that they were victims of the greed of the very men for whom they were fighting.[12]

While such conditions would have negatively affected any soldier, they would have hit harder the second-generation Lutheran son, whose parents had raised him in a pioneer Protestant home based on a moral righteousness that was still not fully attuned to the Southern way. And as a final straw, from 1863 on, "the element of discouragement and hopelessness of the struggle was added to the natural weariness from the strain of the long, bitterly fought war." Lonn writes that "mail bags captured by the United States officers showed already in 1863 that letters of Southern soldiers breathed but one sentiment—weariness of the war. Soldiers saw, despite desperate and heroic efforts, defeat everywhere, saw their toils and sufferings unproductive against apparently inexhaustible numbers."[13]

We need not make more of Hermann Knee's Christmas 1863 desertion, nor search for more plausible explanations for why he left. There is no further record beyond his taking the oath of allegiance to the Union from which his home state had seceded. It is doubtful that he was aware of what had become of his older brother: they served in different areas and would have found it difficult to maintain contact. Too many different factors would have affected their respective experiences and attitudes. If John's musical ability kept him alive to experience parole through surrender to the Union armies at Appomattox,

---

11. Phelps, *The Bombardment of Charleston*, 27.

12. Lonn, 17-18.

13. Ibid., 18.

Hermann's desertion and parole by swearing allegiance to the Union kept him alive until the war was over. Thus at the young—but mature—age of twenty-four, Hermann's name, along with that of his father, could be found among those of the white, free citizens of Walhalla on the Oconee and Pickens Counties 1868 Voter Registration list. Walhalla was still the home of the gods, certainly for those who had served and survived. The German-born Frau Knee doubtless despaired in 1861 at the thought of possibly losing two of her sons to the Confederate cause: she had indeed contributed to the Ladies' Gunboat Fund in the spring of 1862,[14] not because she was patriotic, but because she was the mother of two soldiers fighting a war in defense of someone else's cause. It was for the well-being of her sons that the German mother contributed, not for the Confederacy's purpose that would surely put them in harm's way. In 1864, she would have been relieved that at least one of her sons had returned home. That made it easier when, after the final surrender a year later, her other son exchanged his Walhalla home for one across the border in Tennessee. She could be proud that both had served in their fashion, and both were alive.

We recall that Johann Rosenbohm's sister Anna Maria Fehrenbach, with seven children and an out-of-work husband, was not having an easy time of it already by the mid-forties. She and her husband abandoned their attempt to gain a footing in Charleston and headed to the new (1848) state of Wisconsin. But life in Wisconsin turned out to be no more a bed of roses than existence in Charleston had been. As we know from the earlier account, the family broke apart in the 1850s and returned to Charleston, leaving the husband and father to fend for himself among Wisconsin's Germans. Back in Charleston before the war began, Anna Maria and her younger children were under the protection of her son Nicholas Jr., who had married in 1856 and by 1859 was running a successful restaurant operation. Nicholas Jr. and a younger brother would fight in the Confederacy, while their mother and siblings would make do with

---

14. Mehrländer suggests that *patriotism* was particularly strong among German women, citing the statistic that eleven German women from Walhalla contributed to South Carolina's "legendary Ladies' Gunboat Fund (to fund the gunboat *Palmetto State*), doing so not from public pressure, but "because they all had at least one male family member in the ranks of the Confederate army." *The Germans of Charleston, Richmond and New Orleans*, 219.

life on the home front and, once the war began, endure the consequences of secession and the hostilities that followed.

Records indicate that Nicholas Fehrenbach Jr. entered "state service" in November 1861 and served in that capacity for a little more than a month and a half. At that time, he was twenty-eight years old and head of the family. Married since 1856, by 1860 the son of immigrant parents and ex-ward of the Charleston Orphan House had rather quickly become a fairly successful businessman and was well placed to play an important role in the ethnic community. He was a founding member of Captain Cordes's Company of Cavalry, SC Militia, known as the "German Hussars."

When the Hussars were mustered into Confederate service, eleven of them took advantage of the conscription regulation allowing substitutes to serve in their place.[15] Although he was one of the unit's propertied members,[16] Fehrenbach did not initially offer a substitute. In late 1862, however, he offered as his substitute his younger brother Hermann, then just over seventeen years old. After the January 1863 consolidation of several cavalry companies, the records for Nicholas Fehrenbach consistently note his being "present" *by his substitute, H. H. Fehrenbach*. In August of 1863, N. Fehrenbach is listed as "absent without leave since August 10, 1863"—the date his brother Hermann enlisted in his own name after he turned eighteen. The participation of the Fehrenbach brothers in the war was likely not the result of the September 1862 Conscription Act (second), although the Act may have encouraged the re-enlistment of Hermann once he came of age, since it was still in effect in August of 1863.

Why did the elder Fehrenbach brother ultimately take advantage of the substitute policy? It could have been the case that the seventeen-year-old begged for a chance to be in the action. He had been born in Charleston, and at that point in his teens could have been caught up in the pro-secession political

---

15. Mehrländer has thoroughly researched and analyzed the members of the "German Hussars" militia unit. She notes that Cordes' company was "the only mounted antebellum militia of German immigrants in the South" about a third of whom owned real property and almost a fourth owned slaves. *The Germans of Charleston, Richmond, and New Orleans*, 171-72.

16. Mehrländer lists militia member Fehrenbach with $7,400 in real estate, $2,000 in personal property, two slaves, and taxes paid in 1859 of $149.00.

arguments and the initial enthusiasm for putting the North in its place. More likely, however, was the fact that as the older brother and head of the family, Nicholas felt an obligation to keep his mother and siblings supported by remaining at home and carrying on his business—he could hardly leave them unprotected to fend for themselves by some other means: there was not likely any other source of income. Besides, by the time Nicholas enlisted in February 1862, he had suffered the loss of his restaurant and his family's dwelling place in the fire that had burned much of the city the previous December. His personal and business life were in jeopardy and needed his attention. There is evidence, moreover, that Nicholas did not abandon "service" in the Confederate war effort: he was engaged in running the blockade, serving as a steward on the *Margaret and Jessie*, based in Wilmington, North Carolina—another Confederate coastal city heavily involved in defying the Atlantic blockade. On the *Margaret and Jessie*'s thirteenth and final voyage to Wilmington in early November 1863, with a mixed cargo valued at half-a-million dollars, along with eight passengers, and under the command of Charleston's "Captain Lockwood," the ship was captured by the USS *Fulton* and taken to New York. Most of the cargo was destroyed, and the passengers and crew were jailed.[17] The incident made the news in Charleston: both the *Charleston Courier* and the *Mercury* reported on November 16th that "Northern accounts state that the United States steamer *Fulton* reached New York on the 8th instant, having in tow as a prize the steamship *Margaret and Jessie*, from Nassau for Wilmington, N. C."

As it happened, the *Margaret and Jessie* was the property of the Charleston Importing and Exporting Company, an enterprise in which Nicholas Fehrenbach—as well as Frederick Schroeder—was invested, strongly suggesting that it was potential financial reward that inspired the businessman-on-the-make to be thus involved in the war effort. The profits made by such trading companies exporting cotton through Nassau to Europe and bringing in arms, munitions, everyday necessities, as well as luxury goods, were enormous: captains and crews were paid rates that made the risks involved seem minimal compared to the rewards. Confederate citizens captured by federal blockaders were prisoners-of-war and could be jailed—as indeed Fehrenbach was. After

---

17. Maxwell Clayton Orvin, *In South Carolina Waters* (Charleston: Nelsons' Southern Printing & Publishing Co, 1961), 52-53."

his release, Nicholas returned to Charleston and continued his career as restauranteur well into the post-war years.

Nicholas Fehrenbach's Company A had operated in the Port Royal area throughout 1862, primarily in scouting actions and protecting what were thought to be strategic locations, but reportedly did not actually engage enemy forces. The younger Hermann, in contrast, had a different experience in the same Company, which by January 1863 had been reorganized as Company D. In April 1863 the Company was stationed in St. Andrew's Parish and marched to the orders of General P. G. T. Beauregard. When the company moved to Ballouville, South Carolina, for September and October of 1863, Hermann was one of the Privates whose reconnaissance mission behind enemy lines was accorded special credit "for the manner in which their several Scouts and reconnoisances [sic] were conducted & for their boldness & courage." Again in November and December 1863, he received similar praise: "In this month [of] Dec., Lt. Smith, Privates Barton, Seile, Muirhead and Fehrenbach made several trips to Warren's Island. These officers and men deserve much praise for the gallant and valuable services they have thus rendered our cause."[18]

At his muster-in as his brother's substitute in February 1862, Hermann's horse was valued at $375, his equipment at $45. During the period July-August 1863 he was recorded as "absent; sick in hospital." For January and February 1864 he was "courier to Lt. J. Simons Jr., Judge Advocate," and in April of 1864 his Regiment was in Greensboro, North Carolina, on its way to Richmond. From April 30- August 31, 1864, the record shows him "absent; on horse detail." He had been detached to the horse infirmary at Stoney Creek, Virginia, where he was captured on December 1, 1864. He was sent to Point Lookout, Maryland, as a prisoner of war—an experience he likely never forgot: Point Lookout was a federal prison site that may have been only slightly better than the Confederacy's notorious Andersonville prison.

The younger Fehrenbach was fortunate that his stay at Point Lookout was not a long one. He was exchanged along with more than a thousand other soldiers on February 10, 1865. He was likely back in Charleston by April when at Appomattox the war ended. Having survived his war experiences, he too became a Charleston "restauranteur" and operated a tavern, just as his older

---

18. See http://ehistory.osu.edu/uscw/features/regimental/south_carolina/confederate/5thsccav/CoD.cfm

brother did. Neither brother seems to have had second thoughts about their military obligations to the city, the state, or the southern nation they now belonged to. It could be argued that whether out of duty, loyalty, economic gain, or just for the excitement of it all, the members of the immigrant Fehrenbach family were engaged in the defense of the City of Charleston, the State of South Carolina, and the now-defeated Confederacy. Their mother might well have thought her debt to the Charleston Orphan House, incurred years earlier in the name of two Fehrenbach siblings, had been repaid in full.

Johann Rosenbohm's third sister, the widowed Adelheid Bequest, experienced the march to secession, grieved over the premature death of her daughter, Adeline, and those of her daughter's children who died in their infancy. She managed to survive the assault on Charleston, and held on tenaciously during the unsettledness of the Reconstruction years. She lived until 1895, dying at the ripe age of eighty-six. During her years in Charleston, she lived close to, sometimes with, her daughter, married to Frederick Schroeder. After Adeline's death in 1864, she remained in her son-in-law's household, fulfilling her role as grandmother to the couple's surviving son and helpmeet to her widowed son-in-law.

Frederick Schroeder escaped the net of the first Confederate Conscription Act in 1862 that trawled for enlistees between the ages of eighteen and thirty-five: he was aged thirty-nine in 1862. Having served in the Palmetto Riflemen Company in 1858, he was exempt as a member of a State militia from the second Conscription Act of 1862 that extended the age limit to forty-five, as well as the third Act (age extended to fifty) of 1864. Although not as a Confederate soldier in uniform, Frederick Schroeder experienced first-hand the results of South Carolina's secession, a war he would never have anticipated when he first set foot in Charleston in 1849.

The Schroeder story reveals that a number of businessmen in the German immigrant community participated during the Civil War in the black market and benefitted from the blockade-running enterprise that sustained every-day and mercantile life in a city and country under siege. Records indicate that Frederick Schroeder was one of the Charleston merchants who invested in William Bee's Importing and Exporting Company—one of the five trading companies that were incorporated in South Carolina in 1862-63 for the purpose of defeating the blockade. Mehrländer examines the Bee Company and its investors extensively, particularly the German ones. Her analysis indicates that slightly more than ten percent of the Bee shareholders were German business-men, most of them grocers or dealers in dry goods or spirits. Their combined investment amounted to $79.000, indicating the considerable amount of community wealth controlled by Bee's German investors. Mehrländer states that the German firms' investment in Bee's blockade-running operation "increased their prewar total fortunes by 147.6% to $711,000."[19]

It was also true that Investing funds in blockade-running had the *appearance* of patriotism: the Confederacy urgently needed to import weapons and ammunition, and the cotton piled on Charleston's wharves needed to be sold to Europe, where, if it made it through the blockade, it could be sold at considerable profit. It is safe to assume that German investors took the risks inherent in participating in the efforts to escape the Union's hold more in the interest of the profit they could reap than in demonstrating patriotism to the government they were just getting used to. In Schroeder's case, Mehrländer reports that his investment with Bee was one share valued at $1,000, making him a relatively small player in this game. He was nonetheless a successful businessman and belonged at the time to what would have been considered the comfortable merchant class. He had every reason to want to increase his financial base. He had, after all, invested in his adoptive city and state, and the Union blockade now threatened both entities, as well as his financial footing. The fact that he held a number of enslaved domestics may have affected his sense of loyalty or patriotism to a government intent on defending that kind of property—a government the immigrant had little choice but to accept. It is safe to assume, however, that Schroeder took the risk of investing in Bee's company more for financial gain rather than to demonstrate support for the new government's resistance to the blockade. Havana cigars would have been considered luxury goods, and importing them through the blockade would hardly have been viewed as supportive of the Confederate war effort.

Frederick Schroeder's involvement with Bee's I & E Company demonstrates that members of the German immigrant community were determined to carry on their personal and business lives during the war in Charleston, despite the city's vulnerability. After his wife's death, the widower made every effort to maintain his business in imported cigars, stay connected to the

---

19. For the extensive analysis of the Bee operation, see Mehrländer, *The Germans of Charleston, Richmond and New Orleans,* 219-33.

German ethnic community, weather the throes of Reconstruction, and experience all the ups and downs of the post-war decades. Like Hermann Knee and his wife's cousin, Nicholas Fehrenbach Jr., Frederick Schroeder had become a respected member of the German Lutheran community, a community that, despite the tribulations of the war years, was determined to survive and prosper through the remaining years of the century. The Schroeder story, like that of numerous other, by-now-settled, North German immigrants, demonstrates the immigrant's successful maneuvering through a half century of Charleston life. When Schroeder died in 1901, he had been as determined as any other acculturated German-Charlestonian to persevere. They all had had little choice but to move with the city as it experienced the changes that would come with Reconstruction, to be followed by the last, somewhat anticlimactic, decades of the century.

In general, it seems fair to say that even if the individual German immigrant had been of one mind with the secessionists, felt unconditionally threatened by the Yankee abolitionists, convinced that slavery was sanctioned by God and the natural way of things on earth, of staunch conviction that separation from the Union meant freedom to maintain the *status quo* under the aegis of a new government, the war as it came to Charleston might have changed his mind. After the excitement of taking Fort Sumter and initiating the hostilities, Charlestonians had few options other than to accept what came their way. "Troops came and went. Men from other Southern states who had never traveled more than a few miles from home now took up residence in military camps in and about the city. Fortifications were built all over the area; on James Island, on the Charleston neck, and on the islands around the city."[20] When the Union almost immediately blockaded the port city with warships, Charleston's economy was seriously threatened. The initial response was to run the blockade, and Charleston was transformed into a center of privateering. The blockade made life unpleasant for Southerners generally and for Charlestonians in particular. "Early in the war a merchant wrote that the 'blockade is still carried on and every article of consumption particularly in the way of groceries … [is] getting very high.'"[21] The numerous German grocers

---

20. Robert N. Rosen, *Confederate Charleston: An Illustrated History of the City and the People during the Civil War* (Columbia, SC: University of South Carolina Press, 1994), 78.

21. Ibid., 81.

would have questioned what they had done to deserve this state of affairs, but doubtless considered running the blockade a necessary undertaking on their behalf. Before long, federal forces occupied Port Royal, no more than fifty miles south of Charleston. General Lee was in town by November of 1861 for the purpose of getting defenses readied along the Georgia and South Carolina coasts. Despite Lee's efforts, the mood in Charleston was not a happy one. "Everything looks very dark and gloomy," Jacob Schirmer wrote in his diary in November 1861. "Our enemies appear to be increasing their forces all around us." Within a month, a depressed Schirmer confided: "There has not been any year of our life that has passed, that has been fraught with so many events which will ever be remembered and which should indelibly imprint on our minds the instability and uncertainty of all our hopes and expectations."[22] The acerbic Emma Holmes wrote: "The fiercest wrath and bitterest indignation are directed towards Charleston, by 'our dearly beloved brethren of the north.' They say 'the rebellion commenced where Charleston *is*, and shall *end*, where Charleston *was*.'" Other Charlestonians worried about the city they loved. In May 1862, Harriet Middleton commiserated with her cousin: "Do you not hope that Charleston may be saved. I don't mind our house but I can't bear to give up the old streets and buildings, and the churches. I feel such a strong personal love of the old place."[23] From a long-established Charleston family, Harriet Middleton could leave town for the safety of Flat Rock, North Carolina.[24] Her sentiments were undoubtedly shared by many of the old

---

22. Quoted in Rosen, 86. Schirmer was a member of a prominent family of German descent. A successful businessman, he was the treasurer of the German Friendly Society from 1838 to 1880 and served as president of St. John's Lutheran Church from 1855 to 1869. His registry of Charleston marriages and deaths, in addition to the personal journals he kept, are considered a remarkable record of daily life in Charleston. *South Carolina Historical Society, Schirmer family journals and registers, 1806-1929*, SCHS 1149.00, 1.

23. Holmes and Middleton quotes from Rosen, 85.

24. Many of the wealthier native-born families became refugees, leaving their plantations to wander throughout the state in search of safer places. That, of course, was not an option for most of the immigrants who lacked relatives located elsewhere, much less the financial wherewithal to pick up and leave where they had just settled. For the German Lutheran immigrant, Walhalla would have been the only option to escape the *hotbed of*

families who had inherited Charleston's charm and Southern ways. Immigrant residents, however, could hardly afford to feel quite so sentimental, literally or figuratively, about the old streets and buildings. They would have been worried about the roofs over their heads, whether or not they actually owned them. By the time the Civil War ended, everyone's world had changed.

With regard to the general ethnic community, a change in certain aspects of its character could be noticed already during the decade preceding the Civil War. According to Michael Bell, the number of the city's Germans was noticeably on the increase: "Family members of the German-born added another 1,106 persons to the German community, raising the size of the total German community in Charleston to 3,020 persons in 1860." In fact, the ethnic community was expanding "at twice the rate of the American-born whites in the city between 1850 and I860."[25] Bell accounts statistically for the changes in family structure, living arrangements, and occupational choice that occurred during the decade between 1850 and 1860. As stated previously, such changes indicate that by 1860 the community had come into its own and was recognized by the city's natives with considerable respect and admiration. The Germans were regarded, for the most part, as industrious, well-behaved, economically stable, and independent. "They filled niches in mercantile trades which had been opened for them by their early nineteenth century German predecessors, and began to expand into the skilled and semi-skilled trades by 1860, which was a new and competitive arena for them. German immigrants married into the native white community, and bought real and slave property when they had the means to do so."[26] They worked hard to acclimate themselves and to accommodate the host community's prejudices and social norms. A significant number of them, such as John Andreas Wagener and his younger brother, Frederick, rose to prominence as leaders in the civic community. The elder Wagener would serve a two-year term (1871-73) as the city's mayor.[27] His younger brother would become such a successful businessman that he would

---

*rebellion*—but only if one numbered among the few who had a welcoming relative or friend in the upstate refuge.

25. Bell, *"Hurrah . . ,* 148.

26. Ibid., 146.

27. Charleston had already been served by two German-American mayors, Jacob Mintzing (1840-42) and John Schnierle (1842-46 and 1850-52).

have a section of Charleston named after him. Like the larger host community, Charleston's German community, despite its ethnic homogeneity, comprised a large group of individuals who could be described as average and a smaller cadre of those who in time would earn distinction as leaders of one sort or another. If the two Wagener brothers and select others fully engaged the Charleston political scene, the typical German immigrant enjoyed a kind of anonymity by going about his own business and, for most at least, overcoming the odds that the city brought to bear. This amalgam in the ethnic community had lent a distinct and identifiable tone to Charleston's cultural, economic, and political life before the war started and would continue to do so long after the hostilities were over.

The four long years of the Civil War would test the resilience of Charleston's entire weary population. Some of the Germans, both first- and second-generation, would already consider themselves Charlestonians—with no advantage accorded by their ethnic heritage; others were still in the process of becoming German-American southerners. By the time the war ended at Appomattox, it had leveled the city's cultural playing field, and few survivors were any better off than their neighbor, whether of immigrant or of native background. The entire Charleston community would have sensed that everybody had lost something, that almost everybody had lost someone. Most of those who survived the war years had to start again from scratch, even those who before the war had amassed something like a fortune. Some of the city's older German-born immigrants, despite their long struggle, would die just short of impoverishment. Others would witness their homes and businesses affected by both natural and man-made disasters that transformed the city into something more derelict than they would have expected. After the war, those who carried on would be altered to some degree by participating, willingly or not, in the efforts of the emancipated to right the wrongs of the past. Each actively or passively would become a citizen of a redeemed South once they had experienced the upcoming decade of societal changes brought about by Reconstruction.

# CHAPTER 5:

## INTO THE TWENTIETH CENTURY WITH THREE BROTHERS

A decline in immigration had started already in the late 1850s, and the Civil War in the United States had stifled both the number of immigrants and decreased the percentage of those immigrants from German lands choosing America as a destination. Nonetheless, three of Adelheid Bequest's nephews, sons of her late husband's brother Ludwig, would follow on the chain from North Germany to Charleston. The four Bequests would give the rather non-German-sounding name a substantive presence in Charleston's German ethnic community. The first of the three Bequest brothers risked a late departure from Bremerhaven to arrive just as the firing on Fort Sumter signaled the beginning of the war. Seeking his fortune and, it seems, not quite ready to take up residence in Charleston, this young German emigrant immediately took advantage of the Confederacy's war effort to work as a blockade-runner.

According to an account in a volume on Confederate military history authored by a former Confederate Brigadier-General, young Bernhard Bequest "took to the sea" as a teenager. When he arrived in Charleston "two weeks after the capture of Fort Sumter," that is, toward the end of April 1861, he was not yet seventeen years old. The *Gauss,* one of Captain Heinrich Wieting's ships, had departed Bremerhaven on March 14th carrying only eleven passengers—the few intrepid individuals willing to depart for Charleston in the face of reports of tinderbox conditions in the city after the state had seceded the previous December. There is no record of when the ship actually arrived nor a list of the passengers on board.[1] Given his age, however, it is likely that Bernhard Bequest got to Charleston as a member of the crew on Wieting's *Gauss.* According to the biographical sketch by the volume's author, Ellison Capers,[2] "the Confederate flag was flying," and it was only a few months later in 1861 that Bequest

> hid himself on the little blockade-running steamer, Ruby, and on revealing his presence after the boat was at sea, was put to work as coal-passer during the trip to Nassau. At that port he shipped on the blockade-runner Stonewall Jackson, Captain Black commanding, which on the first trip out was sighted and chased by the United States cruiser Tioga, and compelled to throw overboard part of her cargo and put back to Nassau. This unfortunate vessel at her next attempt to reach Charleston was fired upon and struck as she was crossing the bar, and run ashore, where she was burned with the cargo, young Bequest making his way thence to the city with the mail pouch. His next voyage was from Wilmington, and reaching Nassau he shipped on the Fanny, Captain Moore, with which he made four successful trips. Later he was on the Cyrene, but being taken sick at Nassau, he returned to his home in Germany in June, 1864, and remained until September, when he sailed to Nassau by way of New York, and made a trip into Wilmington on the Rosso Castle. Sailing again on the Watson, they reached the Wilmington bar in

---

1.   Passenger lists had earlier been published in the *Deutsche Zeitung,* but the newspaper was not published between 1861 and 1870.

2.   Ellison Capers, "South Carolina," Vol 5 of Clement A. Evans (ed.), *Confederate Military History: a Library of Confederate States History* (Atlanta: Confederate Publishing Co., 1899).

time to witness the terrific bombardment of Fort Fisher, upon the fall of which fort blockade-running came practically to an end. Returning to Nassau, he opened a small store and remained there until October, 1865.[3]

The young blockade-runner's story—so enthusiastically outlined by the Confederate Brigadier-General—together with the completely different life-stories of Bequest's two younger brothers who followed him to Charleston, demonstrate how the post-war ethnic community was evolving during the decades between the war's end and the turn of the century. The Bequest stories vividly portray the character of Charleston's acculturating German community during those times.

## —THE HONORABLE MERCHANT MAYOR

The Capers account that told of Bernhard Heinrich Bequest's blockade-running days suggests that the ex-Confederate was in awe of Bequest's youth and daring. In the course of his crewing on numerous blockade runners, Bernhard Bequest apparently made enough of a name for himself that he was more than an anonymous participant in the Confederacy's efforts to carry out its defiance of the Union blockade. Capers called it a "romantic story" and noted that the German native had begun a "seafaring life" at the age of fourteen. The escapades of Bequest as related by Capers are indeed impressive, even if only cursorily outlined. Each of the ships Capers claims Bequest worked on can be accounted for. The rescue of the mail pouch by young Bequest after the destruction of the *Stonewall Jackson* was noted in a report of the vessel's capture in the Richmond, Virginia, *Daily Dispatch*, with a "Charleston, April 12" (1863) dateline. Capers's *Rosso Castle* is more accurately the ship *Rothersay Castle*, his *Cyrene* is the long-serving *Syren*. The *Watson* was still at work in early 1865 when Wilmington's Fort Fisher fell in January. Maritime records show that the *Watson* sailed for Nassau mid-February 1865, possibly taking Bequest back to Nassau where he purportedly stayed until October of that year.

---

3. Ibid., 455.

The reality of Bequest's blockade-running was likely not all that *romantic*, and it was doubtless not the case that Bequest simply "took to the sea" with the wind behind him, looking for adventure. He came from a family of seafarers in Geestendorf who had for generations lived and worked the North German coast as sailors of one kind or another. His great-grandfather, a Frenchman, was known as a "navigateur"; his grandfather had at one time been employed as a ferryman and sailor; his father worked as a ship's carpenter, a boatman, a skipper, and as a ship pilot.[4] For certain, the sea was in his blood, but when he began his "seafaring life" at age fourteen it was likely because his father had died in 1859, aged thirty-nine. As the eldest of six children, Bernhard would have been expected to assume his position as the head of the family. But these were not the times—in North Germany nor in other German areas—for the younger generation to accept the expectations of tradition. After his father's death, opportunity for advancement in his native Geestendorf—which by this time had been incorporated into the city of Bremerhaven and become the main port of embarkation for emigrants from German lands—would have been overshadowed by the pull of opportunity in the United States, even if the country on the other side of the Atlantic seemed to be headed for fracture. Bequest was born almost a decade after the union of the Kingdom of Hanover with Britain had been dissolved (1837) and grew up during a period of revolutionary changes taking hold on the European continent. Though young in years, he may have been sufficiently prescient at age sixteen in 1861 to sense that before too long Prussia would press its heavy foot on his native soil, demand of its youth some obligatory service to its army, and turn the Hanoverian "Kingdom" into a province of the rising, militant, new European power.

That he should set out across the sea to arrive in Charleston in early 1861 had undoubtedly to do with the fact that he could make the crossing with a fellow Geestendorfer, the well-known immigrant mentor, Heinrich Wieting, plus the fact that he had family in Charleston where Wieting's ship was headed. Wieting's *Gauss* departed Bremerhaven *before* the firing on Fort Sumter, and the fact that it arrived after hostilities had begun was not anything that Wieting or the teen-ager could have planned for. If reports of conditions in the United States were to be believed, young Bequest had every reason to think

---

4. See Erika Friedrichs and Klaus Friedrichs, eds., *Das Familienbuch des Kirchspiels Geestendorf (heute Bremerhaven-Geestemünde), 1689 bis 1874,* Bd. 1 (2003), 47.

that time was running short for him to seize the day and take his chances like others had done before him.

The teenaged Bequest, of course, knew of the other family members already in Charleston—his Aunt Adelheid and his first cousin Adeline and her husband, Frederick Schroeder. Another extended-family connection in Charleston was a fellow Geestendorfer "cousin," Nicholas Fehrenbach Jr.[5] Nicholas was some ten years older than Bernhard, but they were of the same generation. A successful businessman when the war started, a known entity in the Charleston German community, head of his own family, Nicholas, as mentioned earlier, had re-joined the war effort by enlisting as steward on the blockade-runner *Margaret and Jessie*. It is unlikely that Nicholas Fehrenbach encouraged the younger Bernhard to risk involvement in blockade-running, since the former's service on the *Margaret and Jessie* occurred after Bequest had begun his adventurous career. In any case, the risks involved in running the blockade were less for the younger Bernhard than for Charleston-born Nicholas. Confederate citizens captured by federal blockaders were considered prisoners-of-war and could be jailed; the German teenager could not be apprehended in this way and if captured on a blockade-runner would be released.

Bequest continued to work as a blockade runner until virtually the end of the war. He had done quite well for himself on the Charleston-Nassau run and, according to the Capers account, had garnered sufficient financial means to start a business in Nassau. There is little doubt that the blockade-runner knew what he was doing beyond the challenges of the operation. Despite Capers's enthusiastic report that Bequest jumped at the chance to serve the Confederacy, there is every reason to doubt that the young German arrived with a sense of loyalty to the Confederacy, or that he developed one while working to supply it. For the mature teenager, it was more likely the challenge of the dangers involved and the opportunity for financial gain that outweighed any ideological drive to abet the South's rebellion. While the Confederate Brigadier-General might have wishfully thought it to be the case, it is hard to imagine why a young German would have felt compelled to defend the recently-seceded Southern state and its warmongers because of some romanticized patriotism. Bequest was working for himself and whatever ship's captain

---

5. Nicholas Fehrenbach was a first cousin to Bernhard Bequest's first cousin Adeline Bequest Schroeder.

he managed to sign on with. It was not incumbent upon this adventuresome German sailor to become a committed Confederate during the war in order to later become a German-American Charlestonian. That he did indeed become a German-American Charlestonian is confirmed toward the end of the brief biography by Capers. After noting that Bequest "opened a small store" and remained in Nassau until October of 1865, Capers concludes his account saying that Bequest "came to Charleston and engaged in business and planting at the town of Mount Pleasant, on the bay. Since 1885 he has conducted a successful business at Charleston, is a member of the German artillery, and has twice served as king of the German Rifle Club. By his marriage in 1866 he has a daughter living, Teresa L., wife of John Gishen, and by a later marriage he has one son, John F." Capers saw in Bernhard Bequest an adventuresome young German who made his mark on behalf of the defeated Confederacy, and who established himself after the war as a successful, upstanding, German businessman. This summary account by a Confederate Brigadier-General is a broad-brush outline of Bernhard Bequest's second-stage life in Charleston. In the following details, it will become evident that there is a lot more to the Bernhard Bequest story.

After living and operating a small business of an undisclosed nature in Nassau, Bequest decided to return to Charleston. If indeed he had gotten back to Nassau on the *Watson* in mid-February 1865, he would have been at sea when federal troops took both Charleston and Columbia. Only shortly thereafter, on April 14th, Major Robert Anderson raised the U.S. flag over Fort Sumter—four years to the day after he had surrendered in 1861. Two days later, President Lincoln was assassinated. Bequest, having just turned twenty-one, came to Charleston in October.

As the war moved into 1863-64, Bequest had apparently decided to abandon blockade-running and set up his business in Nassau, likely an undertaking that would be less directly, but no less profitably, connected to the blockade. His subsequent decision to forsake his Nassau business to settle in Charleston suggests that he wanted to find a more stable business environment and, as well, that he was responding to the pull of the chain that had been started by Johann Rosenbohm. He would opt for opportunity in Charleston rather than suffer the anticipated decline of conditions in Nassau once the war was over.

Although by late 1865 his Charleston first cousin, Adeline Schroeder, had died, his Aunt Adelheid was still there, as was Adeline's husband and a number of other individuals in the extended family. These individuals all belonged to the group that had originated in Geestendorf and its environs. Young Bequest understood that he was joining a community that had experienced the full force of the war and the turmoil that wracked Charleston, and the decision to come when he did suggests that he recognized the challenges he would face. It was doubtless a combination of his youth and a kind of immigrant courage that allowed him to appreciate that the realities of the ended war had substantively changed the character of the host city that he already knew. In the soon-to-be-reconstructed Southern city where his relatives and fellow-Geestendorfers had settled, there would nonetheless be sufficient opportunity for him to begin a new chapter in his life. The lure of opportunity, combined with the pull of the chain, would have outweighed any inclination to seek his fortune in another location. His relocation to Charleston signaled his intention to become a citizen of the United States—which at that point had not formally been re-united, and which had barely begun the process of healing—and to take advantage of the city's new beginnings.

Less than a year later, in February of 1866, Bequest married a Charleston immigrant (Gesine Rigbers) from a small town not far from his native Geestendorf at St. Matthew's German Lutheran Church. Nine months later, Bernhard's fifteen-year-old brother, Carsten August, joined the young couple's household. Five years later, in 1871, Bernhard's twenty-four-year-old younger brother, Johann Ludwig, who had immigrated to Baltimore in 1864, joined his two brothers to try make a go of it in Charleston. The chain between Geestendorf and Charleston had brought all three brothers to the South Carolina Lowcountry.

The city of Charleston right after the Civil War was a unique *host* community. In May of 1865 General Sherman had visited Charleston and written: "Anyone who is not satisfied with war should go and see Charleston, and he will pray louder and deeper than ever that the country may in the long future be spared any more war." Sidney Andrews, a journalist from Massachusetts who reported on conditions in the post-war South, began the first chapter of his *The South Since the War* with the words: "A city of ruins, of desolation, of vacant houses, of widowed women, of rotting wharves, of deserted warehouses, of weed-wild gardens, of miles of grass-grown streets, of acres of pitiful and voiceful barrenness, —that is Charleston ... Henceforth let us rest content in this faith; for here is enough of woe and want and ruin and ravage to satisfy the most insatiate heart, —enough of sore humiliation and bitter overthrow to appease the desire of the most vengeful spirit."[6]

*Meeting Street looking south toward St. Michael's Church and the ruins of the Circular Congregational Church and Institute Hall. By the end of the war, the city had been devastated both by the 1861 fire and military action.*

By 1866, however, things had begun to look up somewhat, and Bernhard Heinrich's vision of resurgent opportunity might well have had some basis in reality. In any case, in July of 1868 he purchased property in the rural village

6.  Boston: Ticknor and Fields, 1866; reprinted New York: Arno Press and The New York Times, 1969. Andrews states in his introductory note that he "spent the month of September, October, and November, 1865, in the States of North Carolina, South Carolina, and Georgia, as the Correspondent of the Boston Advertiser and the Chicago Tribune … ".

of Mount Pleasant across the Cooper River from the Charleston peninsula. At age twenty-three, almost exactly three years after his arrival, Bernhard Bequest was naturalized a U.S. citizen.

Bernhard and his wife promptly began the process of becoming Charlestonians: the 1870 federal census shows him with the anglicized name of "Benjamin," aged twenty-five, a merchant; she is "Sarah," aged twenty-two, "keeping house." Both are officially registered as of German birth, both with parents "of foreign birth." The census record shows the value of Bequest's real estate as $1200 (c. $24,000 currently) and his personal estate worth $500. It was almost to be expected that Bequest would initially try to establish himself as a merchant operating a "store," as he had done in Nassau: that had been the antebellum pattern for many of the North German immigrants to Charleston. It seems likely, however, that he considered the Mount Pleasant village at that time to be a limited market and thus opened a store in the city proper. He would become an early commuter, crossing to Charleston by boat from the village "across the bay."

During these first few years, it would have been natural for the eldest brother, while working to establish his own domestic and mercantile footing, to mentor his two younger brothers who followed him to South Carolina. Nonetheless, however much or little they initially relied on each other, they each had to make their own way. John had arrived in Baltimore as a "seaman," and would ultimately work in Charleston in a job suited to his maritime roots. He was still a young twenty-eight-year-old when he was naturalized in October of 1875. For his first five years in Charleston, the youngest brother, Carsten August, worked as a clerk in his elder brother's store. In January of 1872 he followed the footsteps of the immigrants who had moved to up-state South Carolina and set himself up as a merchant in Abbeville, South Carolina, where he remained until he returned to Charleston in 1879.

Bernhard and his wife were married only six years before she died in 1872, shortly after giving birth to the daughter mentioned in the Capers account.[7] Less than a year later, he married the daughter (eleven years his junior) of a family that had immigrated from the vicinity of Geestendorf to Charleston prior to the war. This second Bequest family lost a seventeen-month old son

---

7. Theresa Louise Bequest married John Henry Gieschen—not "John Gischen" as reported by the English-speaking Brigadier-General.

in 1878 to diphtheria and a daughter to scarlet fever before her third birthday. In census records, Bequest is listed as a *planter*, essentially a farmer, doubtless raising produce to be sold in his store. During the years between 1867 and 1879, records of the Register of Mesne Conveyance show him involved in a number of real estate transactions. In the decade following his decision to settle in Charleston, he became a citizen of sufficient civic stature in Mount Pleasant to hold public office as a town councilman, then as the town's *Intendant* (mayor). Throughout the extended period of residence in Mount Pleasant, the family remained in Charleston's St. Matthew's German Lutheran congregation. In 1882, the couple left the rural Mount Pleasant location to move into the city proper, close to where Bernhard had operated his in-town store. The one surviving child of this German-born couple—like his half-sister—was an American born in Charleston.

Bernhard Bequest's story as briefly outlined here leaves plenty of room for details—the daily pursuit of "health and happiness" as an immigrant to Charleston. While those immigrants who had come to Charleston during the years prior to the Civil War had to accommodate themselves to the peculiar institutions of the antebellum city, the first years of the Bequest brothers' existence in the defeated South coincided with the complete revision of everyday life under the aegis of Reconstruction. When Bernhard Bequest relocated to Charleston in late 1865, he would try gain his footing in Charleston as a grocer and a farmer in Mount Pleasant at the same time South Carolina was to be resurrected from its ashes. His beginnings after the war coincided with the implementation of Presidential Reconstruction, Andrew Johnson's questionable efforts to carry out what Lincoln had initiated with the emancipation proclamation. South Carolina was under U.S. military command. A month before he came, a convention had met in Columbia and had drawn up the state's new Constitution—adopting its version of the Black Codes—and state offices in Charleston were closed and the government resettled in Columbia.[8]

---

8. George C. Rogers, Jr. and C. James Taylor, *A South Carolina Chronology 1497-1992*. 2nd ed. (Columbia: University of South Carolina Press, 1994), 102. "The Black Codes, passed by the former Confederate states during Presidential Reconstruction, were part of a complex web of postwar economic, legal, and extralegal restraints designed by white conservatives to maintain broad control over the freedpeople." *Encyclopedia of the*

Most would have thought it a less-than-propitious time to undertake a new beginning: it took the grit and the mind-set of a young North German immigrant to find opportunity in the deplorable conditions that prevailed.

The following timeline[9] demonstrates how the cultural shift underway at this time intersected with the "Benjamin" Bequest immigrant family as the couple negotiated their way through the post-war period of new rules governing everyday life:

—*1865: November 13*: South Carolina ratifies the Thirteenth Amendment, which freed the slaves.

—*1866, February 8*: Bernhard Heinrich Bequest and Gesine Margarethe Rigbers marry.

—*1866, December 19*: South Carolina rejects the Fourteenth Amendment.

—*1866, December 20*: Legislation passed to establish an immigration commissioner to encourage immigration of European whites to offset the black majority.[10]

—*1867, November 19-20*: The first election to allow the freedmen to participate fully is held to elect state and local officials.

—*1868, January 14-March 18*: A convention draws up the Constitution of 1868. The convention comprises seventy-six blacks and forty-eight whites.

—*1868, June 2-3*: The first general election held under the Constitution of 1868.

—*1868, July 9*: Francis L. Cardozo becomes the state's first black Secretary of State. South Carolina ratifies the Fourteenth Amendment.

---

*Reconstruction Era*. Vol 1: A-L, Richard Zuczek, ed. (Westport, CN: Greenwood Press, 2006), 72.

   9.   Excerpted and adapted from Rogers and Taylor, 101-110.

  10.   Charleston's German leader, John Andreas Wagener, was named to the post in 1867.

—*1868, November 3*: Ulysses S. Grant elected president. South Carolina casts six electoral votes for him.

—*1868, November 9*: Bernhard Heinrich Bequest becomes a naturalized citizen.

—*1870*: U.S. Census [South Carolina]: Whites: 289,667; blacks: 415,814; others: 125; Total: 705,606.

—*1870, February 1*: Jonathan Jasper Wright is the first black elected to the South Carolina Supreme Court, serving until his resignation December 1, 1877.

—*1870, November 28*: Alonzo J. Ransier is the first black South Carolinian to be elected to the office of lieutenant governor.

—*1870, December 12*: Representative Joseph H. Rainey is sworn in as the first black South Carolinian in the U.S. Congress.

—*1871, October 17*: President Ulysses S. Grant issues proclamation suspending the writ of habeas corpus in nine South Carolina counties.

—*1871, December 24*: Birth of Theresa Louise Bequest.

—*1872, July 19*: Death of Gesine Margarethe Bequest, née Rigbers.

—*1872, November 5*: Ulysses S. Grant reelected president. South Carolina casts seven electoral votes for him.

—*1873*, July 3: Bernhard Heinrich Bequest and Catherine Mehrtens marry.

—*1873, October 7*: Henry E. Hayne enrolls as the first black student at the University of South Carolina.

—*1876: April 19*: Bernhard Heinrich Bequest is elected Intendant of Mount Pleasant, SC.

*—1876, July 8*: At least one white and four blacks are killed in a race riot in the industrial town of Hamburg, South Carolina.

*—1876, September 9*: Birth of Bernhard Heinrich Ludwig Bequest.

*—1876, September 16*-19: At least one white and about forty blacks are killed in race riots at Ellenton in Aiken County.

*—1876, October 17*: President Grant issues a proclamation to place federal troops at the call of Governor Chamberlain.

*—1876, November*: In South Carolina, the tempestuous and disputed gubernatorial election between the incumbent Chamberlain and Wade Hampton takes place. In the national election, Rutherford B. Hayes is elected president. South Carolina's seven electoral votes are disputed but eventually are counted for Hayes.

*—1876, November 28*: Federal troops occupy the State House in Columbia.

*—1876, December 14*: Wade Hampton, disputing Chamberlain's election, takes the oath of office as governor.

*—1877: April 10*: President Hayes orders federal troops withdrawn from Columbia. Chamberlain concedes the gubernatorial dispute, leaving Hampton as governor.

*—1877, March 1*: The General Assembly passes legislation to end public executions.

*—1877, March*: The University of South Carolina is divided into two branches: whites attend in Columbia, blacks in Orangeburg.

*—1877, December 10*: Wade Hampton is elected to the U.S. Senate.

*—1878, February 10*: Death of Bernhard Heinrich Ludwig Bequest.

—*1878, September 16*: Birth of Anna Meta Adeline Bequest.

—*1879: April*: Bernhard Heinrich Bequest's Intendancy of Mount Pleasant ends.

—*1880*: U.S. Census [South Carolina]: White: 391,105; Black: 604,332; Other: 140; Total: 995,577.

—*1881, April 19*: Death of Anna Meta Adeline Bequest.

—*1882, September 9*: Birth of John Frederick Bequest.

Historians are agreed that the South did not take Presidential—or any other—Reconstruction efforts lying down. The indignities Southerners had to suffer only strengthened their resolve to resist every modification that was to be made to their sacred past. Their defeat made Southern elites increasingly more defensive about their right to exercise white supremacy and radicalized their response to being told how they should accept their loss and accommodate the new order. While there was a gradually increasing effort in other states of the Confederacy to accommodate the new order, South Carolinians were recognized as the most profoundly resistant. The numerous efforts throughout the South to suppress the rights of the emancipated black population were so mean and in violation of the reigning ideology of free labor that they went unenforced or were declared void.

A sense of what life was like in the small island village of Mount Pleasant at that time can be culled from a letter written by Henry Slade Tew to his daughter in February 1865. Henry Tew was a storekeeper and, at the time, the mayor of Mount Pleasant.[11] Three mayors would serve the town between Henry Tew and Bernhard Bequest. The character of the town, however, changed much more slowly than its mayoral incumbents. The Tew letter was written approximately eight months before Bequest arrived in Charleston and gives an account of the occupation of Mount Pleasant by Union troops. The passages excerpted below provide an inside view to the general sensibilities of the time and describe the cultural framework Bequest would meet when he opted to settle in rural Mount Pleasant—not that it was any different there than in the city itself.

---

11. Henry Tew would serve a second term from 1868-1870.

Dear Daughter,

Your absence from home at the time of the evacuation by our troops and the taking possession of those of the U.S. was a great relief to our minds, as our apprehension of insults and violence had been excited by the reports of such conduct elsewhere, and I have prepared this narrative or sort of diary to put you in possession of such facts as transpired and in some of which I was an actor, as may prove of interest to you at some future time may be referred to as part of the history of these eventful times…

While these scenes were transpiring over here, those of Charleston must have beggared description—to us was visible only the awful magnificence of the scene, while the terror, confusion, suffering and crime must have been appalling to the dwellers in the doomed city. The burning buildings public and private, the repeated explosions, the gun boats and other vessels burning in the harbor all presented such a scene as but few ever witness in a lifetime, and surely one which none would ever desire to see repeated. Oh God! What a night of horror that memorable 17th of February was…

About 12 o'clock Saturday three barges landed from the fleet and as I had been elected Intendant by the people on Friday, in that official capacity attended by some of the citizens I surrendered the town submitting to the military authority of the U.S. and was promised protection to persons and private property. The boats were commanded by Lieut. Gifford from the Flagship—they brought a small U.S. Flag ashore and hoisted it for a while on the Light house. The officers were courteous and the men quite peaceful. Many from the fleet were ashore on Saturday and Sunday but we had not yet seen any from the Army from whom we feared violence and insult. All our own blacks boisterous in their reception of the visitors but none that I am aware of had yet left their work or homes. Monday 20th we heard that the troops that had landed at Bull's Bay were marching down and about 11 o'clock the shouts of the negroes apprised us of their arrival. There were three regiments of U.S. colored troops all under the command of Col. A. S. Hartwell, who took his quarters temporarily at the light house. I called on him, told him my name and position and asked protection for the persons and property of the citizens who were mostly women and children and were greatly apprehensive at the presence of the coloured troops... Colonel Hartwell then entered into conversation with me, asked me if I was connected with the Tews of Rhode Island, and if I was favorable to secession as he had received so many assurances from people that they were not, that he was at a loss what to think and could only judge by the manner and not the language. I told him I would reply with the upmost frankness, that if more than one man in South Carolina out of fifty told him he had opposed secession they lied, and that for myself, tho a Union man in 1832 and in 1850, yet on the election of Mr. Lincoln I thought all hope of justice to the South in the Union was lost, and I went for secession with vote and voice. He thanked me for the frankness of my reply and said it would be better if all would be equally so... Many of the negroes from the Plantations came down in the Army train, and together with those of the village made quite a multitude of shouting wild creatures whom the thought of freedom had changed from quiet to transports of uproarious joy. I must tell you what I did for my own. A few days before I gave them $50.00 told them the money would soon be worth nothing and advised them to buy whatever they could then. I also told them that when the troops came they knew they were free to go or stay as they pleased—if they stayed, as long as I had anything to eat they should share as they always had done—not one answered a word, and I knew of course they would go—they stayed however until Wednesday and then went off without a word of leave taking—Sary setting the example—Louis is gone also, Margaret and Zoe are still here as Elisa is with William and forbids their leaving, but I suppose they will not stay long... When orders came for the

Brig to move to the City and they left us with only six men as a guard and our negroes noisy, stealing all they could lay hands on and moving into the houses that were vacant. It was a sleepless night to us. We all sat up till 4 o'clock. Wednesday was a quiet day...

March 1

The 52nd Regt. Major Hennessy Com'g now garrison Mount Pleasant. Headquarters are now established at Mr. Whilden's house and the proximity to our own dwelling is the best guaranty we can have of quiet and order. The commander seems to be determined to enforce order and maintains stricter military discipline than we have ever had over here before from the troops of *either* army. He does not appear to have much sympathy or regard for the blacks, at least he does not place them above the whites and make all claims and interest subservient to theirs...

On Sunday 19th went to Church and in the pew before us was a mulatto girl with a white soldier—we heard he married her Saturday 25th. Attended the funeral of Sally Venning and on Sunday 26th that of little Eddy Royall who died of measles. The whole five of Mr. Royall's children having been taken at one time. On that Sunday the Episcopal Church was taken possession of by negro troops. Their regiment is commanded by Col. Beecher the brother of H. Ward Beecher and Mrs. H. B. Stowe, and we hear that his wife who is with him declines all acquaintance with the whites, but has called upon the colored ladies and invited them to her quarters—from this time forth until matters are settled I suppose that the Church is to be abandoned by the whites, as no one will care to subject themselves to the annoyance of having a colored gentleman or lady perhaps both walking into your pew and overpowering you with their odor or filling you with vermin... [12]

12. Anonymous, "An Eye Witness Account of the Occupation of Mt. Pleasant: February 1865," *The South Carolina Historical Magazine* 66, no. 1 (January 1965): 8-14.

This testament to the idiosyncrasies of life in Mount Pleasant in 1865 resonates with the biases, antipathies, and prejudices endemic in the South when the end of the war left a vanquished people feeling their way out of chaos and not quite used to the new rules of order. For immigrants such as Bequest it would have been a case of finding himself in a new context in which new rules were being applied. There was little choice but to accede to the demands the host society itself was acceding to.

As soon as he became a citizen, and as if to demonstrate a strong commitment to the native community that he wished to become a part of, Bernhard Bequest ran for the office of Warden in the Mount Pleasant election in November of 1868 when Henry Tew was again elected as Intendant. In the *Charleston Daily News* report of the election results, Bequest was one of eleven candidates for Warden: six were reported as Democrats, four were reported as Republicans and "colored," and Bequest was reported as "white" and Republican. He received one vote—likely his own. The following day, the newspaper ran a retraction: "MOUNT PLEASANT—We are requested to say that the statement in the report of the Mount Pleasant election, published in our last issue, that Mr. Bequest is a Republican, is wholly incorrect."[13] The six democrats had run away with the votes, the black Republicans—doubtless "radical" reconstructionists—were defeated, and the white immigrant with a mistaken political affiliation learned a lesson about playing in Reconstruction politics. In the next election in 1870 Bequest did much better, tying for the second highest number of votes (127) of the six wardens elected. The *Charleston Daily News* of September 13th reported that "the election passed off quietly. The parties chosen were all Reformers except the last." Running as a Reformer was obviously preferable to running as a Republican. By age twenty-six, the German immigrant had assumed a more local identity: as would have been expected, in the course of five years the host community had left its imprint.

Even before he was naturalized in 1868, Bequest joined the *Deutsche Schützengesellschaft*. Recognized as the oldest rifle club in the United States, the Charleston club was founded in 1855 by a small group led by two members of the German triumvirate, John Andreas Wagener and Franz Melchers. The Club was a close-knit German society unto itself within the larger Charleston society. It allowed the immigrant and his family to maintain something of

---

13. "Local Matters," *Charleston Daily News*, November 14, 1868.

their heritage in what, at times, must have seemed like an alien world. The Schützengesellschaft would become a cornerstone of life for many in the ethnic community, a center and nexus of social relationships that would sustain them whatever their personal circumstances might be.

Bequest's acceptance into the Schützengesellschaft would mean much more to him than his political defeat in the election in 1868. Because of the war, the Club's annual festival, the *Schützenfest,* had not been held for eight years. Finally in May of 1868, a month after Bequest was voted in as an active member, the Club, with permission from the federal government in Washington, again put on its festival. The German sharpshooters paraded in full complement down the streets of Charleston amidst the acclamation of the crowds and the lively strains of the music.[14] Participating in the activities of the Schützengesellschaft would become the focal point of Bernhard's social life—actually define him within the German community. As was the case for many of his fellow immigrants, membership in the Rifle Club facilitated the members' goal of establishing themselves within the Charleston community: participation in the Club's activities and the favor the Club found in the community gradually effected the transformation of the German immigrant into a Charlestonian of German heritage.

Even before the war, the annual spring Schützenfest of the German Rifle Club had become a major event for Charleston's inhabitants. Its revival in 1868 signaled that it had not lost any of its popularity in the local community. Effusive praise was the topic of the two-column article on the front page of the *Daily News* of May 8, 1869:

> The fact that yesterday would be the concluding day of the Schuetzenfest, drew together the largest crowd that has ever been seen at the Platz. The trains, omnibuses, private and public vehicles were tasked to the utmost to convey the immense number of visitors. These were not confined to the Teutonic element. All nationalities and all classes flocked to the gay scene

---

14. "…paradirten in voller Anzahl, unter dem Jubel der Bevölkerung und den rauschenden Klängen der Musik durch die Straßen Charlestons." Quoted from Alexander Melchers's address to the membership as printed in the 1872 edition of the club's constitution.

to enjoy the occasion, and witness or participate in its joys and amusements. The city was deserted; many stores were closed, and avenues of trade were as still and quiet as on Sunday.

The morning was spent in various pastimes; the Saengerbund and the Teutonia societies sang; the Turners, adult and juvenile, contorted themselves into indescribable shapes; the music of the band and the harps filled the air with delightful sounds, and even the quivering leaves on the overarching branches were inclined to put on airs. About midday the grounds began to fill up rapidly. Every effort was made to cause the last day to be an epoch in the history of the Charleston Schuetzen. Sugar eating, milk feeding, sack racing, greasy pole climbing, mill walking, and sliding on the waterfall caused dense masses to congregate wherever these sports were in process. The greasy poll [sic] was successfully climbed by a white boy, who cleaned the hoop of its prizes as he did last year.

The very best spirit prevailed, and all seemed to enjoy themselves. It would be unwise even to guess at the amount of lager consumed. Kegs and barrels were emptied and replaced, and these again ran dry. Yet, to the honor of the Schuetzen be it said, there was not one riotous person on the ground. So much for lager, with our good Germans to drink it. No unpleasant incident jarred the harmonies of the day. The participants were all too good humored to get vexed with anybody. In the matter of courtesy, the German hosts were masters of the situation, and dispensed their heartfelt hospitality in a free and whole-souled manner.

The shooting ceased at four o'clock, and a brass howitzer made the fact known in stentorius tones. The committee immediately set to work making out the prize list. It was completed by half-past 5 o'clock, when there was a general assembling around the tribune, where the Saengerbund and the Teutonia and their visiting friends sang a parting song as a prelude to the general distribution of prizes.

Captain Melchers then introduced Professor H. D. Meier … Professor Meier delivered an eloquent address in German, speaking of the festival and the glory of the occasion, and the success that had attended it from beginning to end. He continued for some time in his usually impassioned strain, passing in review the main and incidental features of the festival, not forgetting some handsome allusions to the visiting Schützen, He was frequently and loudly applauded. Filling the Schützen horn, which can hold two bottles of wine, he drank to the health of the King. He then addressed the masses in English, and said he regretted he could not speak that language as fluently as he would like, and give expression to the sentiments that filled his heart. He thanked the people of Charleston for the generous support they had given the festival. They had sustained it in a manner that would never be forgotten. He was glad to meet Germans from all parts of the country under one banner, but the best banner to him was the banner of "free labor." Professor Meier then announced the prizes.

At almost every annual Schützenfest, Bernhard Bequest took a prize in the shooting contests and became a champion among the German sharpshooters: his talent with the rifle earned him first prize at the 1871 Schützenfest, when he became its King for the following year.

While German men were regaled as heroes at the annual Schützenfests, the members of the German Ladies' Society (Charleston Damen Gesellschaft) played an equally important social role in the Charleston community. The report in the *Charleston News* on "The German Fair" put on by the Ladies' Society speaks volumes about how the Germans were regarded by others in Charleston at the time.

THE GERMAN FAIR / A TRIUMPH OF TASTE AND SKILL … The sterling worth and unselfish feeling of the German citizens of Charleston are always displayed to best advantage when charity or religion appeals to the hearts which beat so warmly for God and Fatherland. They are thorough in their amusements. There is no lackadaisical enjoyment in the gala doings of the German. But when the religion of their fathers calls upon them for help and aid, their serious souls are stirred to the depths, and they labor with a zeal and devotion which no people can surpass; Happily, however, the Germans do not deem it necessary to be lugubrious because the object of their work is solemn and severe. They wreathe the garlands of innocent gaiety around the pillars of the Temple of Duty, and light up the stern responsibilities of life with the sunny splendor of their smile. No worthy German calls upon a German and meets with a rebuff. The German, it is true, has no patience in dealing with the drone and laggard; but undeserved misfortune and unavoidable affliction claim and receive that substantial sympathy which finds expression in act more than in word. The Germans are always staunch and true, and never have their finest qualities been shown to better advantage than in the Fair of the German Ladies' Society, whose triumphant opening we chronicle today. The object of the Fair, we need hardly add, is to obtain the means of completing the new German Lutheran Church in King Street, whose tower already rears its head above the neighboring buildings.

After a lengthy description of the new St. Matthew's Church, the offerings at the fair are described in considerable detail, each table's wares sequentially portrayed as more desirable than the preceding one. The women in charge of the tables are named with only their surname, as if that is sufficient to identify them for the ethnic, as well as the general, community. Table No. 5, for example, is "under the management of Mrs. Fischer and Mrs. Bequest, assisted by Mrs. Lilienthal and Mrs. Wagener." The reference to "Mrs. Bequest" confirms that Gesine Bequest had taken her place in the church community equal to the one her husband was acquiring in the Rifle Club. The newspaper reporter concluded that

> the opening night of the Fair of the German Ladies' Society
> was successful beyond expectations, but we desire to see the
> fair more fully attended by the general public. The Germans

of Charleston are never backward in giving their help to any measure which is for the good of the community, and it is due to them that the people at large should assist them in erecting a building which is necessary for the religious accommodation of a large body of our most valuable citizens and will be, besides, an ornament to Charleston.[15]

Despite the hyperbole inherent in newspaper reporting during this period, it is difficult to overlook the fact that there was more than a modicum of *judgment* being passed by the newspaper reporter and, indirectly, by the editor.[16] Charleston and its ruling class have not infrequently been accused of being paternalistic, and there is no lack of that in the passages cited above: "*They*" are a separate entity from "*Us*," viewed and judged from a distance, as if the viewer in the center is looking at something on the periphery, ready and able to comment on "*them*," "*the Germans*," "*their* serious souls," "the sunny splendor of *their* smile," "*their* finest qualities," "*our* most valuable citizens." Obviously, "*the Germans*" had for some time been making a very good impression on the natives, but even though *they* were well-behaved and valuable members of the Charleston community, "old Charleston" would—if only subconsciously— keep these Neudeutsche somewhat marginalized for yet a while.

As we know, the effort of the immigrant to navigate the distance between the margin and the center, where the native-born and the acculturated lived, had begun almost a quarter of a century earlier when immigrant numbers had increased to the point that the Neudeutsche were recognizable as a group. The seemingly frenetic activity on the part of John Andreas Wagener can be

---

15. *The Charleston News*, November 1, 1870.

16. The editor by this time was the Englishman Francis Warrington Dawson. According to a brief summary about the *Charleston Daily News* (*Chronicling America: Historic American Newspapers*), Dawson, along with Bartholomew Riordan, had bought the paper in 1867. As its outspoken editor, Dawson "castigated and cheered developments in South Carolina. He argued that the state's reliance on cash crops like cotton had left its economy too vulnerable to forces beyond its control. He championed manufacturing and immigration and encouraged business and community leaders to diversify their local economies and invest in railroads. He fiercely criticized the Republican-dominated Reconstruction-era government for its perceived corruptness and ineffectiveness."

understood as an effort by an individual with leadership abilities to satisfy certain needs of what had become an immigrant *community*. The clubs and societies served to meld individuals into a mutually supportive body, the newspaper facilitated communication and offered helpful guidance, and a *German* fire company provided a sense of security in view of an already over-taxed civic "service" and signaled the immigrants' willingness to contribute to the well-being of the larger community. That as early as 1840 Wagener and others should work to establish a *German* Lutheran Church was indicative of a genuine need of the ethnic community: the founding of St. Matthew's German Lutheran Church had significance well beyond it being yet another "accomplishment" credited to the indefatigable Wagener.

It was natural enough that individuals in the growing ethnic community in Charleston would expect to be able to practice their religious traditions in their adoptive homeland. For the most part, they were Protestants moving into what was essentially a Protestant community. The United States as a whole, in fact, could consider itself a Protestant country, settled from its very beginnings by Europeans of every description seeking religious freedoms derived from the Reformation and separation from the Church of Rome. Those coming to Charleston in the nineteenth century took up residence in a Protestant city dominated by a long-established English, Episcopal tradition. The German immigrants would know, of course, that there was already a Lutheran church—St. John's—whose minister, John Bachman, was a New Yorker born of German parents. Although of German descent, Bachman had early on become a popular and much admired figure in the Charleston community, and his church had become known locally as the *English* Lutheran church.[17] For the immigrants

---

17. St. John's was in initially known as "the German Lutheran Church," its congregation populated predominantly by Colonial-era German immigrants. It called a German, Jacob Eckhard, to be the organist in 1786, and "doubtless at his instigation, a new hymnal, a *Choralbuch,* in German was obtained for the congregation." Eckhard later became organist at Charleston's St. Michael's Episcopal Church, but "maintained a lively interest in St. John's and remained a member of the corporation until his death. He was appointed to a committee to obtain a new English hymnal for the use of the church in 1809." George W. Williams, *Jacob Eckhard's Choirmaster's Book of 1809* (Columbia: University of South Carolina Press, 1971), xi–xiii. The 1809 date for introducing the English hymnal suggests how subsequently it would be known as the *English* Lutheran Church. Bachman

arriving after Bachman had begun his ministry, the English-based services would not have been all that accessible to those speaking *Platt,* nor would the esteemed civic figure have been the kind of individual the majority of these "new" Germans would readily choose as their religious leader. It was not so much that the Neudeutsch immigrant avoided association with St. John's,[18] but rather that the newer immigrants felt called to found a congregation of their own in support of the growing group of *evangelisch-reformierte* Lutherans now in residence.

Tracing the history of Lutheranism in South Carolina is admittedly beyond the scope of this study. Suffice it say that from its beginnings in the seventeenth century it was anything but the result of a clear and carefully planned mission to establish congregations adhering to a unified confessional body. For years it was nothing but small groups of heterogeneous believers scattered about the hinterlands, served by itinerant pastors who might or might not be trained adequately for their work. Trained and educated pastors rarely accompanied an emigrating group, the clergy unwilling to take on the hardships and penurious rewards in exchange for the more comfortable circumstances they enjoyed in their home community. Such itinerant ministers as were available, as well as the disparate flocks they served, could think themselves *Lutheran* or *Reformed* or *Calvinist*—however much or little those distinctions mattered at the time and in those circumstances. The several groups were held together in recognition of the fact that in their tenuous circumstances it was better to accommodate doctrinal differences rather than accentuate them.

Founded already in 1743, the congregation of St. John's in Charleston would become the largest and most coherent in the state, and Bachman became a leading advocate for unity among the several synodical bodies that had

---

was instrumental in forming in 1819 a society for securing and distributing tracts and books among members of the congregation—*The Tract and Book Society of the Lutheran Church of German Protestants, of Charleston, South Carolina, for the Dissemination of Useful Religious Knowledge.* Thus while the congregation was constituted for some time primarily of German Protestants, its services and Bachman's ministry were conducted in English. Bachman's "English" orientation enabled him to begin his "notable ministry to the Negro population in Charleston" the year after he accepted the call of St. John's. Bachman's ministry at St. John's would last for almost sixty years—from 1815 to 1874.

18. Hermann and Catharina Knee were married at St. John's in 1834.

formed in sections of the country. Synodical matters, however, were of little relevance to the immigrants coming ashore in Charleston from the 1830s on. They were hardly versed on the disputes revolving around the Americanization of the several Lutheran bodies, nor were fine points of doctrine or political/ecclesiastical dispute their concern. Once in Charleston in sufficient number, the German newcomers would have wanted—and needed—a church of their own and a ministry in their own language. In this particular case, they were heirs of the state religion practiced in most of the northern German lands, that is, the one formed through the efforts of Prussia's King Frederick Wilhelm III, who on April 4, 1830, the tricentennial observance of the Augsburg Confession, issued an edict that united the Lutheran and Reformed churches. The records of many of the immigrants who left Geestendorf are contained in the *Kirchenbuch 1715-1852* of the *Evangelisch-Reformierte Kirche Geestendorf (Geestemünde)*.

That European religious heritage which the immigrants brought to Charleston would ultimately be modified by the acculturation process of adopting Charleston ways and attitudes, comparable to the evolution of the congregation of St. John's. But initially, it would have been difficult for these later immigrants to come ashore and fall in with what was becoming an increasingly *Southern* congregation accustomed to its English-based liturgy and hymnody, or for that matter, its Americanized Charlestonian pastor. Rev. Hazelius, the President of the South Carolina Synod, in his annual report of 1839, wrote of the "the first attempt of the native German citizens of Charleston, S.C. in establishing a *second, and altogether German, Lutheran Church* (italics mine)."[19]

It was inevitable, nonetheless, that when John Andreas Wagener and fellow Lutherans moved to found the St. Matthew's *German* Lutheran Church in 1840, it would not be long before it was drawn into the orbit that Bachman and other Lutheran leaders had organized. The increasing numbers of Germans in Charleston and in Columbia were subject to the South Carolina Synod's missionary zeal, and when the St. Matthew's congregation, a year after its founding, joined the Synod, the Synod was more than pleased to add two hundred and twenty-five communicants to its rolls. For the increasing numbers of

19. G. D. Bernheim, *History of the German Settlements and of the Lutheran Church in North and South Carolina* (Philadelphia: Regional, 1872, reprinted Baltimore, 1975), 529-33.

German immigrants in Charleston and in Walhalla—collectively the founders and members of the St. Matthew's congregational fold—belonging to a larger organization provided a certain legitimacy. As good Germans anxious to assimilate themselves into the host culture while honoring their religious heritage, their intentions fit in well with Charleston's Protestant environs. Whether or not purposefully, their alignment with the statewide Synod signaled agreement with the ecclesiastical and political stance of the *Southern* Lutheran Church

Looking again at the 1870 *Charleston News* account quoted earlier, wherein the reporter went to such lengths to provide the context and rationale for the German Ladies' Society fair, it is clear that the German immigrant community had by that point become an important sector of Charleston's populace. Recalling when the cornerstone of the "new German Lutheran Church" had been laid the previous year,[20] the newspaper reported that "all the streets through which the procession passed were densely crowded, and every spot around the site of the new church was occupied by eager spectators." The dimensions of the new and impressive "ornament" to Charleston were furnished in full, as if to signify the extent and importance of the congregation: "It is situated on the west side of King street ... and is 145 feet in length and 65 feet in breadth. The nave is 92 by 54 feet, and the chancel 24 by 14 ... There are three entrance doors in front, and two on the sides ... The steeple will be 232 ½ feet in height, higher, by over 20 feet, than any other in the city ... The church is built in the pure German style of ecclesiastical architecture."[21] The edifice would stamp a German presence on the neighborhood and unmistakably signal the significance of the Germans in the civic and religious life of Charleston.

The importance of the role the German immigrants played was in evidence in the popularity of their annual spring Schützenfests. By the time the

---

20. "With Charleston's German population increasing and the membership of St. Matthew's growing beyond the capacity of its original church, the congregation, in 1868, bought the King Street site on which the cornerstone of the ... edifice was laid on December 22, 1869. Building of the Gothic structure was completed in little more than two years." *A History of the Lutheran Church in South Carolina* (Columbia: The R. L. Bryan Co., 1971), 731.

21. Not incidentally, and not insignificantly, Nicholas Fehrenbach, Bernhard's companion in blockade-running, was one of the five members of the Building Committee, all of whom are named on the cornerstone laid in 1867.

Schützenfest was announced in 1874, the newspapers were calling it "The People's Festival." "What was once known in Charleston as the German Schutzenfest[22] has, of late years, assumed so cosmopolitan a character that it is now more appropriately called the People's festival." The "People's Festival" was described in the sub-headline as "a Grand Military Pageant." The parade, it seems, included every paramilitary organization in the City of Charleston and then some:

> In the following order: social Mounted Club, German Hussars, The Fusilier Band, Carolina Rifle Club, Charleston Rifleman, Washington Artillery, Sumter Rifle Club, Palmetto Guard, Washington Light Infantry, Wagener Artillery, Irish Volunteer Rifle Club, Color Guard, National Zouaves, Irish Volunteers, German Fusiliers, Montgomery Guards, Guard of Honor, the chariot containing the eagle target. Then the various carriages: in the second carriage behind the eagle target rode Major Melchers, editor of the Zeitung, and Ex-Kings Melchers, Dunnemann and Bequest, of the Charleston Schutzen Club, and visiting Schutzen in citizens' dress ... The streets through which the pageant passed were thronged with spectators, who occupied windows, balconies and the sidewalks.[23]

This blatant military pageant/display marching through the streets of Charleston had by this time—during some of the darkest days of Reconstruction—taken on the character of a white show of force. The jovial, well-behaved, civic picnic that had been re-started in 1868 had taken on a different attitude, and the Germans were very much in the center of the action. Whatever role they had played before the war, Charleston's German immigrants were now major actors in the performances staged by the city being reconstructed.

The Schützenfest had become a Charleston institution when Bernhard Bequest reigned as king in 1871-72. Four years later, he would again—by

---

22. The umlaut has been dropped.

23. *News and Courier*, April 21, 1874. The *News and Courier* was the successor to the combined [1873] *Charleston Daily News* and the *Charleston Courier*.

virtue of his marksmanship—hold the kingship of the Schützenfest and, as well—by virtue of his having become prominent among the community's *German* businessmen—be elected *Intendant* of the town of Mount Pleasant. The office involved considerable responsibility, and Bernhard Bequest's election says a lot about how in a short time he had won the respect of his fellow citizens—a trustworthy immigrant businessman and property owner with leadership capabilities chosen to manage the affairs of the town. There is nothing of record to indicate that his administration during the years 1876-79 was anything other than routine. But beyond the village, the year Bequest was elected would turn out to be anything but routine. The Mount Pleasant mayoral election took place just prior to the disputed presidential election of Rutherford B. Hayes, during which South Carolina was embroiled in a disputed gubernatorial election that pitted the Democrat Wade Hampton against the sitting Republican Governor Daniel Chamberlain. The determined efforts of the Democrats in 1876 to oust the Republicans' Chamberlain effectively marked the state's "redemption" from the throes of Reconstruction.

It has been noted as part of Mount Pleasant's historic landscape that "in 1876, an election which overturned Black Republicanism and restored white Democrats to power in the district, state, and region so inflamed the town that black Republicans seized the streets for an entire night and fearful white Democrats along with a handful of black political allies barricaded themselves in their homes."[24] We might legitimately question how much of a role the former immigrant Bernhard Bequest played in "overturning" Black Republicanism and "restoring" white Democrats to power: was he, eleven years after his immigration, elected to office because he had become a *white* Charleston Democrat?

One historian's analysis of "how the Germans became white southerners"[25] claims that German immigrants were "a middleman minority community, occupying a middle tier on the racial and ethnic hierarchy below white southerners and above African Americans," who after the Civil War "increasingly exhibited their desire to become white southerners." As a postwar resident landowner in Mount Pleasant since his immigration, Bequest fit

---

24. *The Historic Landscape of Mount Pleasant: Proceedings of the First Forum on the History of Mount Pleasant*. Amy McCandless, ed., (Mt. Pleasant, SC, 1993).

25. Strickland, "How the Germans Became White Southerners," 52-69.

this pattern perfectly. By the latter years of Reconstruction, most native white Charlestonians could acknowledge that it was the mercantile Germans who were the backbone of the city's economic revival after the war. Bequest would number among the successful members of that merchant league, in the same company with Oskar Aichel (John Hurkamp & Co., wholesale and retail grocery), Otto F. Wieters (wholesale liquor business), J. C. H. Claussen (baker), and Frederick W. Wagener (wholesaler in naval stores and cotton). From his naturalization in 1868 to his election to the Mount Pleasant's mayoralty during the years that the Democrat Wade Hampton represented and monopolized the South Carolina political scene, Bequest typifies the acculturation process of the German immigrant becoming a "white southerner."

As the Germans had gone through stages of asserting their cultural heritage on the local scene, for example, establishing the Schützengesellschaft and other paramilitary "social" organizations, they had occupied a middle ground by inviting the attendance and participation of the enslaved and free-black population, while at the same time displaying martial uniforms and guns in their exhibitionistic parades—the latter affirming the sense of white superiority assumed by the mostly-native white crowds in attendance. By virtue of their increasing social and financial ascendancy, the Germans by 1868 were becoming increasingly attuned to the platform of the Democratic Party. By 1871 they were sufficiently politically organized to nominate one of their own—none other than "former Confederate general and slaveholder" John A. Wagener—to run for mayor of Charleston. In that election, enough white southerners would endorse Wagener's candidacy that he would win a two-year term. By that point in the middle of Reconstruction, the Germans were standing on a somewhat modified footing. African-American Republican politicians lashed out at the Germans for their efforts on behalf of the Democratic Party. The state's Republican, African-American, Lieutenant Governor Alonzo Ransier proclaimed it "the basest ingratitude in General Wagener and the Germans to support a ticket in opposition to the rights of the colored people." Ransier argued that the Germans had betrayed the African-American community: "So far as the negro is concerned—let the Germans remember when they came here in their blue shirts—you patronized them, traded with them, and through your patronage they are enabled to-day to raise their heads and now desire to govern us."[26]

MONUMENT TO GEN. JOHN A. WAGENER, MAGNOLIA CEMETERY.

*The memorial honoring John Andreas Wagener, ethnic community leader, founder of St. Matthew's German Lutheran Church, founder of the town of Walhalla, Civil War veteran, Charleston's 43rd mayor. This early photo is miscaptioned: Wagener's monument and gravestone are in Bethany Cemetery.*

In 1876, Mount Pleasant Intendant Bequest was doubtless a small fish in the much larger political pond. Nonetheless, he was elected as a *democrat* and his electors would have thought of him as a southerner. As an immigrant German grocer turned white southerner, he could enjoy certain perquisites. For example, he could take advantage of the lien laws that existed at the time.[27]

———————————

26. Strickland, 62.

27. The crop lien system of credit that "allowed the farmer to place a mortgage on his future crop with the person or persons who advanced him supplies for his operations.

There is record of him—a kind of "sharecropper" himself, farming a leased 1½-acre plot—in his capacity as store owner providing supplies on credit to one, Frank Wallace, a less fortunate sharecropping citizen of the postbellum New South. As *furnishing merchant*, Bequest represented the way the lien laws were made to work as a source of credit and banking for a community, with his Mount Pleasant store both a source of credit and supply. At this point, Bequest was a man of his time in South Carolina, a merchant playing a role that was expected of him. Economically, the German farmer/merchant Bequest occupied a higher position on the social ladder than the native southern sharecropper Wallace.

As was the case with most of his fellow immigrant businessmen, Bequest was always on the lookout for additional opportunity that would improve his financial base and solidify his position in the community. By the time political reconstruction was on the wane, he had established a wood- and lumber-yard business in the city, knowing that wood and wood products were, and would be, in demand by a city in the business of physically constructing and/or reconstructing private and public structures that had been destroyed during the war. The increasingly-acculturated immigrant Bequest's business acumen—or else his readiness to take risks—is attested, for example, by the financial maneuvers he undertook to transition from Mount Pleasant storekeeper to the owner of a lumber business in the city itself. The sale of properties that he had earlier acquired verifies the immigrant's driving desire to own property, as well as his ability to manage his affairs to his advantage. Bequest sold three lots, plus five cotton gins, a grist mill, a 10 hp engine, and a sloop, as well as another store that he owned, known as the "Seven-Mile Store on the Georgetown Road."[28] Then he purchased four parcels of land of substantial acreage from an "old Charleston" resident: a parcel of 2,758 acres known as "Clayfield Plantation," an adjacent 170-acre property known as "Baldwin's Old Field," a neighboring parcel of 1,455 acres known as "Hampton," and finally, a one-acre plot with a

---

Normally those who made advances only accepted liens on an easily salable crop which was inedible and difficult to steal ... No other crop planted in the lower South so completely satisfied these requirements as did cotton." Thomas D. Clark, "The Furnishing and Supply System in Southern Agriculture since 1865," *The Journal of Southern History* 12, no. 1 (February 1946): 44.

28. This was not his store in Mount Pleasant's center, opposite the Courthouse.

barn. It is likely that when Bequest acquired these properties in 1881 he envisioned the pine-forested land as a source of the wood he would be retailing from his wood yard on Charleston's East Bay Street.[29] Although these substantial purchases appeared to be part of a viable business plan, the public record reveals that a decade later all this property was lost to Bequest in a Master's Sale auction in 1891 through a suit in the Charleston Court of Common Pleas brought against "Bernhard Bequest and others" by the Germania Savings Bank. The undertaking had obviously been a joint venture with other investors—most likely fellow immigrants—that had ultimately come to naught. Nonetheless, Bequest's wood business was established by the end of the decade, and he and his wife moved from the village of Mount Pleasant to become residents in Charleston proper, purchasing a house not far from his original in-town store.

Given the general agricultural depression that affected everything and everyone in the postbellum South, the move had been Bequest's purposeful transition from merchandizing in the rural, agriculture-based environs of Mount Pleasant to the more urban setting in the city. In Charleston, he could merchandize a commodity for re-building a city doing its best to recover from the past and take its place in the "New South." The move to Charleston to establish a new business was nevertheless not without personal trauma. Between 1878 and 1881, the Bequest couple lost two young children. Ten-year-old Theresa Louise, Bernhard's daughter by his first wife, was an only child when the couple's son, John Frederick, was born in 1882.

In spite of personal tragedies and the stress of making a go of his new business, the German wood-dealer—as might have been expected—continued his involvement with the Schützen. The *News and Courier* of May 9, 1885, reported that Bequest had won a box of cigars at that year's *Fest* and commented on how much the men of the rifle club had become integrated into their *home, sweet home* of Charleston:

> The prizes, the total value of which was 2600, were awarded by
> Capt. Alex Melchers, who briefly thanked the company for the

---

29. The plantations in Christ Church and St. Thomas Parishes were known from colonial times for the lumber that could be harvested there and sold on the Charleston market. Suzannah Smith Miles, *East Cooper Gazetteer* (Charleston: The History Press, 2004), 75.

interest they had taken in the festival. It was thirty-one years, he said, since the Schutzenfest was introduced into the United States. Though for centuries it had been observed in Germany, to Charleston belonged the honor of forming the first rifle club in this country. After the distribution of the prizes, the games were proceeded with until sundown. The cadets were about the last to leave the grounds, and on their way to town in their wagon regaled all who came within sound of their voices with 'Way down in North Carolina,' 'Barney McCoy,' 'Wait till the clouds roll by,' the German ditty 'Schnick, Schnack der doodle sack,' 'Der Deutscher Rhein,' and as they neared town, 'Home Sweet Home'.

As one of Charleston's several wood merchants, managing the demands of the business may nonetheless have diminished the almost-middle-aged Bequest's involvement with his fellow Schützen. For a number of years, the Bequest name is noticeably missing from the list of prizewinners in the annual Schützenfest shooting contests. His all-but-complete disappearance from the annual target contests suggests that something had changed. Had something personal occurred so that he purposefully avoided the company of his compatriots? Had he felt that his skill as a marksman was not what it had been earlier? Whatever the reason for Bequest's absence—at least in the shooting competitions—it might have been the case that the Club itself was changing and losing some of its aura. While the Schützenfest continued to be the major spring festival in Charleston during the years up to the turn of the century, the newspaper accounts of each year's celebrations grew shorter, the enthusiasm somewhat formulaic. Capt. Alexander Melchers's (brother of Franz Adolph Melchers) "well-planned program" gradually, but inevitably, gave way to new entertainments. New names—a younger crowd—would take over responsibility for the *Platz* and its up-dated programs. It was not surprising that after twenty years, the city and its citizens, including its Germans, were in a different place and of a different mindset than earlier.

Not entirely incidentally, in 1886 a new company (Palmetto) of the Fraternal Order of Knights of Pythias was formed in Charleston. In January 1887, the new company held an organizational meeting where the main order of business was taking measurements for the members' uniforms—black frock coats and pants, white helmets and plumes, gilded belts, and swords and side arms. B. H. Bequest served among the company's officers as "Sir Knight treasurer." His service as the company's treasurer suggests that he was not so much downplaying his affiliation with the Schützen fraternity, but rather expanding his circle of contacts and involving himself in what might have been considered a more "American" fraternal association than his German-oriented rifle club. His involvement in this second "fraternity" was likely responsible for his absence from the annual shooting contests sponsored by the German Rifle Club.

At first glance, nonetheless, the similarities between the Schützen and the Pythians are striking. The previous year's Schützenfest was reported to have begun with "becoming military and Terpsichorean honors"—no doubt featuring splendidly impressive (to both spectators and "performers") uniforms. The Pythians founding the Palmetto company in 1866 were comparably thrilled with their handsome and imposing uniforms, as well as the prospect of marching in a parade to display their finery, swords, and side arms. It is worth noting that the "military department" of the Pythian Order was referred to as the "Uniform Rank."[30] Bequest's affiliation with this new Pythian Company apparently commanded his attention over the course of the coming years. It was not that there was a distinct separation between the two fraternities—much the same group of individuals belonged to both, so that they were connected in more ways than one. It could be argued that the Pythians and the Schützen were so similarly oriented that becoming a Pythian did not move Bequest much beyond his already recognizable groove. In his close-knit circle there were hardly any of Charleston's Germans with whom he was not acquainted: a strong bond still held Charleston's German community together. But during the years after 1886, Bequest's name is more often in the record in connection with the Pythians than with the Schützen. Was he more comfortable in the company of the one group, dedicated as it was to "friendship, charity and benevolence" as he transitioned into a citizen of Charleston at the end of the century? Did he sense that the arc of popularity the Schützenfest had enjoyed had reached its high point, and that the ethnic-sponsored "mirth"

---

30. The current website (kophistory.com) notes that the Uniform Rank (UR) "came into being in 1878. A great many Pythians were Civil War Veterans and some lodges formed their own military drill teams. This would in time evolve into the Uniformed Ranks. The Pythian UR was sometimes known as the Army of the Lily."

was no longer the best way to become more like a Charlestonian and less like a German? Was he trying to modify his German sharpshooter identity by becoming part of a brotherhood that was less militaristic, more American, in order to be considered one of the city's citizens, who, as a Pythian, was "pledged to the promotion of understanding among men of good will as the surest means of attaining Universal Peace"?

In 1892 the members of the German Artillery—the venerable old and the sentimental young—celebrated the organization's "semi-centennial" in October with an impressive parade, an event that received a lot of coverage in the local press. If the columns in the *News and Courier* are accurate, most of Charleston's citizens turned out to admire the marchers in their very impressive finery, and the adults at least, to reflect on what the German Artillery stood for. The celebration once again certified that the Germans were held in high regard by the local citizenry. In a telling speech before the parade got underway, Theodore Melchers (brother of Franz Adolph Melchers) presented a custom-designed badge to the group's leader, Capt. Frederick Wagener:

> It is your untiring exertion which has made this company what it now is. it is through your influence and your work that to-day it owns this magnificent armory, second to none in the Southern States, and it is your untiring zeal which has made this day such a success. This beautiful jewel has been chosen with special care to commemorate your various services. You here behold the shield or battle flag of the 'Lost Cause,' surrounded by rays of glory, surmounted by the emblem of the Artillery, crossed cannons and the eagle—above which you see our national colors and those of Germany, united and held together by the coat-of-arms of our beloved State, South Carolina. These emblems are to denote that you fought as a true and brave defender of the 'Lost Cause': that you are a true son of the Fatherland, a loyal citizen of the United States, and a prince (a merchant prince) of South Carolina. Wear it near

your heart as a perpetual memento of the love and esteem which your comrades bear you.[31]

On this occasion, Bernhard Bequest rode with three of the German organization's leaders in one of the eight carriages in the torchlight parade spectacle, demonstrably honoring and celebrating the accomplishments of Frederick Wagener, a German Confederate war hero who had fought bravely for the "Lost Cause" and then become one of Charleston's leading businessmen.[32]

While trying to glimpse the nature of Bernhard Bequest's Charleston life during the years leading up to his fiftieth birthday in 1894, not much attention has been paid to the political climate, whether it impacted him, and, if so, to what degree. At the national level, James Garfield was elected president in 1880, but South Carolina had cast its electoral votes for his Democratic rival, Winfield Hancock. In '84, Grover Cleveland came to power with South Carolina's nine electoral votes behind him. South Carolina's democrats were out of step in 1888 when Benjamin Harrison was elected. Cleveland came back in 1892, again with the help of the state's electoral votes. Locally, supremacist southerners were managing the political scene with the "Eight Box Voting law"[33] that was in place by 1882. After that, the most obvious political

---

31. *News and Courier*, October 19, 1892. Frederick Wagener was a younger brother of John Andreas, the leader of the ethnic community's early *triumvirate* that worked so hard to integrate fellow German immigrants into the native community. It is possibly gratuitous to note that the newspaper was sufficiently capable of forgetting the recent past when its reporter casually, but incorrectly, referred to the late German leader as "Julius A. Wagener" in his column's second paragraph.

32. "Frederick W. Wagener's contribution to Charleston's economic development was profound and indisputable. Wagener arrived at the height of German immigration to Charleston. He began his business career as a retail grocer like so many other Germans. Upon returning to Charleston in 1865 after his service in the Confederate Army, he partnered with other Germans to form a wholesale grocery establishment that grew into a significant business in the community." Jeffrey Strickland, "Frederick Wagener, 1832-1921," *Immigrant Entrepreneurship: German-American Biographies 1720 to the Present*, 2015. (http://www.immigrantentrepreneurship.org/entry.php?rec=24)

33. What constituted a literacy test, requiring voters to put ballots in separate ballot boxes. Illiterate voters—the targeted Black population—would require "assistance" to

excitement revolved around renegade Benjamin Tillman, who started making noise already in 1885 when he made "a stunning speech on the plight of the farmer."[34] Tillman was successful in ousting South Carolina's old conservative regime by winning the governor's race in 1890. He was the state's governor from 1890 to 1894, and one of its U.S. senators from 1895 to 1918. His words in his inaugural speech suggest the political road traveled since the end of the Reconstruction era:

> The citizens of this great commonwealth have for the first time in its history demanded and obtained for themselves the right to choose her Governor; and I, as the exponent and leader of the revolution which brought about the change, am here to take the solemn oath of office … Democracy, the rule of the people, has won a victory unparalleled in its magnitude and importance … The triumph of democracy and white supremacy over mongrelism and anarchy, of civilization over barbarism, has been most complete.[35]

It is questionable whether the German immigrant had become so "Southern" that he could, or would, subscribe to such political radicalism, whether he could, or would, be comfortable with this manner of race-based ideology. It was nevertheless the distinctive flavor of the political soup of the time and not easily dismissed.

By the mid-nineties, Bequest had established himself as one of Charleston's reliable businessmen. His wood yard was one of three of the city's "firms" that in 1894 was awarded a federal government contract for furnishing wood to fuel vessels "for use in the 6th light house district." The government contract would have carried with it a modicum of prestige and was an affirmation of his success as a wood merchant. Having accomplished this much, the hard-working immigrant found time for leisure activity: the Americanized expert sharpshooter

---

put their ballot in the proper box.

34. George C. Rogers, Jr. and C. James Taylor, *A South Carolina Chronology*, 111.

35. Francis Butler Simkins, *Pitchfork Ben Tillman, South Carolinian* (Baton Rouge: Louisiana State University Press, 1944), 170-71.

tried his hand at something uniquely American—he started playing baseball. At the time, the sport was a new recreational outlet for the still-recovering city. At first, Bequest played for an amateur baseball club, then for the city's official "Charleston Base Ball Club" that played neighboring towns and was part of the South Atlantic League. The *News and Courier* followed the team closely, reporting enthusiastically on every home- and away-game. Bequest was the Club's secretary and treasurer.

1895 would turn out to be an important year for fifty-one-year-old B. H. Bequest: he still had it in himself to undertake a new business enterprise, demonstrating an entrepreneurship similar to that of many of his German colleagues who were bringing new ideas to the Charleston community. In December, the *News and Courier* featured a rather lengthy column describing what the German-American Mr. Bequest was up to:

> Mr. B. H. Bequest, a progressive and enterprising citizen of Charleston, who has for a long time been engaged in the wood business on East Bay, had recently visited his old home at Bremerhaven, Germany, and there discovered a process of smoking fish that he thought could be worked to advantage in Charleston. Upon his return to the city Mr. Bequest went to work at once and yesterday turned out the first batch of smoked whiting from his new smoke house. The fish were caught on Tuesday, cleaned and placed in pickle Tuesday night and smoked four hours yesterday. They were then taken out on the long spits and hung up on frames to cool. A reporter for The News and Courier tasted one of this first batch half an hour after it was taken out and found that they had lost none of the delicate flavor, the flesh being firm and white. The skin of the whiting is tinged a golden brown by the smoke and it is ready for the table after being warmed.
>
> Whiting, the most delicious of pan fish, are not easily kept after being taken from the water, unless packed on ice, but by this process of smoking they will be easily transported, dry, into the country and kept for a week if necessary.
>
> The smoke house is located on Mr. Bequest's premises, 335 East Bay, and is a neat and substantial two-story brick

structure. On the first floor are a set of seven large smoking ovens, with double iron doors 4 by 6 feet. In these ovens are racks and the fish spitted through the heads, hung in rows of a dozen to twenty. In the bottom of each oven a fire is kept up with hickory chips and large flues carry off the smoke after it has passed through the pendant tiers of fish.

Mr. Bequest has not yet fully arranged the other parts of the building, but there will be a cooling and packing room and other accessories.

The industry bids fair to be a prosperous and successful one, and Mr. Bequest is to be congratulated upon introducing it in Charleston. He will probably have the fish on sale in a few days at the principal grocers, and will also be ready for orders from the country. The capacity of the smoke house is several hundred pounds of fish per day, and several varieties, other than whiting, will also be available. The price will likely be 10 to 12 ½ cents a pound for smoked fish, which is comparatively cheaper than the undressed fish, which have to be used the day caught or kept on ice.[36]

To all appearances, behind this new business venture lay a brilliant concept. Fish—most noticeably what the locals referred to as "whiting"[37]—had long been a staple in the coastal city, prepared in a variety of ways, but never smoked. It took a European immigrant to see the advantages of pairing an abundant local resource with a method of preservation long practiced on the North German seacoast. Putting the idea to work took capital, as well as ingenuity: the wood dealer had found a new use for the material he had on hand; he had planned the space to locate the ovens; had conceptualized how they were to be built; had investigated and recruited the sources of supply; engineered the production operation and schedule; and was prepared to undertake the

---

36. *News and Courier*, December 5, 1895.

37. *Menticirrhus americanus* (Carolina whiting), abundant along the Atlantic and Gulf coasts, was similar to *Merlangius merlangus* (English whiting) known to inhabitants along the North Sea and the east coast of Britain.

marketing and distribution operation for what was to be a thriving wholesale business. By the end of the year, the newspaper announced:

> The European Fish Smokery, 335 East Bay / The public can now be supplied with all kinds of smoked fish / Florida Mullet, Whiting, &c, smoked fresh every day / F. W. Cappelmann, J. H. Hesse, C. Muller, P. von Oven, F. Heinsohn, are now supplied with Fish from this smokery / B. H. Bequest / Proprietor / Telephone 272.[38]

Bequest's outlets were obviously some of his German grocer-friends who were happy to lend their support. The operation immediately got the attention of those who advocated any new undertakings that might stimulate the local economy, and for the first year, success seemed imminent:

> Mr. B. H. Bequest, who has recently put up a set of smoking ovens on his premises, 335 East Bay, and begun the drying and smoking of fish, etc. said to a reporter yesterday that the ovens were proving a success and he had every reason to be gratified with his work.
>
> Just at this season, he said, that fish suitable for smoking and drying were not plentiful in the Charleston market, and his supply came mostly from Florida. Besides smoking fish Mr. Bequest has cured and smoked hams and tongues most successfully.
>
> As yet Mr. Bequest has sent but little fish out of the city, the local trade having taken all he could furnish. In a short time, however, he will begin to cure and smoke sturgeon, and this can be secured in such quantities that he will have plenty for out of town shipments and will likely send a good deal to New York. The process used by Mr. Bequest is one learned by him in Germany last summer.[39]

---

38. *News and Courier*, December 9, 1895.
39. *News and Courier*, January 13, 1896.

Despite the enthusiastic advertising in the local newspaper (not in the *Deutsche Zeitung*), by 1897 Bequest's fish-smoking business was demoted to, at best, a sideline operation. The new undertaking that initially held so much promise was only briefly successful. In hindsight, the entire venture may not have been such a brilliant idea. Had Bequest thought through the seasonal nature of his supply? How often would he have to get the fish from Florida, rather than from local waters? Other than his ethnic neighbors, were local housewives likely to stop frying freshly caught whiting to plan meals around the smoked version? Were commercial fishermen going to sell their catch to other markets so that there would be no competition for the new delicacy? How complicated could the distribution of the new product become? It was one thing to deliver an order of wood chips to a buyer, quite another to get a perishable commodity to a widely distributed network of retail markets on a schedule determined by supply and demand. How much labor would it involve to generate the supply sufficient to the demand? If the wood lot had been manageable by a single proprietor, a production line would entail a number of employees and require a different kind of management. These and other matters may have been beyond the business acumen of the single entrepreneur of foreign birth bringing a new commercial idea into a culture almost paralytic by nature—more than one man, however honest and enterprising, could handle. The newspaper had in fact suggested that Bequest's initiative could be scaled up only with the backing of "enterprising business men" interested in "the comfort and profit of all concerned." In truth, Charleston in the 1890s was not the place to find an abundance of enterprising businessmen interested in capitalizing a new business in smoked fish.[40] Whatever forethought was lacking in Bequest's entrepreneurial spirit, his European smokery fell victim to the soft economy that prevailed at the time. All factors considered, it turned out that the vision behind the Bequest fish smokery had not materialized in the right place at the right time.

With the fish smokery on questionable footing, Bequest kept the wood lot going as in the past and kept his good name and reputation. In June of 1898, the *Evening Post* carried a condensed biography of the wood dealer:

---

40. In contrast, as will be seen, to the undertakings of his brother August.

In mentioning our citizens who have made a success by energy and business ability the name of B. H. Bequest stands among the leaders of Charleston's prosperous men.

Mr. Bequest is a native of Germany, where he was reared and educated. In 1861 he entered Charleston harbor in the bark Goss under Capt. Vieting, that well known seaman (now deceased). The morning he entered the harbor the confederate flag was flying over Fort Sumter, and a short time after, Mr. Bequest, true to the cause he believed right, entered the Confederate service and experienced some thrilling adventures in the blockade service under Capt. Moore steamer Fannie. He was on the Stonewall Jackson/Sirene with Capt. Black, and others.

Mr. Bequest is an old and tried seaman, having serviced in England, Scotland, Russia, Mexico, West Indies, etc.

After the war Mr. Bequest started in the grocery business on a very small scale at Mount Pleasant, remaining there for sixteen years. He was one of the leading citizens and enjoyed the confidence of the people. He was honored by the people, serving in the city council and four years as mayor.

In 1885 he came to Charleston and established his present business, which at that time was on a very small scale. But when, as before, hustling, coupled with untiring energy, and strict honest business principles won, and Mr. Bequest was enabled gradually to build up his now large and lucrative business. His plant is large and commodious, covering an acre of ground. He is wholesale and retail dealer in oak and pine wood, oak and pine blocks, gravel and white sand, wood sawed and delivered to any part of the city. Vessels supplied at low rates. Mr. Bequest has all the modern conveniences for the successful prosecution of his work, the capacity of the plant being fifteen cords per diem.

Eight wagons are run and ten men given employment. To say that he has made a success is but to read the above.

Mr. Bequest stands high both commercially and socially in the city. He is a member of the German Artillery, a K. of

P Uniform rank, having been treasurer for many years. He is also a member of the German Rifle Club, having been king twice.

Mr. Bequest is also a member of several other organizations of the city, and a public spirited, progressive gentleman who believes in pushing Charleston and the Palmetto State to the front.[41]

At the risk of repeating what has been stated previously, this summary of the German immigrant's industry and entrepreneurship, together with the emphasis on the esteem he had earned from others, illustrates the way many in the German ethnic community approached the process of becoming one with the host community.

In the early morning hours of October 28, 1899, Bequest died unexpectedly in his home at the age of fifty-five. The brief funeral notice in the *News and Courier* read:

> The funeral services of the late Mr. Bernhard H. Bequest were held at St. Matthew's German Lutheran Church yesterday afternoon, and the remains interred at Bethany Cemetery with Pythian ceremonies. Mr. Bequest was an estimable citizen of Charleston, and had been for many years in business here. His death at his residence on East Bay street Saturday morning was a surprise and a shock to his friend [*sic*], for he had been at his office quite recently and was not thought to be seriously ill. He was a member of Stonewall Lodge, Knights of Pythias,

---

41. *Evening Post*, June 11, 1898. The article incorporates many of the details in the account by Brigadier General Ellison Capers cited earlier, suggesting that the reporter here was privy to that account before it was published in 1899. The reporter includes some additional far-flung adventures that are unverified, and he misstates the date Bequest "came to Charleston" to start the wood yard. As an English speaker, the reporter might be forgiven for misspelling the name of Heinrich Wieting's ship, the *Gauss,* that brought Bequest to Charleston, as well as the name of the Captain himself. Those were details that belonged to the fading, not-too distant past.

and also a member of Palmetto Company, U.R.K.P. Both of these organizations attended the funeral yesterday.

A number of creditors came forward in response to the published notice of probate: $6.75 worth of groceries had been charged at G. Abrams's "Choice Groceries"; the Standard Oil Company had delivered a bucket of light axle grease October 25th; E. Wierman's "Ship and Family Groceries" presented a bill for $3.18 for some loads of gravel and white sand; there was $3.50 due to George J. Phillips for five shoeings of horses and mules during October and November; the same horses and mules had been fed in September and October with oats and hay from the C. D. Gartelman Co., whose bill came to $38.93; Albert Bischoff, dealer in "Hay, Grain and Mill Feed" had also delivered "merchandise" in the amount of $14.86 in September and October. These bills were all paid, and two days before Christmas 1899 "the Engine, Boiler, Belting, Shafting, Saws and all machinery appurtenant to the wood yard business carried on by the late B. H. Bequest in said city of Charleston," as well as "the carts, three sets of harness, three horses, one mule, tools, one wagon, wheelbarrows, window shades, desk, stove and office chair, and stock of oak and pine wood" were sold at public auction. The auction included Bequest's buggy and his schooner, *Leonore*.

Bernhard Bequest's German-born widow had lost two children in their infancy and now had one American-born son, aged seventeen, to raise and depend on. Catherine Bequest née Mehrtens lived until 1920. As for her late husband, the liquidation of the successful wood business that had enabled him to become a German-American Charlestonian was but meagre validation of a thirty-four-year-long struggle through the hard times of Reconstruction and the fading of Charleston into the backwash of the New South during the final decades of the century. A life that had begun with daring adventure and a vision of opportunity progressed through service to the public good and dedicated efforts as a landowner, merchant and entrepreneur. In the end, the German immigrant could take comfort in knowing that he had won the praise, respect, and esteem of the Charleston community that had come to regard him as one of its own.

## —THE QUIET SEAMAN

Bernhard Heinrich Bequest's story can be read as that of a typical upstanding, respected, hard-working, entrepreneurial German immigrant to Charleston who experienced the turbulent years between the end of the Civil War and the end of the century. The stories of his two younger brothers provide further examples of the post-war immigrant experience, the one perhaps less entrepreneurial, although just as hard-working, the other, entrepreneurial and hard-working, though less upstanding. Bernhard Heinrich's two younger brothers' stories add detail to the composite picture of the German ethnic community as it evolved past the turn of the century into the years preceding the next (the "Great") war.

Both younger brothers came with fewer resources than their experienced blockade-runner sibling. Given their youth and maritime heritage, they, like their elder brother, probably worked for their passage as members of a ship's crew. Less than three years younger than his older brother, Johann Ludwig Bequest was the second to leave for America—not initially to Charleston, but to Baltimore. He held out there for six-plus years, then in 1871 joined his elder and younger brother in Charleston, the latter having gotten himself to the city already in 1866 as a fifteen-year-old teenager. While there may have been a plan that they should all at some point end up together in the same place where each would benefit from the support of the others, John's six-year stint in Baltimore suggests that Charleston was not considered the only option. In any case, each had a mind of his own and their stories make clear that each of their paths leading to acculturation would take a distinctly different direction.

Of the three, there is every indication that John was the quiet one, an immigrant not demonstrably inclined to either social or political ambitions, nor driven to assume any position of leadership. For the entire decade of Charleston's highly unsettled years of Reconstruction, quiet John Ludwig Bequest lived an undistinguished life, not unlike numerous others in Charleston's late nineteenth-century German immigrant community. But no matter how quietly he, or they, carried on under the public radar, the immigrant would not have been oblivious to the social, economic, and political conditions that defined Charleston and South Carolina at the time. Once in Charleston, John Bequest would experience a good portion of the Reconstruction years. He would see Ulysses S. Grant re-elected to the presidency in 1872, would know that Daniel Chamberlain was elected South Carolina's governor in 1874 as a Republican. In 1875, he willingly, knowingly, purposefully, became a United States citizen in a state in which the white population was unsettled, angry, and again rebellious, and in which the emancipated would exceed sixty percent of the city's population within the next five years.[42]

Taking advantage of family support, John spent his first years in Charleston working for his brother Bernhard as a clerk, living above the elder brother's grocery store. In 1883 he married Bernhard's first (late) wife's sister, Catherine Margarethe Rigbers, in a ceremony performed by the pastor of St. Matthew's. After a dozen years in the city, he was working as a driver for the Palmetto Brewery, a thriving business that belonged to a fellow German immigrant, J. C. H. Claussen. The young couple soon had two children: a daughter, C. Adeline Therese— doubtless named for John's late first cousin, Adeline Bequest Schroeder—and a son, Johann Ludwig. The father of two left his job at the Palmetto Brewery and for a while was employed as a "stableman," then finally found work at the Morris Island lighthouse. That job, at least, was work more attuned to his maritime background and kept him close to the water. Twenty-four years after his arrival in the United States, John Bequest was not yet propertied: the family rented quarters around the corner from the Bernhard Bequest residence. Possibly in pursuit of a more rural environment and likely in order to acquire property, the John Bequest family moved in 1888 across the bay to Mount Pleasant—the reverse of his brother's move into the city almost ten years earlier.

In the newspaper account of an incident that occurred in Mount Pleasant in August, 1889, we get another glimpse of the cultural context presented by the small village community where the John Bequest family and numerous other German immigrants or their descendants lived. The headline read: "Reviving the race issue / An exceedingly ugly affair at Mount Pleasant." Three-and-a-half columns reported on "[t]he accidental shooting of a negro woman by a white boy … the calling out of the State troops, the fiendish work of black viragoes, the law triumphant." As the story went, the Negro woman had made a purchase in the small store owned by Mr. Tiencken (by name, doubtless a German and described as "one of the most prominent, popular and conservative citizens of Mount Pleasant"). The young clerk, Mr. Tiencken's

---

42. 1880 Federal census.

seventeen-year-old brother-in-law, Fred Scharfner (by name, also a German or of German descent), had just cleaned his (loaded) gun that was lying on the counter. Although warned to be careful, the Negro woman accidently brushed against the gun, which discharged and mortally wounded her. The young clerk, with the help of a Negro man with a cart, got her to a doctor, then gave himself up to another village resident, Claus Koeper (by name, a German). It took no time before the public was informed of what had happened:

> The news spread with lightning rapidity, and the truth of the rumor, so far as the sheriff's appeal for aid, was speedily verified. Gen. Huegenin, commanding the 4th brigade, was soon in communication with Governor Richardson, and as the result of the telegraphic correspondence, orders were at once issued to Col. Magrath, commanding the 1st battalion of State Volunteer Troops, to detail two companies of his command with orders to report to Sheriff Hale... The detail was promptly made, the German Fusiliers and the Sumter Guards being designated, with Major J.C. Von Panten to command the battalion.

The military promptly arrived in Mount Pleasant with the afternoon ferry. As excerpts from the newspaper reveal, the accidental shooting turned into a local drama:

> — It is difficult to imagine how any civilized or even semi-civilized people could have made the tragedy the pretext for a threat to lynch...

> — The negro women of Mount Pleasant, however, like their sisters of Cainhoy, Edisto, or other places along the seacoast are very excitable. They at once sounded the war whoop, and in an incredible short space of time had all the black vagabonds of the village in a state of rage that threatened a rupture of the peace...

— [A] number of the white residents of the Village, whose business brings them to the city every day, appeared on the wharf. Most of them were armed with Winchester rifles and were anxious to get to their homes, where their families were comparatively unprotected and at the mercy of the black fiends who were heading the intended riot...

— About half-past ten o'clock the German Fusiliers, about twenty-five strong, marched into the Ferry slip under the command of Lieut. Schroder. The men were attired in the handsome fatigue uniform of army blue and wore patent cartridge belts, each belt lined with twenty rounds of ammunition...

— [T]he Sappho steamed up to the Mount Pleasant wharf. The disembarkation was the work of two minutes, and then the battalion, with fixed bayonets, loaded muskets carried at the right shoulder and at quick step, marching in columns of fours, was on its way to the scene of the supposed battle...

— The jail is at some distance from the Court House... Near it are several houses with double piazzas, all of which were crowded with women—the men in that vicinity being gathered into groups of four or five. They were as sulky, as ugly and as brutal a set as could be gathered together anywhere in the State. The women were engaged in cursing, swearing, blaspheming, shouting, and shrieking; the men stood with lowering looks and sulky mien. It was altogether an ugly, treacherous, brutal crowd, which might, under the tongue lashing of the black viragoes, have caused considerable trouble but for the timely arrival of the soldiers from the city...

— But as was the case on Mount Pleasant, the women were the loudest and the most indecent in their denunciation of the white race. These flaunted their skirts in the faces of every white woman or child who passed them without escort and indulged in obscene and abusive language...

— It will of course be understood that the colored persons who so disgraced their race last night constitute a small and a most disreputable part of the colored population of Charleston, but the crowd that assembled at Market wharf about seven o'clock made no effort to conceal their bitter hatred of the white race. It mattered not to them that there had been no murder done, that the young lad whose gun had accidentally killed a colored woman was as unhappy as he was unfortunate. It simply gave them opportunity of exhibiting their hatred to the white race...

— The people who were arrested yesterday by Sheriff Hale were Maria Alston, Amelia Simons, Handy Washington, the ring leader, John Edwards and Jim Brown. There will be a number of other arrests...

— Mr. Pollte, a prominent colored lawyer, also assisted in quieting the negroes by his coolness. He was aided by the Rev. J. S. Singleton and the Rev. J. F. Lite, both colored preachers. They advised the negroes to keep quiet and obey the law.

This lengthy newspaper account reveals how little had changed in Mount Pleasant and in Charleston between 1865 and 1889, how ineffective the efforts to *reconstruct* the region had been, how endemically the racial divide persisted. In the account we can also note how integral the Germans had become to the communities they lived in. As in Charleston, the Germans were likely Mt. Pleasant's principal merchants, and names like Tiencken, Scharfner, and Koeper were no longer identified as of foreign origin. And no one was surprised that the military forces come to quell the disturbance included the handsomely attired German Fusiliers.

We might wonder at this point why in 1889 the German Fusiliers, organized already in 1775 and recognized as the oldest German militia in the South, were more than a century later still involved in keeping the peace in Charleston; additionally, how it was that the local newspaper reporter could not help but notice that the Fusilier men were "attired in the handsome fatigue uniform of army blue and wore patent cartridge belts, each belt lined with twenty rounds of ammunition."[43] Digressing briefly from the John Bequest story, it is worth noting that ever since their founding, Charleston's German volunteer militias, like other ethnic militias in the "martially charged culture of the South,"[44] had assumed a protectionist role. Functioning as a kind of paramilitary organization, the protectionist role was consonant with that of the original Schützen (German verb *schützen* = to protect), whose function in protecting the local citizenry harks back to the Middle Ages. Charleston's Schützengesellschaft, founded in 1855, initially operated as a paramilitary organization, and it was from those early Schützen that members of Charleston's nineteenth-century German militias were recruited.[45] That such a paramilitary entity like the Fusiliers persisted for so long to play a role in "protecting" Charleston had as much to do with the city's persistent *need* of protection as with the Germans' readiness to function as protectors. As was pointed out in Chapter One, Charleston's native white population had since early on been intent on defending itself against the threat of those under its control. That context, together with a resident ethnic population ready to offer its "military sense" in protecting the larger community against its enemies was a mutually beneficial arrangement.

It was Melchers who identified the "military sense of the Germans" in the *Deutsche Zeitung* in November, 1853, when he wrote about the parading German Riflemen: "The German Riflemen are now without question one of the handsomest and best companies of the city. Clothing and weapons are simple, tasteful, and practical, and the formation as outstanding as can be expected from a German company and completely in harmony with the military sense of the Germans."[46] As in this particular instance, it was rarely the case that mention of any of the city's ethnic militia companies on parade (or, for that matter, in other contexts as well) would fail to take notice of the group's uniform. The parade's spectators, natives and immigrants alike, are always described as impressed by the sharp-looking uniforms of the German

---

43. Mehrländer points out that by 1860 the Fusiliers "were no longer an ethnic German unit ... but rather consisted of Charleston citizens of German ancestry."

44. Mehrländer, *The Germans of Charleston, Richmond, and New Orleans*, 79.

45. Ibid., 84.

46. *Deutsche Zeitung*, November 15, 1853, cited in Mehrländer, *The Germans of Charleston, Richmond and New Orleans*, 83

parade participants, whether or not the individual reporting on the event is a German-American or a "native" Charlestonian.

It is clear that uniforms visibly unify a group and set it somewhat apart as a means to articulate the group's unique identity. In the case of Charleston's ethnic German militias, their uniforms served to preserve the group's ethnic identity and signal its resistance to the pressures of assimilation. At the same time, it showed them off, advertised them, as it were, to non-ethnic observers. In Mehrländer's opinion, the "external" essence of the militia was self-presentation: "magnificent, exotic uniforms, highly polished weapons, and sharp exercise drill at public parades were expressions of the wealth and pride of an ethnic minority.[47] At the same time, these well-outfitted and well-trained ethnic groups' participation in practically every public event or celebration unified them *with* the native populace in attendance, certified them as full-fledged citizens of the larger host community. It would be difficult to decide unequivocally whether their "display" was intended as an indicator of patriotism or whether it was a defense of their ethnicity: it was likely a little of both. That for whatever reason they themselves took pleasure in their "exotic uniforms, highly polished weapons, and sharp exercise drill," to which the public responded in adoration of the same, signifies that the two cultures were able to merge in creating the symbiosis that Michael Bell described as unique to antebellum Charleston

Returning to John Bequest's story and the 1889 incident in Mount Pleasant, it was also reported that the German immigrant had a role to play in the drama: "Early yesterday, when the mob was gathering, Sheriff Hale deputized John Bequest and A. Danton, and they with Charles Lafayette, a colored deputy sheriff, and Isaac H. Harris, the colored jailer, rendered assistance to the sheriff in preserving the peace." [48] John Bequest was never identified as a member of the Schützen, nor did he belong among the elite members of any of the German militias. He had only shortly before moved to Mount Pleasant (1888) where a decade earlier his older brother had served as the town's mayor. He worked during the summer as a mate on the *Sappho*,[49] and was likely on

---

47. Mehrländer, *The Germans of Charleston, Richmond and New Orleans,* 80.

48. *News and Courier*, August 24, 1889.

49. The well-known steamer of the Mount Pleasant ferry company that carried passengers from downtown Charleston to Mount Pleasant.

board when the steamer brought the handsomely-attired German Fusiliers to the wharf in Mount Pleasant. In calming the rowdy crowds threatening the good white citizens of the town, Sheriff Hale did not have to look far to find the German immigrant John Bequest, along with two other protectors (the "colored" deputy sheriff and the town's jailer—risen in status and acting in reverse roles) at the ready to be deputized in preserving the peace.

With peace restored and the "race-issue" quieted, whites and blacks and immigrant and native-born continued to co-exist in Mt. Pleasant. The following year (1890), John and his wife lost their four-month-old son, Johann Frederick (named for John's nephew, Bernhard's son, now eight years old). Two years later, after having borne four children in nine years, the German-born immigrant Catherine Margarethe Rigbers Bequest died, aged thirty-eight, a Charleston resident (as Catherine Mary Sophie) for seventeen years. The family had previously moved back into town to share quarters with Catherine's younger brother Frederick, a grocer and "saloon-keeper"—a further indication that at age forty-five John Bequest still did not own property. Like his elder brother, the widower with three children would soon re-marry, the second time to a U.S.-born younger woman from Pennsylvania. With his new wife, sharing quarters with his former brother-in-law was no longer tenable, and the newly-married couple moved back to Mount Pleasant.

Given his rather checkered employment history, the quiet German seaman finally found his calling as a member of the life-saving crew on Sullivan's Island, a barrier island adjacent to Mount Pleasant. For his late-life, protectionist, occupation, John Bequest could hardly have found a better match for the sea-hankering he had brought with him from his native Geestendorf. It would subsequently turn out that the sea off the coast of Charleston would twice add dimension to the character of John Bequest, whose life would otherwise have gone unnoticed by all but his own family and his closest acquaintances.

Charleston's *News and Courier* of January 24, 1894, under the headline "Cast up by the sea / Small boat with two corpses thrown up on the beach at Morris Island," reported:

> Only meagre details of one of the most distressing accidents that has occurred in the waters around Charleston in many years reached the city yesterday. In this case the victims are all white men, and it is not yet known but that six lives were lost.

Monday afternoon last a small cat-rigged boat left Sullivan's Island with supplies for the Morris Island life-saving station. The passengers were Fred Miller, of Sullivan's Island, Harry R. Campsen, of Charleston, Capt George Campsen, of the life-saving crew, John Bequest, of the life-saving crew, Walter Croft, of Charleston, and a German boy, whose name could not be learned. Nothing more was seen or heard of any of the men till Tuesday afternoon, when a colored fisherman discovered two bodies on the Morris Island beach.

Subsequent reporting offered identifying details of each of the six men feared lost. John Bequest was described as "a member of the crew and in the summer time was mate of the steamer Sappho. He was a brother of Mr. August Bequest, cashier of the German American Trust and Savings Bank."[50]

For Charleston's German community there was some good news, when two days later it was reported that John Bequest was, in fact, not one of the six members of the life-saving crew lost to the sea.

The cheerful information was received yesterday that all of the six men supposed to have been drowned were not lost. Mr. John Bequest and the German boy were not in the ill-fated bateau, but were on duty at the life-saving station. Mr. Bequest was down on the beach Monday night, and he says that a strong wind was blowing and the sea was very high shortly before midnight. This gives a plausible explanation of how the bateau foundered. It is probable that a flaw struck her and in the high sea the crew could not manage her.

Safe and sound, John Bequest was a member of the search party that later discovered the other bodies and brought the drowned victims to the city for their respective inquests.

---

50. It is worth noting that John is identified here in connection with his younger brother, August, rather than with the elder Bernhard, who had served as mayor of the neighboring community. At the time, August Bequest was busy acquiring a reputation in Charleston.

Four years later, he would have another close call with the sea, but again would escape being its victim. As a member of the Coast Guard, he was involved in August of 1898 in saving the life of a young swimmer about to drown in the surf off Sullivan's Island. On August 20, 1898, the *Evening Post* reported the drowning of Charles M. Coste, one of the guards who had tried to save "young Ned Schachte":

LIFE CREW TO THE RESCUE / The cry of distress was heard by the life saving crew and Coste, one of the best swimmers of the crew, made for the water and quickly swam out to Schachte, who was almost exhausted from the terrible struggles with the waves. Guard Coste was followed by Capt. Adams, Guards Bequest and Tapio. Captain Martin, who was out on horseback riding at the time, heard the cries of young Schachte and dismounting he quickly threw off his coat and removing his shoes swam out towards Coste, who had Schachte trying to bring him in, reaching the two men about the same time as Capt. Adams and Tapio. Capt. Adams was the first to relieve Coste, Capt. Martin and Guard Tapio assisting him. They spoke words of encouragement to the boy, telling him they were out for a little fun and would soon reach the beach.

A BATTLE WITH THE WAVES / Suddenly the swimmers reached a point where the current sweeps around the jetties like a mill race. It was a flood tide and the sea was choppy. Ned Schachte became frightened and seized Capt. Adams around the throat with a death like grasp. Capt. Martin released the boy's hold just in time to save them both, as Capt. Adams had become considerably exhausted. In fact all of the men were, as the battle of the waves and strong tides was a terrific one.

Guard Bequest in the meantime came with life belts and Schachte was delivered to him. He had not had the boy long before he cried out that he was being swept out to sea by the strong current. A boat from the life saving station had been launched and in a short time picked the men up and started for the shore.

Tapio had become very weak and was seen to go down once. The boat reached him just in time to save him from a watery grave. The water was only waste [*sic*] deep but the poor fellow had completely worn himself out and his strength had about left him when he was picked up. He was in an unconscious condition when the shore was reached. Some time was spent in restoring him to consciousness. Tapio is an expert swimmer.

COSTE GOES DOWN / Capt. Martin and Capt. Adams, after seeing that young Schachte was all right, made their way for the shore. They gave no thought to Coste, as they knew him to be an expert swimmer and had seen him make for the beach after he had been relieved of Ned Schachte. Instead of following the current, which forms an eddy around the rocks at that point, and swimming to shore, he attempted to swim across and it swept him away.

All of the men who took part in the rescuing of Schachte displayed remarkable bravery and coolness. Not once did any of them lose their head or become nervous, and it is not an easy thing either for a man rolled and tossed by a choppy sea, trying to save the life of another, to keep cool throughout ...

To-day Capt. Martin and Capt. Adams and the life saving crew have been the recipient of many congratulations. [51]

In reporting on the rescue operation that cost the life of one of Bequest's fellow guardsmen, there was no need to mention that one of the life-saving

---

51. One hundred and fifteen years later, the 1898 rescue was commemorated in April 2013 with a ceremony posthumously awarding the Silver Lifesaving Medal for Heroism to James L. Coste, who had drowned in the attempt to save young Ned Schachte. On that occasion it was revealed that the young swimmer who had been rescued was the grandfather of Charleston's long-serving mayor, Joseph P. Riley Jr.

crew was a German immigrant who had assisted in saving the life of a young man of German descent. Both rescuer and rescued were Charlestonians.[52]

The 1910 federal census indicates that John Bequest owned a home in Mount Pleasant and worked "on his own account." By then, he was in his early sixties and doubtless retired. For the five years between 1910 and 1915, he and his wife received small payments for "rent for a white school," paid quarterly by the County treasurer to "Mrs. J. L. Bequest." More than likely, Pennsylvania-born Mary Emma Bequest was teaching school for white children in her home in Mount Pleasant. Surely neither she nor her German-born husband ever reflected on how her employment in the educational system at the time articulated the legacy of the post-Reconstruction era in Mount Pleasant, South Carolina.

The couple's daughter married a ship's carpenter in 1908 and moved to Jacksonville, Florida. Their two sons—both manual laborers (boilermakers)—followed the exodus to Jacksonville[53] where both died young: Heinrich in 1914, John Jr. in 1918, a victim of the influenza pandemic. In his retirement, John Bequest Sr. gardened on his small Mount Pleasant acreage. He would witness the slow march of the United States into the war with his German homeland. Widowed in 1919, he left Charleston within a few years to live with his daughter in Jacksonville, dying aged seventy-eight in 1925. On his death certificate,

---

52. Ned Schachte's father, Capt. Henry Schachte, was a business associate of both of John Bequest's brothers.

53. A large number of Germans in the Southeast, including those in Charleston, migrated to Jacksonville: "Since the 1880's it had been a resort for invalids and vacationers from the northern United States and Europe. Local business leaders had distributed promotional literature advertising the city throughout the country and abroad, so that the city was well known to travelers. Good railroad and steamship line connections to the city made it possible for impecunious immigrants to reach it without too much difficulty. During the 1880's a building boom began, including new home construction and public works projects. In short, the city was neither remote nor unknown, it offered the opportunity for employment in the service sector if not in industry, and unskilled labor might exceed the supply of available blacks." Kathleen Ann Francis Cohen, "Immigrant Jacksonville: A Profile of Immigrant Groups in Jacksonville, Florida, 1890-1920." University of North Florida, 1986.(Graduate Theses and Dissertations. 1. https://digitalcommons.unf.edu/etd/1)

he is *John Louis Bequest*, a widower, a retired *seaman*: the informant, his second-generation daughter, Adeline, was unable to furnish the names of her paternal grandparents, although she certified that they were born in Germany.

In summary, the German immigrant Johann Ludwig Bequest lived quietly among his Charleston hosts and, except for the part he played in the rescue of a young swimmer in the waters off Sullivan's Island and his own near-drowning, unnotably. Perhaps his second marriage to an American woman contributed to the process of erasing his German heritage. Living beyond the end of the First World War when anti-German sentiment made German origins a liability, there was little reason for him to harken back to the past, no reason to celebrate his ethnicity, no reason, even, to connect his children to the heritage stamped on their parents. By the time John left Charleston, his children had already left the coastal city that had allowed a North German seaman to transform himself into a southern American. Charleston would not hold onto them, nor they onto it. At the end of the first quarter of the twentieth century the story of John Bequest as a German immigrant was thus of only minor significance to the native community that had taken him in. Once more, this Bequest's story—individual as it is—reflects the story of the many others whose heritage evaporated in the process of acquiring an American, southern, identity indelibly marked on them by the unique culture of Charleston and its environs.

## —THE BOLD OPERATOR

The course that immigrant Carsten August Bequest took after coming to Charleston suggests that the youngest Bequest brother was cut from different cloth. His life-story brings us farther, and somewhat more dramatically, into the decades leading up to WWI and demonstrates how members of the German ethnic community were adapting to the changing Charleston context.

August—*Carsten* was dropped almost immediately—joined his elder brother in Charleston shortly after the latter had come back to the city with his blockade-running days behind him. If, as proposed earlier, the three had decided to emigrate and, in sequence, all end up in the same place, such a plan would take a number of years to materialize. After an initial period in Charleston, August decided that he needed to be on his own somewhere else.

For five years he worked as a clerk in his elder brother's store,[54] then took himself—an independent twenty-year-old—to up-state South Carolina to open his own grocery store in Abbeville, South Carolina. He may have been influenced to try his luck there in light of the St. Matthew's Lutheran community's missionary zeal to settle immigrants and establish a congregation elsewhere in South Carolina. As we know, German immigrants were encouraged to be even more pioneering by moving to the more rural location in the fertile northwest corner of the state, where competition with the locals for employment was less of an issue. Abbeville was not that far from Charleston nor from the Walhalla settlement, was indeed a more rural, less competitive environment, and given its size, could well accommodate a (another?) dry goods/grocery/liquor store. At the time, one could get there on the Blue Ridge Railway that connected Charleston with the town of Hamburg on the South Carolina-Georgia border, not too distant from Abbeville.

August's effort to establish himself in Abbeville was twice stymied by fires that destroyed his stores. He nonetheless persisted and was advertised in Abbeville's 1876-77 City Directory as "A. Bequest/Dealer in/Dry Goods, Groceries, Provisions & Liquor." By then he had married his second cousin, Augusta Catherine Rohde, at St. Matthew's. Augusta either remained at first in Charleston while her husband operated the store in Abbeville, or else retuned to Charleston to give birth to their first son, Heinrich Christian, in 1877. A second son, Bernhardt—obviously named for his uncle—was born in Abbeville two years later, but lived only sixteen days. By the time a third son, Johann Ludwig (named for his other uncle) arrived in 1881, the couple was back in Charleston. The Abbeville enterprise had run its course, and with a wife and two young sons, August, approaching the age of thirty, went into business operating a grist mill. His opting for this occupation was no doubt determined by a *German* connection: the Hanoverian immigrant couple who owned the Blohme Milling Company manufacturing flour, grist, and meal, were good friends, compatriots, and mentors to the Bequests. The Bequest's fourth son, born in 1883, was named August Blohme Bequest.

---

54. The elder brother put both younger brothers to work in his store until they found their own footing. John left Baltimore to come to Charleston the same year that August left to move to Abbeville.

The couple's Abbeville experience had taken place during the middle years of Reconstruction in rural, up-state South Carolina. The politics there were undoubtedly more straightforward than in either Charleston or Columbia, but the aversion to Radical Reconstruction was no less intense, possibly more so. The activities of the Ku Klux Klan were more demonstrative of the racial divide in rural areas than in the urban setting of the cities. August and Augusta were married just after the disputed gubernatorial and presidential elections of 1876 and would have been witness to the less nuanced rural politics that brought an end to Reconstruction in South Carolina. When they returned to Charleston, August's elder brother was ending his term as mayor of Mount Pleasant, and Charleston, with the rest of the state, was on its way to being redeemed. After 1877, white Democrats—the Redeemers—would take control to effectively banish white and black Republicans from every sphere in which they had previously operated. A new South was taking shape, and the ethnic community would find itself adapting to life among the "redeemed."

Once back in Charleston, August's activities mark him as the more aggressive Bequest brother. If with hindsight we can see Bernhard Heinrich as a methodical, careful, well-respected and entrepreneurial citizen-businessman, and the less organized, less ambitious John following a somewhat directionless course, the immigrant August will be revealed as a Type-A looking to move up, rub shoulders with the bigwigs, and with daring, engage the rapids of the local business and political river. He took quickly and actively to the Democratic camp, although being white, he could hardly have done anything else. The democratization of German immigrants had begun already when John Andreas Wagener was put on the ballot by the Democratic "machine" to run against the Republican party's Pillsbury in the 1871 mayoral election. At the so-called "Taxpayers' Convention" in 1874, the up-state town of Edgefield's cavalry hero, Martin Witherspoon Gary, suggested that the Germans should be used to "shift the voting balance and secure a Democratic victory." Richard Zuczek writes that Gary "had no doubts that Germans would make good Democrats, for he believed the difference between Democrats and Republicans was 'race, not party.' ... Gary argued that since ten South Carolina counties had white majorities, and twelve were split rather closely, 'the introduction of a few hundred immigrants' into each of the marginal ones would bring

Democratic control of the legislature, and possibly even the executive."[55] This sentiment, popular in the early 1870s, does not mean that German immigrants were used for similar political purposes a decade later, but it does suggest how easily August Bequest and other Charleston Germans could find themselves aligned with the resurgent Democratic Party. Since so many aspects of the politics of the time were framed around the "question of race," it was almost impossible for the immigrants in their whiteness not to covenant with the Southern white society they were now a part of. That covenant had been in place already in antebellum times when the immigrant had had few options to cross the racial divide.

The term "mover and shaker"—someone who could "wheel and deal"— would be an apt descriptor for August Bequest during the period after his return from Abbeville into the 1890s. The grist mill operation planted him firmly in the business world, and he had a social circle in which he could extend his connections both within and outside the ethnic community. In 1887, a daughter, Annie Agnes, was added to the family. Now the father of four, the grist mill operator thought it time to shift his footing. He bought a restaurant. As a more up-scale and socially advantageous venue than what the rather pedestrian grist mill operation offered, the restaurant afforded him more opportunity to play a different role on Charleston's business stage. By the end of the year, "Bequest's restaurant" had become a destination in downtown Charleston. The new restaurant owner could continue his involvement in Democratic politics in a more social setting, hosting the downtown crowd at tables, while monitoring the issues of the day. He was one of twelve delegates to the Democrats' 1887 Nominating Convention.

August Bequest became sufficiently financially stable that he could buy and sell property, as well as invest effort and money in anything that promised a positive return. He was making numerous "moves," seizing opportunity when it knocked. Already in 1887 he was elected to the Board of Directors of the new Consumers' Coal Company along with his German friends Henry Schachte, E. H. Jahnz, A. F. C. Cramer, H. A. Heiser, Henry Wohlers, and H. Sahl. This was but an initial step to move into the circle of Germans who were playing a

---

55. Richard Zuczek, *State of Rebellion: Reconstruction in South Carolina* (Columbia, SC: University of South Carolina Press, 1996), 137.

significant role in Charleston's economic development and, in their own way, shaping the city's future.

In 1892 he was elected treasurer of his Democratic ward, positioned at this point to mind a portion of the finances that would be used to reorganize local Democratic forces. To whatever degree the local Democrats needed to reorganize themselves, they were indisputably in charge of the city's politics. August Bequest was frequently a signatory to various actions taken by his Club or the Party on questions or concerns affecting the public. By the early nineties, the Bequest family could afford to spend the summer at the seashore on Sullivan's Island among the large colony of Charleston Germans trying to escape the heat—essentially the ones who had achieved economic success. It was not until 1893 that he was naturalized, twenty-seven years after he had set foot in Charleston. It was as if he had been too busy to declare his intentions earlier.

A month before his naturalization was finalized, he and several of his friends were granted a commission to incorporate The Charleston Improvement Company "doing a general industrial business" and dealing in real estate and personal property. The businessmen/friends in this venture were J. Fred Lilienthal, John D. Cappelmann, and J. C. Blohme. They were all "successful" Germans: Lilienthal was secretary and treasurer of the Germania Bank and Loan Association, John Cappelmann was an attorney, and Blohme was August Bequest's friend, mentor, and one of Charleston's largest grain dealers. The restaurant owner could comfortably call these men his associates: he had sufficient resources to contribute to the capital investment, and the four of them together must have felt confident that they had enough collective acumen to run the newly-formed enterprise. Cappelmann was probably the only one who had been formally trained in a profession—the others were self-made men.

Before long, it was clear that August Bequest intended to do more than just put his toe in Charleston's business waters. In 1893, the South Carolina Secretary of the State granted a commission to I. V. Barden and August Bequest—the "Board of Corporators"—to open the books of subscription to the capital stock of the German-American Trust and Savings Bank.[56] Overnight,

---

56. "Prior to 1886, incorporation of any manufacturing enterprise in South Carolina required a special act of the legislature. In 1886 the legislature, with little fanfare or opposition, enacted a general incorporation law that allowed the South Carolina Secretary of State to grant a charter to any applicant who fulfilled the requirements of the law."

the restaurant owner became a banker. The local press was enthusiastic. This was good news for Charleston: "The board of directors is composed of some of our most progressive and energetic and active citizens, selected especially from the younger generation, wide awake to the true interests of the city."[57] The following week, he was elected cashier of the bank. It was not for lack of ambition that August Bequest had aligned himself with some of Charleston's "most progressive and energetic and active citizens" working for the common good. The newspaper did not mention that so many of those "progressive and energetic and active" businessmen were German immigrants. The charter for the German-American Trust and Savings Bank was granted within two weeks of Bequest's election as cashier.

The bank immediately ran advertisements in the local papers outlining the range of its banking services: "Transacts a general banking business"; "Checks exchanged with all city banks"; "Exchange bought and sold"; "Money to loan on good security at low rates"; "Deposits in small or large sums received"; "Interest allowed on deposits in savings department at 5 per cent per annum semi-annually, or 4 per cent per annum quarterly"; "Interest mailed to non-resident Depositors on receipt of order or Pass Book."[58] The ads ran continuously for the next several years, attesting to the fact that the competition for the city's monies was keen: for a city its size, Charleston had a surfeit of banking institutions, e.g., The First National Bank, People's National Bank, Bank of Charleston, South Carolina Loan and Trust Co, Carolina Savings Bank, Miners' and Merchants' Bank, Exchange Banking and Trust Co., Hibernia Savings Bank, State Savings Bank, Germania Saving Bank, Charleston Savings Institution, Nickel Savings Bank, American Savings Bank, and the Columbian Banking and Trust Co. Through the bank's ads and notices in the newspaper, the Bequest name was continually before the eyes of the reading public, alongside those officers serving other institutions, all of whom were prominent in the community and who commanded the respect of their respective clientele. At the anniversary meeting of the bank's stockholders in February of 1895, August was elected to the board of directors, and at a subsequent meeting he

William J. Cooper Jr., *The Conservative Regime: South Carolina, 1877-1890* (Baltimore: The Johns Hopkins Press, 1968), 121.

57. *News and Courier,* January 20, 1893.

58. *News and Courier,* March 1, 1893.

was elected president "to supersede Mr. J. Fred Lilienthal who on account of his business affairs declined re-election."[59] At the annual meeting in February of the following year, "the financial statement, which was read by President Bequest, showed the bank to be in a most flourishing condition." [60] August was again named as president.

In his capacity as cashier of a Broad Street bank, August Bequest had climbed into the ranks of Charleston's successful businessmen and could leverage that success to get involved in additional enterprises. The corporators A. Bequest, A. F. C. Cramer, E. C. Metz, and John D. Cappelmann received a charter from the Secretary of State to incorporate the Palmetto Soap Manufacturing Company "to manufacture and sell all kinds of soap." Bequest, along with a number of his "energetic" friends, was elected to the Board of Directors. This was indeed a case of some of Charleston's "energetic" businessmen creating an investment opportunity for themselves and other local citizens, as well as offering a stimulus to help the city out of its economic doldrums. In many cases, it was a cohort of Germans who were viewed as Charleston's entrepreneurs. In a list of twenty "new enterprises undertaken in Charleston during the year,"[61] August Bequest was named in three: the German-American Trust and Savings Bank, the Palmetto Soap Manufacturing Co., and the Charleston Improvement Company.

Pausing a moment to take stock of August Bequest's ascendancy into the upper echelon of the Charleston business community, it would be reasonable to suggest that he had leveraged himself into that company with both his money and his mouth. His transitions from grocery/dry goods store proprietor in Abbeville, to grist mill operator, to owner of "Bequest's" on King Street had obviously provided him with sufficient financial resources that—in combination with his extrovert personality—he could transform his numerous friends and acquaintances, the majority of them successful Germans, into business partners willing to acknowledge his financial participation with a position of rank. It was not that he had any particular knowledge, or ability, or training that made him valuable to any of his new ventures—not to the banking industry, not to the local soap manufacturer, nor to the port city's commerce and trade in coal.

---

59. *News and Courier*, February 21, 1895.

60. *Evening Post*, February 20, 1896.

61. *News and Courier*, September 11, 1893.

August Bequest could be numbered among Charleston's "progressive and enterprising business men" because he indeed had talents: he was not risk-averse, he knew in which circles he wanted to move, he aspired to succeed as others with the same German blood had done, and he recognized no limitations on what might be possible. With some—or all—of the balls he managed to keep in the air, he was determined to succeed. Each undertaking represented an opportunity for him to gain even more traction in getting to the top.

On his way there, he put yet another feather in his cap. Early in 1895, the *News and Courier* announced the opportunity to subscribe to the capital stock of the Equitable Fire Insurance Company. August Bequest was one of the three incorporators. This would add another directorship as well as a vice-presidency. A month before the Equitable Fire Insurance Company's organizing meeting, the German-American Trust and Savings Bank had held its anniversary meeting and, as noted previously, elected August president to take the place of J. Fred Lilienthal, who declined re-election. If he was keeping track—and no doubt he was—August had been one of the named corporators of four businesses, was now on the board of five enterprises, and was president or vice-president of three. As if there were not much left for him in Charleston proper, he sought and found a niche in another part of the state as one of the incorporators of the Central Cotton Mills Company. The German Charlestonian, along with his other friends, foresaw the potential of monetary gain in the burgeoning textile industry in up-state South Carolina.[62] Compulsively busy, Bequest continued to plan and negotiate. In July of 1895 he aligned himself with several of his German colleagues to start a piano manufacturing company that proposed to "manufacture, sell and deal in pianos, and all kinds of musical instruments, print and sell sheet music, etc."[63]

All the while he was gathering additional plumage, August Bequest, naturally enough, was taking part in the Democratic machine that was by this time the only game in town. As a member of the German Artillery, he would

---

62. After construction that began the same year that the Central Cotton Mills Company was chartered, the Olympia Mill in Columbia became the world's largest textile mill under one roof. George C. Rogers Jr. and C. James Taylor, *A South Carolina Chronology*, 114.

63. *The State*, August 1, 1895. The *News and Courier* (August 7, 1895) followed with the notice of subscription opening.

have been among those in adulation of the older, but still venerated ex-U.S. Senator, Wade Hampton, who came to Charleston in May 1895 to "deliver the Confederate oration before the 'young Confeds'." August had not been in the war, but he would not have missed the opportunity to mingle among the members of the post-Reconstruction Democratic party still aligned to the "old cause." The democratic fervor was celebrated again at the end of the year with "a great democratic rally": "Mr. A. Bequest" was one of those named in attendance. The rally was in celebration of the passage of the Constitution of 1895—the legacy of Benjamin Tillman who, in his efforts to "transform white supremacy into something more than a slogan," had called for a new state constitution "carefully crafted to exclude most black men and safeguard Anglo-Saxon supremacy, good government, and ... our civilization."[64]

When Reconstruction was considered ended in 1877 as federal troops were withdrawn from the state, South Carolinians could think themselves again masters of their own fate. While moderates such as Wade Hampton and radicals such as Ben Tillman vied for control, the formerly-enslaved were denied every aspect of "progress" that they had briefly enjoyed when the new order had suggested that they were to be considered equal.

> The plight of many blacks appeared worse at this time than it had been under slavery, for they now lived in a society that simply had no jobs for them. Many whites wished that the blacks would simply go away and they embodied their feelings in segregation laws and customs. Acceptance of the black citizens' rights and place in the society was retarded by laws that resulted in their disenfranchisement and segregation. The march toward this segregation of society culminated in the Constitution of 1895 which effectively permitted the blacks to be ruled out of the political life of the state.[65]

Such was the social and political context that had evolved and in which Charleston's nineteenth-century German immigrants—irrespective of whether

---

64. Stephen Kantrowitz, *Ben Tillman & the Reconstruction of White Supremacy* (Chapel Hill: University of North Carolina Press, 2000), 198.

65. George C. Rogers, Jr. & C. James Taylor, *A South Carolina Chronology*, 95.

they arrived before or after the Civil War—participated. For the individual German immigrant, it was nearly impossible to swim against the current if one wanted to get ahead or even just manage to stay afloat. It was necessary, as it were, to forfeit one's German past in order to function in Charleston's present. If some struggled mightily against the ideas then current, August Bequest seems to have embraced them.

The positive commentaries accompanying the newspapers' reporting on new enterprises—many in which August Bequest participated—signaled the somewhat desperate need for the city to expand its economic horizons and to deal with its declining economic status. By the end of the nineties, efforts were made to improve the state of things, and attention was already being paid to the tourist trade as part of an economic stimulus. The *News and Courier* reported enthusiastically that "there have also been marked improvements on the waterfront, the most recent being by the Consumers' Coal Company, on Central wharf, and of all the points noted in the list of building permits the one most to be lauded and giving the greatest cause for gratification is that so large a number of people are building comfortable and convenient houses for themselves, costing from $500 to $5,000 each."[66] In mid-1895, both Bernhard and August Bequest were praised in the *News and Courier* as "men who have done much to build up Charleston's credit at home and abroad."[67] However differently, the two German brothers were firmly established as Charleston businessmen in the New South, each operating at the top of his game. Bernhard's life would be over in four years: August's would start to unravel.

August was prominently in the public eye in mid-January 1896, when he was appointed by a state court judge as receiver to manage the affairs of the insolvent Palmetto Brewery, founded by his German friend, J. C. H. Claussen. Almost immediately he found himself embroiled in a courtroom drama that would last for the better part of the year. Bequest's appointment by the state court was challenged by the appointment of his friend, A. F. C. Kramer, by a federal court judge. Awkwardly, both men at the time were corporators of the Palmetto Soap Manufacturing Company, co-corporators of the Wenzel Piano Company, and close friends of J. C. Blohme. Cramer was a director of the Germania Saving Bank, August, the president of the German-American

---

66. *News and Courier*, September 14, 1895.

67. *News and Courier*, December 21, 1895.

Trust and Savings. The judicial argument about jurisdiction went back and forth until April of 1897 when the State Supreme Court ruled against the state judge "in one, two, three order," by which time August's name and role in the dispute had faded into the background. Although he was on the losing side in this instance, he had gained exposure as someone known to the local community—his name frequently referenced among the city's leading businessmen.

Involved only tangentially in the lengthy courtroom proceedings determining the future of the Palmetto Brewery, August continued to "operate." He and his friend Cramer could not afford to let the earlier judicial dispute come between them or to take the issue personally. Their cooperation was needed on several fronts: for example, on the board of the Equitable Fire Insurance Company. In mid-May 1896, the company was reported to be flourishing, "with branches soon to be established in Georgia and Tennessee,"[68] and both men were re-elected as directors. August was still vice-president.

A month later, however, August Bequest's coat of many colors began to unravel. The headline in the *Evening Post* of June 18, 1896 was ominous: "Stockholders will meet. The failure of the German-American bank. Effort to reorganize will be made on Saturday—President Pringle of the Charleston [Bank] to be co-receiver—bank's condition unknown." The details followed:

> The doors of the German-American Trust and Savings bank at 58 Broad street are closed to-day. Business has been suspended and the affairs are in the hands of Capt. James F. Redding who was appointed receiver by Judge Brawley last afternoon.
>
> The inability of the bank to meet maturing papers has caused the embarrassment or failure. The exact condition of affairs of the bank are unknown and cannot be ascertained for several days until a thorough examination, which has already been instituted by the receiver is completed.
>
> The defunct bank was organized three years ago, on the 19th of January in 1893, with an authorized capital of $1,000,000, but the capital stock paid up was $60,000. The bank has a very large deposit account and the depositors are on the anxious bench to know if they will get all or a part of

---

68. *Evening Post*, May 15, 1896.

their money back. There will be no answer to that question until the examination of the affairs is concluded.

Under the state law the stockholders of the bank are responsible for the amount of their stock and 5 per cent. The alarm of the depositors was precipitated when it became known that several checks had been refused payment during yesterday.

To-day it was agreed that President Pringle of the Charleston Bank should be appointed co-receiver with Capt. Redding, and a petition will be presented to Judge Brawley sometime this afternoon. Bequest is president of the bank, B. I. Simmons, vice-president and J. A. Patjens, cashier.

The petition for a receiver was filed in the United States circuit court late yesterday afternoon, and in the absence of Judge Simonton District Judge Brawley granted the prayer and fixed the 23$^{rd}$ inst. as the date for the hearing on a question of permanent receivership. The petition was filed by Attorneys Mordecai and Gadsden, representing Van Wych Horton, of . . . Massachusetts. He states that he has a deposit account of 6,000 in the bank and alleges that the institution is unable to meet its debts, that the bank has been mismanaged, has suspended payment and failed. He prays the court's protection by the appointment of a receiver to manage its affairs properly.

It will be seen from the advertising columns of The Post that a meeting of the stockholders of the bank will be held at noon on Saturday with a view to the reorganization of the bank. It goes without saying that there will be a large attendance. It is hoped and believed that a plan for the successful reorganization of the bank will be suggested and this financial institution which has done in many respects a prosperous business will not be lost to the city.

The subsequent, extensive, coverage in the *Evening Post* revealed that a plan to save the bank had been devised and approved by the stockholders. The investigating committee that had been formed presented its report, and a number of new details came to light. Recounting the bank's founding history, the committee acknowledged that a minute book had not been kept, so that it had had to rely on "loose memoranda" in its investigation of what had gone wrong. But the following "facts" had been ascertained:

> On the first of February, 1895, J. F. Lilienthal resigned as president and A. Bequest was elected a director in the place of Mr. Hunt who at some previous time had declined re-election. Subsequently Mr. Bequest was elected president of the bank... The bank ledger shows that on the 1$^{st}$ of March, 1896, Bequest's account was overdrawn $9,821.46 and that subsequently this was enhanced by his notes for $1,600, $1,400 and a memorandum check for $251.56, making $13,100.60, to this must be added an overdraft of $4,363.95, and a note of A. C. Bequest for $2500 and a note on which he is endorser and which is prorated for $2,730 making the Bequest indebtedness $22,956.[69] To secure the payment of this sum it is alleged that Bequest surrendered as collateral 25 shares of a "Guaranty and Investment Co.," 14 shares of German-American Trust and Savings bank stock, and three life insurance policies payable on death of the assured. That all of such collateral have not yet been found by the receivers. None of the life policies are in our opinion properly assigned, and in the case of two of them there is no evidence of any attempts to assign.
>
> It would appear from the books that J. F. Lilienthal has made call loans for (est. J. F. Lilienthal) $3,000 and for $2,500, and personal memorandum checks dated March 1896 for $1,500, $1,670.91, $363.37, $236.83 (aggregating $9,361.11), and he is an endorser on a note for $3,800 due next month. (The drawer of this note has recently died). Amount of this indebtedness is $12,743.96. The only attempt to secure this sum that we hear of is 60 shares of the Southern Prepared Flour and Grain Co. stock, 3 shares Palmetto Brewery stock and 6 shares of the German-American Trust and Savings bank

---

69. The numbers do not add up exactly as reported, the inaccuracy likely attributable to the newspaper reporter, not the committee of stockholders.

stock. In addition to this Lilienthal also gave a mortgage on property in Thomas street for $7,000, dated May 2, 1895. This mortgage was not recorded until the 10th of June, 1896 when the receivers took possession of the bank and it was then found that a prior mortgage existed on the same property dated May 1st, for $3,000.

Of the present board of directors it does not appear that Messrs Simmons, Norris, or Hesse ever used the bank for their own advantage.

We also note that loans have been made by the bank on stocks of merchandise, the goods remaining in the hands of borrowing firms, in one case for $15,000, and in another instance for $12,000. We have further to report the existence of notes discounted which were drawn by firms and endorsed by some young men in their employ apparently without means. One of these notes is for $3,000 and has been protected for non-payment. Another note for which $2,500 was paid is drawn for $2,500 in figures, but the amount is written in the body of the note is twenty-five dollars.

We have had no funds to use in consulting a lawyer, but we find in the "Acts of 1893" an act to affirm, amend and extend the charter of the "German-American Trust and Savings Bank," which states "that no director or other officers of said corporation shall borrow any money from said corporation. If any director or other officer shall be convicted on indictment of directly or indirectly violating this section, he shall be punished by fine or imprisonment at the discretion of the court."[70]

Such evidence laid out before the public was utterly damning. Neither August Bequest nor Fred Lilienthal would ever recover the name they had before June 18, 1896. And this was just the beginning.

Within a week, the "All around town" column in the *News and Courier* would gossip that Vice-president A. Bequest had resigned from the board of the

---

70. *Evening Post*, June 26, 1896.

Equitable Fire Insurance Company.[71] There was no further news until August. In the interim it was likely that the Bequests were skipping the summer trip to Sullivan's Island and keeping a very low profile, they and the Lilienthals waiting to see what would follow on the heels of their embarrassment and wondering how their friends and associates would pursue them for the crimes they had committed. The agonizing suspense ended on August 7: "Mr. August Bequest, former president and director of the German-American Trust and Savings Bank was arrested at one o'clock this afternoon under three warrants issued by Magistrate Rouse." No longer amicable, former friends and business colleagues had taken out the warrants:

> The first warrant charges Mr. Bequest that on the 22nd day of April, 1895, he fraudulently and feloniously obtained $1,400 from the German-American Trust and Savings Bank by falsely representing that he had deposited with the bank as collateral security fourteen shares of the stock of the German-American Trust and Savings Bank and that he knew his pretense and representation was false and untrue. The second warrant charges him with borrowing $9,797.15 from the bank for which he gave his note, while his personal account with the bank was credited with the amount. The third warrant accuses him of having on the 4th of May, 1895 taken a Northeastern Railroad coupon bond of the value of $500, the property of Edmund Ravenel, which had been deposited with the bank as collateral on a note for $165. Bequest is charged with committing a breach of trust in committing the bond to his own use and that he feloniously carried the bond away from the bank.
>
> Constable Duke was given the warrant to execute and he went direct to Mr. Bequest's house on Society street and found him there. The officer took charge of the ex-bank president and escorted him to Magistrate Rouse's office where he is now held. Mr. Bequest took his arrest coolly and when he reached the magistrate's office he went to a private adjoining room and sat quietly by himself and commenced reading the New York

---

71. *News and Courier*, July 2, 1896.

World. He smiled as he read the warrants. He spoke about sending for his attorney, Mr. Bryan, but when the reporter left the court room at 2 o'clock no lawyer or friends had then called. It is expected that Mr. Bequest will have to give a $5,000 bond in each case and unless he can raise the $15,000 surety before night he will be committed to jail.[72]

Whether or not deservedly, J. Fred Lilienthal fared a little better and appeared the lesser scoundrel:

At 2:15 o'clock this afternoon Alderman J. Fred Lilienthal was arrested by Constable Duke in Mordecai & Gadsden's office in connection with the case against Bequest. The warrant was sworn out by the same parties. Mr. Lilienthal is charged with borrowing from the German-American Trust and Savings Bank, of which he was a director, by overdraft $582.83, which is in violation of the state law, a bank officer borrowing from his own bank. It is classed as a misdemeanor. Mr. Lilienthal was represented by Mr. P. H. Gadsden. Judge Rouse fixed his bond at $300[73], and Mr. F. W. Wagener was offered as security, which was accepted. Judge Rouse fixed the bond for Mr. Bequest in the three cases at $9,500. Mr. Buist asked Mr. J. P. K. Bryan, who represented Mr. Bequest, who he offered as bondsmen. Mr. Bryan was not at that hour, 3 o'clock, prepared to say who would become surety for his client. Mr. Bequest is still in the custody of the magistrate.[74]

The reported attitude of August Bequest in his predicament would have done nothing to endear him to the colleagues who had sworn to the warrants for his arrest. Nor does his "coolness" add much to the character portrait that at this point has only been partially analyzed. From details in the next day's

---

72. *Evening Post*, August 7, 1896.

73. Subsequent accounts indicate that this amount is erroneous: the bond was fixed at $3,000.

74. *Evening Post*, August 7, 1896.

*News and Courier* report, it was clear that the vultures were circling: "The arrests have been looked forward to by all those knowing the circumstances surrounding the failure of the German-American Trust and Savings Bank. Last Saturday Messrs Bequest and Lilienthal were sent cards telling them to appear at the bank by noon Wednesday and settle their indebtedness. This was definitively a notice from the directors of the bank that it was a case of "pay up" or be arrested.[75]

No doubt was left to the seriousness of the charges. Affidavits were detailed, charging Bequest with breach of trust with fraudulent intent and grand larceny. When found at his home, the "cool" Mr. Bequest "remarked to the constable while getting ready that some remarkable things would happen after his arrest ... several others connected with the bank would find themselves explaining things." Fred Lilienthal apparently heard that a deputy had been sent for him and more forthrightly appeared at the Magistrate's office on his own. The Magistrate set Lilienthal's bond at $3,000. The prominent Frederick Wagener signed for him, and Lilienthal was released from custody. For the three cases against Bequest, bond was set at $10,000 ($500 more than the *Evening Post* had reported). "During the afternoon Mr. A. S. Emerson went on one bond for Mr. Bequest to the extent of $5,000 and upon this Mr. Bequest was released until today when he will be returned to give two more bonds, one of $2,000 and another of $3,000."[76]

August went home for the night and did indeed show up the following morning to post the $2,000 bond: his wife Augusta and his brother Bernhard each posted $1,000. The evening paper reported that Bequest expected the $3,000 bond to be paid by Augusta's brother-in-law, Christian Amme, a director of the Germania Bank, married to Augusta's sister. Relishing the melodrama, the *News and Courier* the next day reported that Bequest's son "a young man of 20 was with him at the Magistrate's office, and worked industriously for him."[77] Finally,

---

75. *News and Courier*, August 8, 1896.

76. *News and Courier*, August 8, 1896. One of Bernhard Bequest's competitors in the wood business, A. S. Emerson owned the Emerson Steam Laundry and must have been one of August's most loyal friends.

77. His first-born, Heinrich Christian.

As the time came for closing up the office Magistrate Rouse took from his desk a little blue paper and commenced to fill it out. It was the commitment paper and was to put in jail the man who was once the president of the German-American Trust and Savings Bank. Mr. Bequest seemed a little gloomy, but was perfectly cool and collected. The magistrate informed him that he would take his release papers home with him, and if the bond was secured during the night he would send them to Capt. Kelly. There was nothing else to do. Mr. Bequest's buggy was outside and the constable rode with him to the jail.[78]

Amme and another German friend, D. W. Gotjen, posted the bond the next morning, and August Bequest had survived his overnight stay in the jail. Not that he was entirely free: he was released under a $19,990 bond for trial in the Court of Sessions on the original three charges. That experience did not begin until almost three months later, when in November the grand jury found "true bills" against both Lilienthal and Bequest. The hearing date was set for November 25, but—for whatever judicial reason—was continued.

Less than a month later, on December 17th the *New York Tribune*, *The State* (Columbia, SC) the *Baton Rouge Daily Advocate*, the *Charlotte Observer*, and the *Columbus Daily Enquirer* all reported under a "Charleston December 16" dateline that

Fred Lilienthal and August Bequest, former officials of the German American Trust and Savings Bank, were arrested here to-day and charged with a conspiracy to defraud that institution last May. Lilienthal was president and Bequest cashier of the bank at the time. It is alleged that Lilienthal as president, drew a check that had been given to him with fraudulent intent by Bequest. Both men waived the preliminary examination and gave bond in the sum of $10,000. The same men have been arrested before on similar charges and cases are now pending against them in the court of sessions.

78. *News and Courier*, August 9, 1896.

This second arrest and prolongation of the agony had come about when the new cashier at the German-American Trust and Savings went over the books and discovered the alleged conspiracy. The *News and Courier* explained:

> August Bequest and J. Fred Lilienthal were arrested by Constable Dukes of Magistrate Rouse's court, yesterday afternoon at 7 o'clock on a warrant charging them with a conspiracy to defraud. The warrant was sworn out in the morning before Magistrate Rouse by Mr. W. Richmond Pinckney, cashier of the German-American Trust and Savings Bank. The discovery of the alleged conspiracy was made about a month ago by Mr. Pinckney, while going over the books and passes of the bank. The officers and directors of the bank are determined to push this last case as vigorously as the others. Mr. Pinckney said yesterday that there were some of the bank's patrons who did not believe that Messrs Bequest and Lilienthal would have the charge pressed against them as they should, and that there were others who were dissatisfied on account of the continuances at the last term of court of the cases first made against them. As soon as this last transaction was discovered the officers of the bank decided to carry it into the courts, and the warrant yesterday was the result.
>
> Mr. Bequest was found at home by the constable. He expressed a desire that he be allowed to wait until the next morning, but the constable could not grant such a request. Mr. Lilienthal showed some agitation when the warrant was shown him at his home and wanted to go to see his lawyer, but this request had also to be refused.

Pinckney claimed that Bequest had drawn a check on the bank in the amount of $793.14 and given it to Lilienthal, who cashed it: "August Bequest, not being authorized to give said check, and he, the said Lilienthal, not being entitled to receive the same. But said transaction was done by them unlawfully and fraudulently and without the knowledge or consent of the board of directors and with intent to defraud the said bank."[79] Augusta came to her husband's rescue and posted the $1,000 bond. Fred Lilienthal's mother, Mrs. Lucy Lilienthal, did the same for her son.

By the end of this eventful year, August Bequest and Fred Lilienthal had been dealt twice-earned, near-fatal blows. Christmas 1896 was doubtless not a festive occasion for either man, nor for their respective families—immediate and extended. Whether or not quiet John Bequest on Mount Pleasant suffered any embarrassment because of his brother's infamy, August's fall from grace surely would have left a bad taste in his elder brother's mouth. There was no doubt that August's scandal had brought the Bequest name into question just when Bernhard Heinrich was trying to get his new European Fish Smokery established. It is not unreasonable to think that the arrest and humiliation of August took years off the life of his brother.

It was not until February 1897 that the cases reached the Court of Sessions, by which time they had lost any hint of scandalous white-collar crime. The defendants were treated like ordinary criminals. The *Evening Post* reported on the Court's convening on the twenty-second and objectively commented that "in addition to these, besides quite a number of minor cases, there are two murder cases which have not been passed upon by the grand jury as yet; five cases against Mr. August Bequest for breach of trust, one similar case against Mr. J. Fred Lilienthal, a rape case against Henry Simmons, colored, and rape cases against Wm Campbell as principal, and John Brooks as accessory."[80]

As might have been expected, negotiations and plea bargaining between the accused and their former associates were carried out as the days and months of 1897 dragged on. It was an awkward affair among friends, relatives, acquaintances, partners and associates, of the ethnic community trying to save face while meting out appropriate punishment to some of their own. The "sentences" of Bequest and Lilienthal seemed to fade into the complexities of the recent past with the hope by everyone concerned that the whole thing might be forgotten. *The State* reported in early July that "the grand jury demurs against the not processing and compromising against J. F. Lilienthal and August Bequest, against whom were found true bills."[81] Nothing more

79. *News and Courier*, December 17, 1896.
80. *Evening Post*, February 22, 1897.
81. *The State*, July 2, 1897.

revealing found its way into the Charleston newspapers. Whatever the final disposition,[82] August Bequest, for one, would have to start a new life, cast down as he was from the peak on which he had enjoyed a brief existence, undone by the crimes he had intentionally or unwittingly committed.

After fending off disgrace for two years, it was imperative that August find other employment if he was to keep his family together. According to the Charleston 1897 City Directory, the family was still at their residence, despite August not having any occupation specified. Sometime that year, August and his son John took off for California—both to escape the embarrassment of life in Charleston and to find work. The 1898 San Francisco City Directory lists "Bequest August, bartender, B. N. Rohde" and "Bequest John L., clerk Henry A. Wuhrmann." Clearly, B. N. Rohde was one of Augusta's relatives—she had a brother Bernhard—who had come to the rescue to provide subsistence employment. John had apparently found a position with the relative of one of Charleston's German merchants. August remained in San Francisco only for a year, but John stayed on for a period, taking over his father's bartending position at Bernhard Rohde's San Francisco establishment.

After his elder brother's death in 1899, August managed to find work as a "special agent" with the Mutual Life Insurance Company of New York. He worked initially out of Wilmington, then Charlotte, NC, while the family remained in Charleston. He apparently had been successful in shaking off the scandal that had all but finished him in South Carolina four years earlier: the 1901 Charleston City Directory confirms him as an insurance agent with the family living at a different address. One of the repercussions of the bank scandal was that their residence on Charleston's Society Street that had been purchased in Augusta's name was conveyed in 1897 to "D. Rohde" (Augusta's first cousin who had immigrated to Charleston already in 1849), either under financial duress or as a means of keeping the property in the family until things improved.

While continuing to sell insurance, August undertook a partnership with "Smith" in Columbia, South Carolina, to sell Fay-Sho typewriters—"the

---

82. While the grand jury demurred against the "not processing and compromising" against the two, the lack of any further reporting of legal action against them suggests that they were never sentenced, but also never formally declared "not guilty."

leading typewriter in the market." By April of 1903 he found additional work as an agent for the Piedmont Fire Insurance Company of Charlotte, while the partnership/firm of "Bequest & Smith" in new and rebuilt typewriters continued to operate out of Columbia. This dual life in Charlotte and Columbia put him back in the fast-paced mode that he thrived in, juggling more than a few balls in the air and working in several spheres at once. He clearly always had the talents of a salesman who could talk fast and convincingly. That he was always moving quickly and not infrequently a little out of (figurative) breath is evident in a letter to his former business partner and now his attorney, John Cappelmann.[83] Written hurriedly in October 1904 on the letterhead of the National Life Insurance Company, Montpelier, Vermont, listing A. Bequest as "General Agent" and C. A. Smith as "Cashier," the letter displays his fluency in English—not surprising by this time—as well as the quick pace of his thoughts. It is written (verbatim) in a fairly legible hand:

> Dear Sir/Please make the effort to have Bond transferred from C. Bart & Co as indicated in your letter ascertain from Mordecai the principle and int, I have been delayed in Columbia on account of the chief medical director of our Co making a trip through the territory the cost of services of $50.00 I will bring for you when I come down next week or as soon he leaves I fear M_ may take steps for another fee you know what I mean you can phone me tomorrow over the long distance phone #722 at Columbia reverse charges, when the will charge our offices for the call after you ascertain the amt you can prepare proper paper for Mrs. Bequest to sign acknowledge the amt to be due under the Bond the rest such as the title from D. Rohde we will get in proper form when I come down/with kind regards/Verry truly/A. Bequest[84]

---

83. The attorney for the German-American Trust and Savings Bank and other businesses with whom Bequest had earlier been involved.

84. One of the few Bequest documents in the South Carolina Historical Society's archives (Simons, Siegling and Cappelmann Collection).

The letter concerns a transaction that almost certainly involved getting the title on the Society Street house transferred back from "D. Rohde" to Augusta. Cappelmann would have to keep the other lawyer at bay for much longer than a few days: the arrangements Bequest promised to make when he got back to Charleston, as well as others made in connection with the matter, were postponed for years. Nonetheless, Cappelmann was successful in fulfilling August's request, and the Bequests were able to occupy the house on Society Street by 1905.[85]

August's peripatetic activity on several fronts in an effort to achieve a semblance of financial stability was a struggle, and if one thing got fixed, another did not. A personal blow came in 1905 when the couple's daughter, Agnes, died, five months short of her eighteenth birthday. Augusta was left in Charleston with the couple's two sons, August Blohme working as a collector for the Consumers' Coal Company that his father had helped incorporate, and his older brother John (returned from San Francisco) working as a clerk. The eldest son had left to go to college the year all the bank trouble had started and had been living in New York City since 1900. In the 1908 Charleston City Directory, August is listed as a traveling salesman. To all appearances, he had worked for at least a decade to put his past mistakes behind him. He had been sent out of town on the rails, but now it looked as though he had been able to restore his name by staying clear of Charleston and accepting a less vaulted role in the business world.

As if through a character flaw in combination with the pressure felt by the aging immigrant determined to succeed, August Bequest fell once again into the hands of the authorities. The *Charlotte Observer* ran the following story in May 1908 under the headline "Alleged accomplice of Mills arrested in Athens, Ga":

> Insurance Commissioner Young is notified by Deputy Commissioner Scott of the arrest by the latter, at Athens, Ga., after a hot pursuit, of A. Bequest, an insurance agent who jointly with W. J. Mills, perpetrated upon a lady at Laurinburg five years ago the biggest insurance fraud ever known in North

---

85. Not a little irony in the name of the street where the Bequests lived: the Bequests would never again be accepted in Charleston's "society."

Carolina. Mills was arrested at Philadelphia a few days ago after a year's chase, and is in jail at Laurinburg, where his accomplice was taken to-night. They five years ago represented the Mutual Life at Charlotte, and as its agents perpetrated most of the fraud. The company made good its part.[86]

Once again, Augusta's husband was accused of fraud and this time jailed in North Carolina. No doubt the details of the scandal and the circumstances of August's arrest reached Charleston quickly, so that it is not surprising that Augusta would write to John Cappelmann—in German—to register her dismay that attorney Mordecai was acting unmercifully (*unbarmherzig*) in demanding interest payments on the mortgage for the home on Society Street. She hopes he (Cappelmann) appreciates how difficult it is for her to be paying this obligation. She refers to Cappelmann as "old friend," and signs her letter "Relying on your good graces, I remain, Your friend, Augusta C. Rohde."[87] In the context of her husband's second criminal offense, Augusta appears to be the victim. Yet her affront at their legal obligations—complicated as they were by her husband's felonious activities—suggests that while she was utterly embarrassed by her husband's purported criminal behavior, she was a somewhat defiant partner. Signing her letter with her maiden name signals that she was trying to separate herself from her husband's scandals while doing her best to hold up her head in Charleston's German community. A letter from Attorney Mordecai to a colleague offers an explanation for why he might have been short on patience and, to Augusta's mind, acting *unbarmherzig*:

Dear Sir: in the matter of Bart & Co. v. Bequest

I have received your message, through our Mr. Pearlstein, that this matter will be settled immediately after the first of July.

If it is proposed to settle this on July 2nd,—which is next Thursday—and I have your guarantee to that effect, I of course will proceed no further; but as we have had so many promises

---

86. *Charlotte Observer*, May 6, 1908.

87. "Mich ganz auf Ihren Güte verlassend verbleibe ich in aller Freundschaft, Augusta C. Rohde."

from your clients which have been ruthlessly broken, I cannot accept anything in this matter except your guarantee to me, which of course is all I ask. Mr. Bequest has been promising me for four years to close this matter up, and I have learned to take these promises at their true value.

Yours very truly,

T. Moultrie Mordecai

Attorney Cappelmann in Charleston doubtless found it awkward to negotiate any matter connected with his client August Bequest in Laurinburg, North Carolina charged with embezzlement.

What started in 1908 with Bequest's arrest went through two courtroom trials in the course of the following year. The *Charlotte Observer* made sure everyone was informed of the details:

> Just a little over seven years after the time of the commission of the alleged crime, W. J. Mills and A. Bequest, were placed on trial here to-day charged with having embezzled about $1,400 belonging to the Mutual Life Insurance Company, of New York. The crime is alleged to have been committed about November 11th, 1901, while they were its agents in this territory. The alleged embezzlements were discovered during the last of November, 1906, some five years after their perpetration. At that time complaint was made to Insurance Commissioner Young and as a result of such both Mills and Bequest were indicted, finally apprehended about the first of May and brought here for trial … They also stand indicted jointly on a charge of conspiracy to cheat and defraud Mrs. Hattie McLaughlin in the same insurance transaction. Mills stands further indicted on a charge of having embezzled $1,400 on December 5th, 1901, belonging to Mrs. McLaughlin.

During the judicial deliberations, August was described for the public as "a man of some 50 years, very plain and simple in his manners and dress, [who] sits quietly by and shows not the greatest interest in what is going on."[88] After the evidence was concluded, the judge ordered a verdict of "not guilty" for Mills. Bequest testified on his own behalf, and by the time the trial was concluded, the jury was sufficiently confused that it could not agree in "the case against Bequest." The judge ultimately ordered a mistrial. The Insurance Commissioner, however, had brought other, i.e., *additional*, cases against Mills and Bequest which had earlier been postponed. Bond was fixed at $2,500 and $2,000 for Mills and Bequest respectively, so that neither man was in the clear after the case against Bequest ended in a mistrial. For five more months the axe would hang over their heads.

While out on bail, August would have had a hard time functioning as a salesman if his reputation at this point was preceding him wherever he went. To add to his travail, his son, John L., aged twenty-seven, died of a chronic heart condition in July. With her son Henry living in New York, Augusta was left with her youngest son, August Blohme, her only support during these troubled times.

Her husband's second appearance in court loomed already toward the end of April 1909, when the *Observer* of May 4th would replay the courtroom melodrama. In Mills's trial, August took the stand for the State. "Mr. Bequest produced his accounts to corroborate his statement. The defense made a fierce attack upon the books and the character of Mr. Bequest." The case against Mills was subsequently declared a mistrial and the defendant was sent to jail until his bond could be renewed.[89] The trial of Bequest for embezzlement of funds from the Mutual Life Insurance Company of New York was postponed until the next term. Although the *Observer* reported on June 1st that Commissioner Young had again left for Laurinburg to testify "in the case against two former insurance agents, Mills and Bequest, on a charge of swindling," there was subsequently no further mention of the Mills/Bequest cases in North- or South Carolina newspapers. It is likely that the final disposition of the case was a mistrial, and doubtful that Bequest spent any more time in jail.

Despite having had his name repeatedly dragged through the public mud, by the summer of 1910 August Bequest had become more famous than infamous. His name was frequently mentioned in the Charleston *News and*

---

88. *Charlotte Observer*, June 3, 1908.
89. *Charlotte Observer*, May 5, 1909.

*Courier*'s "Among the travelling Men" column as "one of the most popular men on the road." That would be August Bequest's final claim to fame. The *News and Courier* columnist who regularly reported on the whereabouts and activities of the "travelling men" during the early decades of the twentieth century—when newfangled consumer goods were peddled door-to-door to the rising middle class—seems to have taken special notice of the former bank president who had fallen several steps down the ladder. Possibly it was because Bequest had a past that still dogged him that "news" about him had an appeal for the local readers. Perhaps it was genuine empathy on the part of the columnist for a man who had demonstrated an ability to pick himself up, dust himself off, and continue to run the race. There was nonetheless a hint of sarcasm, a little *Schadenfreude*, when the columnist repeatedly paired the German Bequest "who sells scales, refrigerators and things"[90] with the Irish "'Little Willie' Keenan, the crockery and chinaware man, from Charleston." Having survived the Laurinburg scandal, Bequest had managed to talk himself into a new sales position, so that by 1910 he had become "the Scale man." The *News and Courier*'s columnist would have fun with August Bequest and Willie Keenan as subjects for his column for the next several years. The newspaper's readers apparently enjoyed hearing that

> Mr. A. Bequest, the Scale man, suffered rather a severe but short illness on Thursday night of last week and had to "run in home" for a week. It practically "done him up," and he is able to be out on the road again, but he "slipped up" on getting to Conway yesterday, No. 54, the Wilmington train having "skidooed" out just as he reached the station. Ask him now about "Little Willie Keenan" and the "Fish" if you want to get up a scrap.[91]

Or, a couple of weeks later:

> Mr. A. Bequest, who has about recovered from his recent illness from having eaten too much fish and from keeping

---

90. *News and Courier*, August 1, 1910.

91. *News and Courier*, August 8, 1910.

company with "Little Willie Keenan," was in town to-day. Mr. Bequest said that he had been carried out to Magnolia Cemetery and the keeper was clearing away a place to make an excavation for "A. Request" and that "A Bequest" made a "Request" of the keeper that he wait with time and patience until a later day. The "Request" was granted and "A. Bequest" was the happier when he awoke and found that he was really alive and could continue to sell scales.[92]

If the columnist seemed frequently to be lightheartedly—if sarcastically—joking about the travelling salesmen, he was also capable of lecturing them on how they should stop contributing to the "tale of woe" that was depressing the business atmosphere in South Carolina. In a November 1910 column, he questioned what "a long-faced drummer" could sell to a "merchant inclined to be blue":

> Travelling men on the trains, in hotels and in the stores are talking hard times. There seems to be a depression among the merchants and business people, generally surprising when the prices of all farm products are considered. This cry of hard times in South Carolina is imaginary to a great extent, but it is a fact that must be faced by the men on the road, and faced with a smile and a boost instead of a long face … A stiff upper-lip and a cheerful face go a long ways on the road, and if the travelling man will begin to boost the business conditions instead of pulling the other way, business will begin to look brighter and the merchant will begin to get busy and everything will pick up.[93]

Whether August Bequest was one of the long-faced drummers on the move throughout the state—he would have had ample reason to display a frown rather than the called-for smile—his *modus operandi* likely enabled him to put a happy face on the job he had to do.

---

92. *News and Courier*, August 22, 1910.

93. *News and Courier*, November 21, 1910.

As a travelling salesman, August could believe he was performing an important civic role. Post E of the Charleston Travellers' Protective Association held a meeting in February, 1911, during which the chapter reorganized in an effort to "upbuild" the city, and to make the organization "a force in itself beneficial to its membership and forming another agency for boosting Charleston." In connection with the Association's meeting, the reporter thought it newsworthy to mention that Bequest was doing his part in boosting the city: "Mr. A. Bequest, the Southern Scale Company's representative in this section, who spent Sunday with his family in Charleston, was out for business this week, and he got it. Mr. Bequest says that when the Irish and Dutch, 'Little Willie Keenan' and 'A. Bequest,' go after 'biz' there's going to be 'something doing.'" Making "biz" happen could not have been easy: August and Willie were two of some four hundred travelling salesmen operating out of Charleston.[94]

This particular report was not the first in which Bequest had been identified as a "Dutchman," a term, not necessarily of endearment, that had come into the local vernacular to accommodate the transition of the *Deutsche* into Charlestonians of a particular heritage. It was the lazy tongue of the Southerner who found it easier to use that term even if it had nothing to do with the inhabitants of the "other" Low Countries. But if August was the Dutchman one week, the next week he might be referred to in the newspaper with various military titles[95] as "Major" or "Lieut." or "Capt." or some other "honorific" label:

> Lieut. A. Bequest, the scale, furniture and fixture man, who sells refrigerators and all kinds of nice looking things, was in Florence last week, but he left "Little Willie" behind him. The "Lieutenant" says that it won't do for the Dutch and the Irish to hit Florence together too often for fear the "fish" won't bite...[96]

---

94. *News and Courier*, February 6, 1911.

95. Were these titles taken from the U.S. military vocabulary, or were they remnants of Charleston's German "military" tradition aptly applied to this "Dutchman"? The Irishman was always "Little Willie Keenan."

96. *News and Courier*, March 20, 1911.

Capt. A. Bequest, the genial Charleston Dutchman, was here this week, doing business for the Southern Scales and Fixtures people. Capt. Bequest is greatly attached to Florence and his friend, Jim Muldrow, and he's thinking of moving up to the "Little Gate City" from Charleston, so that he will not have to lose time to "run in" on Saturday nights … [97]

There was a reunion of the Dutch and Irish in Florence during the past week. Uncle A. Bequest and Little Willie Keenan met here and enjoyed one of their "fish dinners" at a certain local hotel. Their friends were with them and enjoyed the evening as much as the two gentlemen alluded to above did … [98]

This constant reporting on the activity of her husband, more often than not incorporating some sarcasm between the lines, understandably might have gotten the best of Augusta Bequest, even though her husband's out-of-town activities were the lifeline of financial support for her in Charleston. In June 1911, she left New York on the North German Lloyd steamship *Kronprinz Wilhelm* for Bremen to spend three months in Germany—away from it all.[99]

While she was gone, her husband settled "officially" in mid-state Florence— described as "the coming city of South Carolina." He resigned his job with the Southern Scales and Fixture Company of Columbia and opened his own business in partnership with his son to carry a "full line of fixtures, refrigerators and scales." In December 1912, the Florence Scale and Fixture Company was commissioned as one of the State's new enterprises. August was once again an incorporator, this time with his son, August Blohme, as his partner.

With father and son working in Florence, the decision was made at some point to put the Society Street property in the senior son's name, even though he was still living in New York. Whether Augusta was relieved of this legal responsibility by a helpful son or whether the property was transferred out of her name by a calculating husband is of little consequence to the story that is about to end. The new Florence Scale and Fixture Company had become a

97. *News and Courier*, May 8, 1911.
98. *News and Courier*, May 22, 1911.
99. *Evening Post*, June 9, 1911.

family affair: the Florence City Directory for 1913 shows A. Blohme Bequest as vice-president and treasurer (but "residing" in Charleston); Augusta is listed as president of the company, "boarding" at the Central Hotel and travelling back and forth between Charleston and Florence in her new capacity. Son August Blohme, while he was "in business" with his father, chose to remain a Charleston resident in the house on Society Street that was now in the name of his older brother.

By the middle of the second decade of the twentieth century, August Sr. was sufficiently removed from his past embarrassments that he could resurrect something of his political self and participate in local Democratic party activities. The Columbia newspaper, *The State,* quoted A. Bequest as the "Florence man" reporting on one occasion to the editor that "Richard I. Manning is gaining strength in every section throughout the Pee Dee and Florence county."[100] Although not in any official capacity, as he travelled throughout his region Bequest kept his political ear to the ground, and his assessment of the political temperature was sufficiently well regarded that the newspaper editor found it worth mentioning. August Sr.'s democratic leanings flowed naturally enough to his son August Blohme. The younger Bequest's name—along with that of his first cousin, John Frederick Bequest—consistently appeared in the *News and Courier's* listings of those enrolled in the Democratic Club. The junior August advanced to be a "manager" for his Ward 5, Precinct 1 in the November election of 1918. His "membership" in the Democratic Party was in no way surprising. He was a second-generation German-American and Charleston was a one-party town.

After the cursory mention of the "Florence man" in *The State* in 1914, the senior August Bequest disappeared from the media's radar screen. Whatever his activities or involvements, they were no longer of any interest to South Carolina newspaper reporters or editors. In these years, August lived in the shadow of the increasingly hostile anti-German sentiment that was in evidence. If he had entered the salesmen's race as a middle-aged man handicapped by a history of bad decisions, there was little the "Dutchman" with a past could do to escape his German heritage. He died in 1923 of "chronic nephritis and arterial hypertension," his condition exacerbated by an enlarged heart. There

---

100. *The State*, August 24, 1914. Manning was running for the governorship and was elected.

was a single funeral notice in the *News and Courier* of Sunday, March 4, 1923: "The relatives and friends of Mr. and Mrs. August Bequest are invited to attend the funeral services of the former at his late residence, No. 56 Society street, this afternoon, 3:30 o'clock. Interment Bethany Cemetery." A similarly cursory funeral notice announced Augusta's death the following year.[101]

The elder son, Henry, had apparently been a regular visitor to Charleston ever since moving to New York. On his visit in 1914, he was described by the *News and Courier* as "a Charlestonian who has made good in New York … making a visit to friends and relatives in Charleston, his birth place. He is now employed by the great American Locomotive Works as supervising inspector of automobile parts and accessories, a very respectable position."[102] Henry Bequest never returned to Charleston to live there permanently. There was no issue from his marriage, and when he registered for the draft in 1918, he was forty years old. Despite his "very respectable position" in New York, the 1940 federal census showed the childless couple renting a house. Having left the place of his birth, he apparently had forgotten his birth year and reported his age to the census taker as fifty-eight: born in 1877, he was actually sixty-three and clearly did not identify as a Charlestonian.

The bachelor August Blohme and his first cousin John Frederick are the two native, Charleston-born, scions whose graves in Charleston's Bethany Cemetery, the resting place of Charleston's immigrant, Lutheran, German families, carry the Bequest name. Both of their immigrant fathers, one of whom brought shame and embarrassment to the Geestendorf name of German-French origin, lie in unmarked graves in the cemetery's lowcountry sandy soil.

---

101. There was something of a message in the fact that neither's funeral was held at St. Matthew's.

102. *News and Courier*, August 14, 1914.

# CHAPTER 6:

## INCREASING VULNERABILITY

The life stories of these individual immigrants—some described only cursorily, others purposefully revealed in considerable detail—collectively portray the diverse ways the newcomers approached life in the new country. We have looked at these representatives from Charleston's German community from the mid-nineteenth century up to the first decades of the twentieth in order to assess the character of the ethnic group. As it was absorbed into the native community, it inevitably evolved to become less noticeably German. If it was initially possible for the native society to look on "the Germans" as distinct from themselves, by around 1910 it was rarely necessary to distinguish a "Dutchman" from a Charlestonian.

During the years between 1880 and 1900, the German community's younger generations—already second- and third-generation Americans—would find their lives socially and economically diminished by the slow deterioration of Charleston into a not-so-special place. Without exception, these later generations would continue the process that had transformed their first-generation parents and grandparents into semi-Charlestonians, but now with considerably less regard for the ethnic heritage. As could be expected, the foreign-born population would be edged out by those born and raised in the host culture, confirming E. P. Hutchinson's assessment that "with the passage of time a given immigrant family or group goes through a cycle of change, first being made up entirely of members of the immigrant generation but eventually being represented only by the children of the original immigrants; and in the following generation the family or group loses its national identity in the census record, for the native born of native parents are no longer traced to country of origin but are merged in the native stock."[1] In this regard, the Charleston situation was not unique. Jeffery Strickland, however, adds another dimension: "The Charleston-born German American population was larger than the first generation, but its members largely identified with white southerners—they were southern whites first and German Americans second."[2] Both historians thus agree that the earlier "German" culture embodied in the ethnic community would be perceptibly diluted after reaching its zenith in the years prior to the Civil War. This diminution of the original ethnic identity in Charleston was no different than what was happening throughout the United States. Any sense of a distinctly German heritage was challenged by the fact that so many of German descent had already become Americans.

A look at the "news" as published in the post-war years by the *Deutsche Zeitung* provides additional insight into the nature of the ethnic community as it slowly changed over the course of years. In 1873 when Reconstruction was well underway, for example, the *Zeitung*'s editor was acknowledging that the ethnic community had achieved the status of a political block when he encouraged every German in the city to vote in the mayoral election for John Andreas Wagener, telling his audience that "die Amerikaner" were depending on "die Deutschen" to save the city. On the same page, the editor felt free to lament that many University of South Carolina professors had been replaced, *unfortunately*, by Negroes, something that would certainly be to the detriment of "die Weißen" and accomplish nothing for the blacks. Editorial commentary such as this suggested that the paper's German readership was as intolerant of blacks who were assuming positions previously held by whites as were others among Charleston's distraught, frustrated, white population.

Inasmuch as it was routine in every issue to announce the upcoming meetings of the various ethnic clubs and associations, for example, the upcoming

---

1. *Immigrants and their Children, 1850-1950* (New York: John Wiley & Sons, 1956), 12.

2. Strickland, "How the Germans Became White Southerners," 53-54.

parade and weapons practice of the German Hussars, such announcements were obviously meant to keep the German public informed of "their" social obligations. At the same time, these notices served to spread the word to others that what the Germans were up to was of interest to the larger community. The "schedule" was an open invitation for all to participate and enjoy. In 1874, the paper was unabashedly partisan in proposing that if certain candidates were elected, the state would then have something like an *honorable* government, even if were a Republican one. The future of the state, the newspaper assured its readers, lay in the hands of the conservatives. The editor left little doubt that his fellow Germans identified as conservative Democrats.

After ten years of "reconstruction," the *Zeitung* assumed that its German readers were attuned to southern humor: they would undoubtedly enjoy the joke in a 1876 "Miscellaneous" column that told of a fictional Negro who accidentally shot himself in the head: after the flattened bullet was subsequently removed, it was clear to all that a Negro head held neither reason nor lead. Like other locals, the Charleston German would smile and agree. A decade after the war, the *Zeitung's* editor was still in the habit of addressing its German readership as a monolithic entity: he spoke for the ethnic community when it was reported later that year (1876) that there were some German "radicals" in Kingstree, South Carolina. One, Phillip Heller, the County Treasurer, had called the Germans in Charleston fools. The *Zeitung's* editor parried by saying that the Germans in Charleston, thank you, knew what was good for them and did not need to be lectured by the radical Heller. Ten years after the war, Charleston's Germans—at least as far as the *Deutsche Zeitung* was concerned—were one with each other and, as a group, perfectly capable of navigating the local political waters.

In an issue in 1878, the reading public was informed that the German Fire Company had celebrated its fortieth anniversary, elected its officers for the coming year, and sponsored a well-attended dance that was so enthusiastically enjoyed by everyone in attendance that the festivities had lasted until the early morning hours. Here was another instance of letting the entire Charleston community know that the Germans had been their civic friends for almost a half-century and that the ethnic group's organizations were there to be, and were, enjoyed by everyone.

For the 1879 celebration of George Washington's birthday, editor Franz Melchers enthusiastically noted how the Germans reveled in the splendor of the uniforms on display: the 130-man *Deutsche Artillerie,* he opined, was most impressive, accompanied as they were by some twenty veterans of the Civil War. The uniforms of the companies of German Fusiliers and German Hussars thrilled the thousands of spectators as they watched the parade of marching Germans playing their paramilitary part in the grand civic celebration. The German newspaper's commentary on the American holiday festivities cele-brated the ethnic "military sense" on display for an enthralled public. It was testimony that the two cultures were becoming one: through their uniformed paramilitarism, the Artillerie, the Hussars, and the Fusiliers could signal their ethnicity at the same time they were demonstrating their patriotic participation in a singularly *American* celebration.[3] And in showing their appreciation for the "protection" these marching soldiers represented, the approbation of the mostly-native spectators signaled their acceptance of the foreigners, the latter now well on their way to no longer being considered foreign.

On the eve of the 1880s, the ethnic community had evolved to recognize that it cohered as a group that could stand on its own, no longer needed to suffer marginalization or paternalism, convinced that its ethnicity was valid at the same time it was integrated with the native community. Reporting in late 1879 on a speech by "Dr. Wigner" visiting from Baltimore, the *Zeitung*'s Melchers felt called upon to endorse the change of attitude that was surfacing in the German community. He told his readership that the speaker had ad-dressed the local audience in "golden, relevant" terms that precisely defined the position of German-Americans at that time. In his address, Dr. Wigner had arguing that the Germans should not organize as a separate group if they wanted to assume effective political power rather than be used as a tool at the disposal of the two Parties. They should strive for equal, integrated status in the society: they were, after all, full-fledged American citizens, many of them born in the United States, who deserved the same rights as those of a different heritage such as English-speaking natives and immigrants. "Equal Obligations, Equal Rights" should be their slogan.

Almost ten years later, the newspaper's editor would still address his fellow Germans as a group of unique citizens in regard to a local issue that especially affected "die Deutschen der Stadt": the matter of city taxes.[4] In this instance, he

---

3. See earlier analysis in Chapter Five.

4. *Deutsche Zeitung,* January 13, 1887.

brought to their attention that the ethnic community was split between those who were successful and sufficiently well-off that they did not feel burdened by increased taxation, and those with less, who were inclined to protest strongly. Those who demonstrated little concern for the plight of the less fortunate would one day find the tables turned. The editor explained that after the Civil War, the Germans by their diligence had risen in the ranks of society and purchased a considerable number of the older houses that had fallen into disrepair. These they had subsequently rehabilitated—as was their nature—only to currently find their taxes disproportionally high in comparison with those of other citizens inhabiting lesser quarters. Given that the German was a dutiful taxpayer and not very active politically, it would seem that previous municipal administrations had regularly placed an increasingly higher tax burden on German real-estate holders than on others. The opinion of the editor was that there was no ready solution to the matter: it was every German for himself.

The property tax issue that the *Zeitung*'s editor brought to the attention of the German community was an acknowledgment that there were at this point perceptible class distinctions within the ethnic community, moreover, that the Germans who had risen to the top in terms of wealth and living conditions seemed inured to the problems of the less fortunate, less successful, whom they had left behind. But it was not a situation the Germans had created, nor was it a problem that they themselves could solve. The editor's "preaching to the choir" on the matter nonetheless makes clear that toward the end of the century many of the Germans had successfully formed, and were part of, a middle class that had earlier been missing in the civic hierarchy.

As a sign of the immigrant community's slippage into the culture of the majority, a contrived "letter to the editor" published in December, 1895, encouraged German parents to make a better effort at preserving the native language. It was argued that children born to Germans in Charleston were growing up speaking more English than German, even if the parents still spoke German in the home, and that if the children were forced to speak German, it was likely to be a mishmash of German and English. Even more unsettling was the fact that native-born parents were encouraging their children to learn another language—namely German. It had gotten to the point that Americans of German descent could be heard lamenting "Oh, if I could only speak German!" There was something of a consensus that the ethnic community was being eroded by pressures from the outside.

Fully aware by 1910 that the ethnic community was capable of playing a meaningful role in local elections, the *Zeitung*'s editor did not hesitate to offer advice to his fellow German-Americans who would vote in the upcoming gubernatorial and congressional races. It was assumed that even after a half century of acculturation, the German-American Charlestonian still paid attention to the newspaper that considered itself the "Voice of German Societies and Clubs of the South" (*Organ der Deutschen Gesellschaften und Vereine des Südens*) and claimed to be the "Weekly for Safeguarding German Interests" (*Wöchentliche Zeitung zur Wahrung deutscher Interessen*). The German-language newspaper still considered it its purpose to advise and instruct its ethnic readers. even if by this point they had slipped beyond its control.

On the surface, the German Day celebration of 1891 and the one celebrated twenty years later in 1910, appear not very dissimilar. In 1891, the main event had taken place in the Germans' own Artillery Hall on Wentworth Street. The pastor of the German Lutheran Church had offered the invocation. There was an address in German by another pastor on "a religious perspective on the effects of German immigration" and another by the *Zeitung*'s editor, Franz Melchers, on "the history of German immigration to South Carolina and its influence on the nation's history." The German men's chorus sang the *Deutschlandlied*, and a local German attorney spoke in English on the "German legacy and its effects on the prosperity of the nation." There was a "festival march" followed by folk songs. The evening had ended with ballroom dancing.

The columns in the October 7, 1910, issue of the *News and Courier* under a headline "Deutscher Tag is Celebrated by City's German-Americans / Anniversary of the landing of the first settlers from the fatherland is fittingly observed in Charleston" acknowledged the long-standing tradition of this civic event and the importance of the German ethnic community in the city's heritage. There was much ado about the parade of the automobiles and the cadets from the German training ship *Freya* to the music provided by the Navy Yard Band. Notably, "a number of the *Freya*'s German officers expressed their appreciation when they noticed on many intervals along the route large German and American flags displayed from doorways." At one point in the day's program, the Governor-elect, Cole L. Blease, made rather rambling, politically-tuned remarks:

He felt, he said, that the German element of Charleston believe that they have in him a man who will stand by them,
and that they are correct in this opinion, that he will always
stand by men who stand by him ... South Carolina has no citizens of which she should be more proud than of her German
citizens. He opposed immigration, but he never had opposed
the immigration of the class from which such citizens of [*sic*]
these have sprung.

According to the newspaper account, Blease then suggested that the men
of the *Freya* should spend the winter in Charleston, but if that were not possible "when you go back home, tell your people to come over and let us make
of them American citizens. We will do for them what Germany could never
do." After Blease, the Hon. John Cappelmann, Southern vice president of the
German-American Alliance, introduced Mr. Emil Jahnz, the Imperial German
Consul, "who addressed the crowd in German. Mr. Jahnz's address dealt
principally with the military power of Germany, and more especially with the
naval branch. His remarks were especially interesting to the young cadets, as
he spoke of loyalty of all Germans to the Fatherland. Mr. Jahnz was frequently
interrupted by applause."

Despite the similarities, some of the commentary in the newspaper account of the 1910 German Day celebration suggests that the status of the city's
Germans was under some strain. Did the comment about the German sailors
responding to crowds of Germans holding two flags imply a dual loyalty of
Charleston's Germans-Americans? Was the governor-elect playing politics with
an electorate that was feeling somewhat insecure? This German Day celebration might well have been a festive occasion for Charleston's Germans, but as
well, it might have ruffled a few feathers among the native population ready to
question whether these German-American German-Day celebrants might not
be overly loyal to the[ir] Fatherland and feeling a little superior.

The pages of the *Deutsche Zeitung* suggest that as the first decade of the
new century drew to a close, the character of the community of Germans in
Charleston had indeed changed from what it had been before the Civil War.
By the end of the nineteenth century, most of the immigrants whose life stories
were told in previous chapters were dead. It had been evident for some time that
citizens still identifiable as "die Deutschen" were second-, in some instances,

third-generation individuals of German descent. These descendants of immigrants were themselves no longer immigrants bent on fulfilling a "rags-to-riches" mission in a new homeland. They had no direct connection to the "Fatherland" and were unlikely to feel a strong allegiance to the Hohenzollern Kaiser or an increasingly militant Prussia. They had experienced markedly different childhoods while growing up among English speakers, and were not a little resistant to the publicly-displayed and privately-practiced conservatism of their parents. Each generation after the first had relinquished some of its ability to speak and/or read German. The preference for using English rather than German was something that had been evident ever since the first settlers had arrived. Almost from its founding, for example, the *German* Friendly Society did not require of its members the ability to speak German.

Federal census data for 1910 indicates that the *foreign-born white* population of Charleston numbered 2,404 (4.1% of the city's total population); 891 (37%) of those *foreign-born whites* were born in Germany. The *native-white of foreign or mixed parentage* numbered 4,902 (8.3% of the total population); 1,253 (25%) of them were children of parents, both of whom were born in Germany. While these figures indicate the larger number of native-born persons vs. foreign-born persons, census data reveal that between 1900 and 1910, the number and percentage of first- and second-generation immigrants decreased relative to the number of *native-born of native parentage*. The population of native-born white of native parentage was 20,458 (34.8% of the total population) in 1910. These numbers support the earlier suggestion that the second-generation was becoming the face of the German community and indicate that the community's minority status in Charleston was increasing. By 1920, there were only 527 foreign-born whites born in Germany, some seven hundred fewer than ten years earlier.

In 1910, only .9% of the native white population was illiterate, compared to 6.3% of the foreign-born. 81.1% of Charleston's native whites with native parentage were attending school, while 85.7% of second-generation children of foreign or mixed parentage—possibly more avid to learn—were attending. The data for 1920 shows that 0.8% of the total native whites were illiterate, compared to 3.3% of the foreign-born. The gap between the two cultures was narrowing. The ethnic community was increasingly being absorbed into the city's host society by virtue of language erosion, by intermarriage between the native-born second generation of foreign or mixed parentage with the native-born of native parentage, by an educational system geared toward literacy in English, and by the insistent pressures to accommodate and adapt to the values of the dominant English-speaking culture.

At the same time, other forces beyond the Charleston context were coming into play. There had been something of a rift between Great Britain, Germany, and the United States back in 1889 over the Samoan islands: a treaty had been signed and the dispute "passed without any serious results." But, as Clara Schieber explains, it marked "the first definite friction with Germany and the earliest appearance of any general American sentiment of distrust and suspicion against Germany."[5] In years following, as Germany exerted its militarism and imperialism, and the more the Hohenzollern Kaiser asserted his "divine" rights, the American public would become increasingly wary of the "Hun." The nativist sentiment may have been very low-key in well-integrated (white with white) Charleston, but the *Zeitung* of May 6, 1911, reported on the now-evident antipathy between England and Germany, publicly acknowledging that the matter was relevant to the mixed English-German population in Charleston. The newspaper blamed the tension between the two countries on England's resentment at Germany's remarkable industrial growth and advances in other areas during the previous twenty years—growth that had put England in second place. The overt mistrust between the two nations was clearly England's fault: Germany and its people—and by association, the Charleston Germans—were innocent of any wrongdoing. The final comment, "So be it. There's nothing we can do about it," relieved Charleston's German-Americans of any responsibility to mediate the tension or regret its existence, should any of them have taken notice or sensed any repercussions at the local level.

Later that year, the *Zeitung* ran a long editorial copied from the Savannah German newspaper, praising Kaiser Wilhelm II—his military acumen, his foreign policy, his diplomacy, his desire for peace, his stature as an individual—"a model for his countrymen in every sense" (*ein Vorbild seines Volkes in jeder Beziehung*). It was due to the Kaiser's leadership that mighty Germany had the best-prepared army in number and quality, was the leading industrial power, its teachers and its school system the best in the world. This three-column editorial in defense of the Kaiser suggests that by the end of 1911 there was a perceptible

5. Clara Eva Schieber, "The Transformation of American Sentiment towards Germany, 1870-1914," *Journal of International Relations* 12, no. 1 (1921): 58.

need to avert any negative feelings toward the German people that may have surfaced as the German leader began to take a leading role on the world stage.

Charleston's German-Americans were well aware of a national organization dedicated to advancing the interests of German-America. The well-known "Hon. John Cappelmann" who introduced the German Imperial Consul at the 1910 German-Day ceremonies had been identified in the newspaper account of the ceremonies as "Southern vice president of the German-American Alliance." For some time, there had been a concerted effort to promote an appreciation of German-Americans and all that those of German heritage had contributed to the nation. The effort had been initiated in 1901 with the founding of the National German-American Alliance (*Deutsch-Amerikanischer National-Bund*) in Philadelphia. Charles John Hexamer was elected president and would serve in that capacity for sixteen years. The Alliance's mission was stated in the preamble to its constitution:

> The German-American Alliance aims to awaken and strengthen the sense of unity among the people of German origin in America with a view to promote the useful and healthy development of the power inherent in them as a united body for the mutual energetic protection of such legitimate desires and interests not inconsistent with the common good of the country, and the rights and duties of good citizens; to check nativistic encroachments; to maintain and safeguard the good friendly relations existing between America and the old German fatherland.[6]

The organization's purpose was to "promote and preserve German culture in America" by resisting the Americanization of Germans who had immigrated to the United States. It counted every member of its local chapters, as well as members of recognized German organizations, in constituting its purported membership of 2.5 million. It promoted German language instruction in schools and encouraged the founding of educational societies, such as the German American Historical Society. The Alliance focused on

---

6. Charles T. Johnson, *Culture at Twilight: the National German-American Alliance, 1901-1918* (New York: Peter Lang, 1999), 11.

demonstrating the role German-Americans had played in the development of the United States.

It has been argued that the organization was not founded as a *defense* against the anti-German sentiment that would be evidenced later on, but rather because German immigrants and their descendants were genuinely proud of what they had accomplished: they justifiably could be proud of their homeland's achievements in science, art, music, education, and philosophy. If Americans and others were slow to recognize this, there was a consensus among the ethnic group that it would not be untoward, or in any way inappropriate, to remind them of those accomplishments. In some sense, however, it was indeed a "resistance" movement—a *defense* against total acculturation and the loss of an ethnic identity. Thus this rather soft-spoken, unobtrusive, work by a national organization chartered by the U.S. Congress had been on-going since early in the twentieth century across the country, carried out through socially-acceptable channels by local chapters of the larger organization. In 1915, it was shocked into a somewhat more aggressive stance as Germans and German organizations sensed a growing antipathy grounded in nativist sentiment against hyphenated minorities.

Not surprisingly, Charleston had its chapter, part of the NGAA's "South Atlantic League of German Societies, Lodges and Singers," that was organized in 1906 in Savannah. The letterhead of the League is indicative of the ubiquity of the German "element" in the coastal Southeast: the League's president was C. Toussaint of Savannah; its First Vice President was F. H. Hanne in Jacksonville; two of Charleston's Germans were Second (Paul Suren) and Third (E. Albenesius) Vice Presidents; acting as Secretary was F. H. Opper of Savannah, as Treasurer, C. Brickwedel of Jacksonville; Charleston's John D. Cappelmann was Chairman of the Committee on Judiciary. The letterhead's listing of the various organizations that constituted the League suggests that not *every* German organization—in Charleston or elsewhere in the region—was officially connected with the League, heavily weighted as it was with the fraternal lodges organized by the "Order of the Sons of Herman"—whose Charleston Lodge (o.d.H.S. [Der O̲rden de̲r H̲ermanns-S̲öhne]) was founded in 1908. Together with Cappelmann, Charleston's Paul Suren and E. Albenesius functioned to connect the local lodge with the regional League.

It is difficult to determine how many of Charleston's Germans were actively engaged in the efforts of the National German-American Alliance. There can be little doubt, however, that the work of the South Atlantic League's chapters and of the larger national organization was subscribed to by a number of individuals in the local ethnic community. The *Deutsche Zeitung* was the League's official newspaper, and for years, attorney John Cappelmann served as the Charleston chapter's president.[7] The Charleston chapter cannot have been acting in any sense covertly: in an October 18, 1907, letter from the NGAA's president Hexamer to the local chapter's Capplemann, the national president praised Cappelmann's work: "Dear Sir: I read your interview with much pleasure. You are on the right track—constant agitation and propaganda in the English papers of our country for a better understanding of our work is what we need."

If there had been any suggestion of covert dual loyalties in the ethnic community during the 1910 German Day celebration when the *Freya* was in the harbor, there was more than a suggestion already in 1908 that an overt anti-German sentiment existed in this part of the South. That year, the *Augusta Chronicle* published a lengthy letter by the Executive Committee of the South Atlantic League addressed to the Rev. Len G. Broughton, D.D. of Atlanta:

Dear Sir:

During a political address which you delivered in your church on Sunday, May 17, you made a most scurrilous attack upon the German-American Alliance and its members. Your charges were so utterly devoid of truth, and your statements, in general, were so extravagant that at first we hardly deemed them worthy of notice or reply; but upon more careful consideration we feel that there are people in Georgia who are ever ready to accept the statement of a clergyman at its face value, and unless we answer you, many will think that it was impossible for us to deny the allegations... You characterized us all as, "beer-bellies, brewers, bartenders, race track touts, apostles of beer and booze, enemies of Southern chivalry and civilization, Sabbath desecrators, debauchers of young men and women,

---

7.  Previously mentioned John Cappelmann was an attorney of German descent, known to every German in Charleston.

enemies of the government, wreckers of homes, moral lepers, dive runners, extortioners, thieves and bums."... If the American citizens of German descent in this country were as intemperate in their habits as you are in your speech, we would all have been sent to the penitentiary, hung, or consigned to the chain gang long ago.[8]

The six-page remonstration that followed was a valiant attempt by the Executive Committee to defend the organization and its members against such reactionist anti-German sentiment preached from a pulpit. In great detail, the Committee reminded the clergyman of all that the Germans had done for themselves and for America. At the end of the letter, the committee threw down the gauntlet by questioning what the clergyman's real intent had been: "Were you seeking to advertise yourself? Did you hope by such means to achieve international fame, and that your address might possibly become subject of consideration in the Departments of State of Germany and America?"

This is but one instance of the back-and-forth arguments that were increasingly in evidence between those who had, for whatever reason, taken a dislike to the Germans in their midst, and ethnic organizations intent on defending a cultural heritage they could justifiably be proud of. It is more than probable that it was that pride itself that stuck in the craw of the natives, particularly in "Southerners," who never liked to have it suggested that "their" heritage and traditions were secondary to anyone or anything. It is safe to assume that Atlanta's Rev. Broughton did not feel any obligation to offer an apology, nor that he took kindly to his comeuppance by beer-loving foreigners.

That there was something of a "divide" between the Germans and everyone else in regard to the relationship between the U.S. and the European powers can be read in a letter that John Cappelmann wrote in January 1912 to "Pitchfork Ben" Tillman, former South Carolina Governor, and at this time serving as one of the state's senators in Washington. Cappelmann writes:

I am required by a resolution of the South Carolina Branch of the National German American Alliance... adopted

---

8. *Augusta Chronicle,* May 31, 1908. The Rev. Broughton was a well-known Baptist minister and vocally rabid prohibitionist.

unanimously last night, to write to respectfully urge upon the part of your good self and your colleague hearty cooperation in the ratification of the pending treaties between United States, England and France ... The reports that there is serious opposition here to the pending treaties you may safely disregard. I feel at any rate that the Citizens here of German Extraction do not oppose but sincerely desire them and also a similar treaty as soon as possible with Germany ... It was not understood here on the part of many of us as American Citizens why the treaties contemplated did not embrace Germany and we honestly felt that it would be best for the United States to have a similar treaty with Germany also. It is now fully understood that negotiations to this end are underway and whatever you can do towards furthering the ratification thereof also (at the proper time) will be appreciated.[9]

Cappelmann had apparently quashed any opposition in the local ranks to the United States ratifying pending treaties with England and France without also establishing a similar relationship with Germany. He explains the misunderstanding and confirms that local sentiment favors equal treatment of the three European powers. As head of the local NGAA chapter, Cappelmann was in a somewhat awkward position in that he could not assume that Charleston's Germans were as united as the NGAA would have wished when it came to deciding whether militant Germany deserved the same status as the other two "allies." It is questionable how many of the city's German-American citizens in 1912 were conflicted by strong feelings for the ancestral homeland that would have compromised their professed allegiance to the United States.

The growing tension between the U.S. and Germany would only exacerbate the situation, nationally and locally. Shortly after Germany declared war on France on August 3, 1914, Hexamer wrote to Cappelmann (August 18, 1914) as follows:

---

9. Capitalizing "Citizens" was doubtless intentional.

My dear Mr. Cappelmann:

In reply to your favor of the 15th inst., I thank you very much for your prompt and excellent activity. All over the United States we have the support of every German-American in this serious crisis confronting German thought and German culture, and I know that over in your part of the country, the work for Germany and our National Alliance is in the best of hands, and if anything should occur I will let you know immediately … With kindest regards to you and all my dear friends, brothers and sisters in South Carolina, who are uniting in this hour of need in their wishes for Germany's success, I remain

With kindest regards, / Yours sincerely, / C. J. Hexamer

Another letter from Hexamer followed on the 19th, thanking Cappelmann for sending him a clipping from the *News and Courier* the day before: "This is excellent work, and what we must do all over the country. Even after these present fearful times have given place to peaceful ones, which I hope will redound to the honor of Germany, we must not let up any more, but try and have the English speaking Americans fully informed of the German-American side of things." The "clipping" from the *News and Courier* ("German-American Meeting is held / Efforts of German Red Cross Aid society endorsed / German side of the war / Public asked to wait before forming opinions about the European struggle") was a one-and-a-half-column account of a meeting of the South Carolina branch of the German-American Alliance in the German Artillery Hall on the 17th. Called to order by Cappelmann, several resolutions were passed, one of which stated:

[W]e as American citizens courteously ask that the American press present all information as to the present war in Europe in an unbiased and impartial manner and that the editorials as far as possible may be without prejudice towards any class of American citizens, this though an English speaking country, is not an English Nation, and it is but fair in these stirring times that that American spirit of fair play shall be exercised to the fullest extent so as to further good feeling among American citizens of every extraction and creed.

The organization passed another resolution calling for the opening remarks by Cappelmann to be published. In those remarks Cappelmann had questioned whether contributions to the German Red Cross should be viewed as being at variance with citizens' loyalty or the national effort to remain neutral:

> To afford to those in our community who desire to help in the care of the wounded and suffering, there has been organized here an Aid Society to the Red Cross... This Society will receive and forward through the proper medium all contributions so that they may be applied and used in accordance with the wishes of the givers. In this way timely and helpful service can be rendered to the stricken families and soldiers of the Fatherland, without in the slightest degree being at variance with our American neutrality.

It is fair to conclude that such remarks by Cappelmann in defense of the potentially conflicted sensibilities of Charlestonians "of German extraction" confirm that in the summer of 1914 there had arisen a significant degree of tension between the "natives" and the "foreigners" in the genteel, Southern, coastal city.

The physical distance between the United States and Europe when WWI began in the summer of 1914 effectively separated those of German heritage in the U.S. from their European brethren. Charleston's German-Americans, as elsewhere, nonetheless still felt connected to Germans in Germany. Through the local chapter of the National German-American Alliance, Charleston's Germans were active early on in the local Alliance chapter's campaign to raise money for Germany's war victims. As early as August 1914, Cappelmann was planning how his group could effectively cooperate with the German Red Cross Aid Society, whose president was E. H. Jahnz, the German Consul. It was noted that "many non-Germans had shown interest in and had contributed to the work of the society who[se] success has been very gratifying so far."[10] *Evening Post* issues listed for all to see the names of the donors on record, as well as the amounts they had individually contributed. At a chapter meeting, Consul Jahnz reminisced about his experience during the Franco-Prussian War and admonished that since it was impracticable for German-Americans to enlist in Germany's armed forces, it was incumbent upon those who sympathized with Germany to contribute liberally to aid those suffering in the Fatherland. The *Evening Post* of September 21, 1914, announced that "local Fatherland organizers" were organizing an ambitious German Day celebration in October:

> The German Day celebration will be no war celebration, but German Day has been celebrated in the United States for a number of years in order to chronicle from year to year the achievements of German culture, and salutary effects of such culture and civilization on the material and intellectual progress of the United States. It was pointed out that German Day is the one day of every year set apart to rejoice in the part German science, German integrity, German honesty and good morals have played in the intellectual, commercial, industrial and moral development of the world in general and of the United States especially. "Such blessed influence," stated one of the speakers, "would remain for all ages even if Germany should fall prey to the overwhelming odds she is at present engaged in overcoming. A German Day during the perilous days of the Fatherland is right now more appropriate than ever."

The local/foreign connection was equally clear in the announcement that "the local German Red Cross Aid Association has ordered through their secretary, Paul Wierse, all the German casualty lists. Many Germans in Charleston have relatives in the war and are anxious to know their fate. The lists show every man slightly or seriously wounded, dead or missing."[11] In an early 1916 article about the German Red Cross Association's collections, the newspaper

---

10. *Evening Post*, August 15, 1914.
11. *Evening Post*, November 21, 1914.

described those who belonged to the group as "former subjects of the Kaiser and their descendants."[12]

Since the United States initially stood aside from the hostilities, the German press could monitor and report on the situation abroad with apparent objectivity and lack of bias. In December 1914, for example, the *Zeitung* reported the drama at Dunkirk with purposeful equanimity: the Allies had gotten the art treasures at city hall removed to safety, the German army along the Ostend-Ypres line was estimated at 700,000; the French had suffered heavy losses and were expecting a major onslaught; ambulances and field hospitals were taking every precaution; England was forcing Norway to violate its neutrality.[13] The next month, the tone was slightly different. A lengthy article in the *Zeitung*'s English edition[14] expressed satisfaction that the U.S. seemed finally willing to speak out against England regarding the latter's hegemony on the world's trade routes:

> At the same time, the Washington government's "note of warning" should serve to open the eyes of the American people to the "true inwardness" of the European war; at least, in so far as it affects themselves and their interests. They have been, already, too long blinded by sentiment; by talk of "our cousins" or threats of "German militarism." They may, now, begin to see that they have been made to suffer far more, and have much more to fear, from British "navalism." The European nations may have cause to watch and fear Germany's growth; but as for America, she needs only to watch England, on the east, and Japan, on the west—but to fear neither.

An article on the front page of the *Zeitung*'s English edition of March 3, 1915, posed the question "Which is the more efficient / The English or the German Navy?" Listing the ship-type, size, speed, and age of both navies' destroyed vessels, the vote went to Germany: "Which is the most effective, the

---

12. *Evening Post*, February 4, 1916.

13. December 5, 1914.

14. "The Worm has turned at last," re-printed from the *Atlanta Chronicle* of January 2, 1915.

gigantic English navy or the small German navy? It's here, like everywhere, 'the man behind the gun' who counts."

If Charleston's German newspaper had thus far been side-stepping a budding negative opinion of Germany's role in the European conflict in contrast to that of England and its United States "cousin," the negativity toward Germans in the U.S. broke to the surface with "Col." Teddy Roosevelt's questioning the loyalty of those he referred to as "hyphenated citizens." The *Zeitung's* May-Day[15] English edition carried a letter by Paul Wierse, the editorial writer and editor of the Charleston pro-German newspaper, the *American,* that had been sent to the editor (at the time, Theodore Roosevelt) of the *Metropolitan* magazine in which Roosevelt had published his own article entitled "When is an American not an American?" The letter had been returned to Wierse by Roosevelt with the remark "thanks for letting me see it"—a clear message that he had no intention of publishing the Wierse letter. The headline in the *Zeitung* read "An Open Letter to Col. Theodore Roosevelt," and the paper encouraged "all true American square-dealing" papers to kindly copy it. Wierse wrote defensively on behalf of his fellow "hyphenated" Americans:

> This is the time of aspersions being cast upon the patriotism of hyphenated Americans. History repeats itself. We have had the "Know Nothing Movement" which finally was drowned effectively in the heart blood of hyphenated Americans who fought in the ranks of the North with equal patriotism as they fought in the Southern ranks. The Irish-Americans, the German-Americans and the Jewish-Americans have been tested in the furnace of war and reconstruction, and they came forth as pure gold as genuine "dyed in the wool" American patriots, having sacrificed substance and life unhesitatingly for the country of their adoption even to the point of fighting brother against brother—North against South … Slowly it dawned on our intelligent citizens that the United States had utterly failed in its policy of a square deal. Slowly they realized the hypocrisy of those who cunningly hide their origin under the amalgamation of "unhyphenated Americans." It is

---

15. May 1, 1915.

a grave error and an injustice as well to say that the German-Americans would put the interests of Germany above those of the United States. It is the interest of the United States they really have at heart ... They have been told by politicians of every shade of "their citizens' rights" and they feel that at least it should be exerted for the square deal principle and much praised democracy ... Put Germany's interest above the interests of the United States? It is a foul calumny. Not one single German-American would ever be guilty of it. Not a single German-American would like to see this country involved in war, not even on the side of Germany. From no German source has ever come any frantic and perversive invitation to "join in" like it has come from English authors and as it is in an underhand way promulgated by a large percentage of our English and French press, notably the Herald and others ... The German-Americans naturally would like to see a continuation of the friendship that has ever existed between the United States and Germany, but they don't want to see it at the cost of a violation of our neutrality. This again is more than can be said for the hypercritical unhyphenated Americans ... The German-Americans have ever fought for the best interest of this country, although they have modestly refused to take any prominent part in politics. If now they take the initiative, let us hail this as a sign for a better future of American independence.

Similarly strong denials of any suggestion of disloyalty on the part of Americans with a foreign heritage would become increasingly louder as the German community observed the pronounced one-sided stance of neutrality taken by the United States vis à vis the European belligerents.

Wierse understood Roosevelt's anti-hyphenism as evidence of the same nativism that had characterized the earlier Know-Nothing movement. And although, as Michael Bell has suggested, the mid-nineteenth-century Know-Nothing movement ("agitation for temperance, an intolerance of Catholics, and an ethic of extreme Puritanism") had had little success in Charleston—the city's citizens "were too tolerant of both Catholics and foreigners to be swayed into the nativist camp"—Charles Johnson contends that nativism is always present just beneath the surface. In a society comprised of minority nationalities existing among an Anglo majority, waves of Anglo-influenced prejudice against the "other" have frequently surfaced at times of local or national stress. Johnson acknowledges that "the reasons for this nativism are complex. For example, in the early 1890's they were economic—based on the fear that immigrants would take jobs away from native-born Americans. In other circumstances they reflected a belief that certain races, such as eastern Europeans, were intellectually and morally inferior. A final reason, especially in the case of the Irish, was the fear of Catholicism and its influence in Protestant America."[16]

If for the most part German-Americans, including those in Charleston, had not been targeted in these earlier nativist attacks against other ethnic groups, it was apparent after about 1910 that their time had come, as relations between the United States and Germany grew increasingly more complicated. Charleston's Germans could not remain immune to what was going on elsewhere. It might be argued that Charleston in these early decades of the twentieth century was somewhat cut off from other parts of the country: there was a very pronounced sectionalism between southern states and the rest of the nation—the latter itself not yet a coherent concept for many who had survived the Civil War. There were still local "pockets" operating within their limited horizons, and what transpired in one place did not necessarily happen in another. Nonetheless, the German-Americans in the Lowcountry port could not have slept comfortably with their heads in the proverbial sand, ignorant of the social and economic developments affecting the country as a whole.

Long before the war began in 1914, it was obvious to all that since its unification in 1871, Germany had come to dominate the European stage, a truth that put Germans in America in the unenviable position of straddling the lines that were being drawn between their ancestral and their adopted homeland. The work of the NGAA to promote the German heritage ran bluntly into a suspicious nativism ready to question which homeland "the Germans" were ready to defend should the United States decide to get involved in the European dispute. It would become clear that during the years leading up to the war, and, once the war was underway, during the three years of U.S. neutrality, that German-Americans were damned if they professed their loyalty to the United

---

16. *Culture at Twilight*, 137.

States and damned if they did not. In many ways, the activism of the NGAA was responsible for putting German-Americans in the spotlight. Practicing what they thought was their sanctioned right to be pro-active in their own interests, German-American descendants of nineteenth-century immigrants encountered nativist reactions of suspicion and doubt. German-American pride in the ancestral country's past achievements and current status did nothing but raise the hackles of Anglo descendants who gave no quarter to anyone suggesting superiority. In the glare of the spotlight, German-Americans were stereotyped, as Atlanta's Rev. Broughton had done, as beer-loving potential enemies of the government, puppets of a hegemonic Germany carrying out a Pan-German agenda. Each camp would offend the other, each took umbrage of the offense. As Frederick Luebke put it in his *Bonds of Loyalty: German-Americans and World War I,* "[b]y 1914 most of the ingredients for an explosive mix were present."[17]

In the following chapters we will learn that anti-German sentiment was less overtly manifest in Charleston than in other parts of the country. This was, after all, the city where the Deutsche Schützengesellschaft had established the oldest rifle club in America, the city where "German Day" was celebrated annually, the home of the *Deutsche Zeitung,* a city ornamented with the bold German-style architecture of its centrally located St. Matthew's *German* Lutheran Church. But something was in the air. In spite of its history, Charleston was said to be genteel and tolerant. How would it deal with "the German problem"?

---

17. Dekalb: Northern Illinois University Press, 1974, 78.

# CHAPTER 7:

# AFTER THE LUSITANIA

The sinking of the *Lusitania* on May 7, 1915, changed the dynamic between Americans and German-Americans for the worse. The torpedoing of the Cunard steamship by a German submarine that cost the lives of 1,128 people—among them 128 Americans—in the waters off England "greatly reduced much of the remaining tolerance that American society had towards German-Americans. And although the war was avoided in the weeks following the crisis, the war on all things German in the United States gained new momentum. Many German-Americans, at this point … renounced any further loyalty to Germany, and expressed their complete support to the United States Government."[1]

Charleston's *Deutsche Zeitung*, the voice of the now somewhat-diluted-by-the-passage-of-time German-American community, continued to express how unfortunate it was that the loyalty of Germans to the United States was in doubt. Americans' doubt about U.S. Germans' loyalty was expressed in the consistently negative public reactions to Germany's war plans, in combination with the obvious-to-all pro-English prejudice that had taken hold in the U.S.

---

1. Erik Kirschbaum, *The Eradication of German Culture in the United States, 1917-1918* (Stuttgart: H. D. Heinz, 1986), 57.

government. The German newspaper could acknowledge the tragedy for which America, England, and Germany were all responsible in one way or another; could agree that, yes, the United States would have to respond to Germany's aggressive policies; could, in the same breath, remind the readership that Germany had indeed given explicit warning to Americans that there was risk sailing on the Cunard liner; could argue that, no matter the parameters of the crisis, German-Americans were innocent bystanders whose loyalties should never be questioned. The *Deutsche Zeitung* argued that the response to the half-challenging question put to German-Americans, "Where do you stand?" had always been a straightforward and unanimous one: "We know but one flag and will follow it, wherever it may lead to; we know only the Stars and Stripes as our flag and resent the very idea that we could ever be disloyal to it."[2]

While the German newspaper continued to function in these years as it had always done, never giving up its dual role as a source of information and as a guide for the physical, psychological, and social well-being of its primary audience, it could not control external events that impacted—however benignly—the local population. That the German embassy, for example, the day before the *Lusitania* was sunk, had published a warning to passengers expecting to sail on British vessels—an action that would lead to an increase in accusations of German guilt—was a fact that could not be denied. Rumors about what had happened were rampant and spread like wildfire. Conspiracy theories focused on the network of official and unofficial operatives of the Reich. Any potential public defense of Germany's actions was precluded by the publication of *The Report on the Committee of Alleged German Outrages* by Viscount James Bryce, who had been commissioned by the British government to investigate reports of German atrocities in Belgium. When the Bryce Report came out a week after the sinking of the *Lusitania*, British propaganda sources made sure it was sent to virtually every newspaper in the United States. Bryce's report on the atrocities was "a huge propaganda victory for the British" and showed the Germans in the worst possible light. It served to convince millions of American and other neutrals that the Germans were beasts in human form.[3]

---

2. *Deutsche Zeitung*, May 22, 1915.

3. See Frank Trommler, "The Lusitania Effect: America's Mobilization against Germany in World War I," *German Studies Review* 32, no. 2 (2009): 246.

Additionally, and again beyond the control of the *Zeitung*, the German government's propaganda efforts more often than not misfired, resulting in the opposite effect of what was intended. Germany's attempt to control the news was "extremely counterproductive ... undermining the claims of German Americans to be patriotic Americans while maintaining their traditional ties to Germany and German culture ... [T]he German government had rarely understood the precarious position of German Americans—either exaggerating their influence on American politics or dismissing their stance after 1914 as disappointing in the battle for American neutrality."[4]

Against this background, it was not so much their vulnerability to growing expressions of doubt about their loyalty that brought German-Americans into the foreground during the pre-war years, but rather their defensiveness. On the defensive for some time, Germans and their organizations evidenced a heightened sense of self-worth and, as suggested earlier, a tendency to argue their right as American citizens to express the unappreciated, indeed superior, nature of their German-ness. On the national stage, German-Americans themselves behaved in ways detrimental to their efforts to defend their case:

> Doubts about the loyalty of the country's large foreign-born population were accentuated by the great number of German-American rallies in which solidarity with a foreign power was used to enhance cohesiveness, activism, and ethnic pride. The often irritating expressions of self-assertion of an otherwise well integrated segment of the population stirred new questions "about the nation's assimilative capacities and the impact of ethnocultural diversity on American security" with the result that "politicians and opinion leaders increasingly called for government policies promoting national conformity."[5]

Locally, the behavior of Charleston's acculturated Germans was rarely in dispute. Nonetheless, the larger Charleston community was keenly aware of the NGAA's activities through the publicity it was receiving, as well as through the involvement of the local chapter's leader, John Cappelmann.

---

4. Trommler, 246..
5. Ibid., 247-48.

Lacking evidence to the contrary, there were probably relatively few Charleston German-Americans who actively subscribed to the program of the National German-American Alliance, whose work was promoted primarily by members of the Order of the Sons of Hermann. It was likely that only a minority of the Charleston ethnic community cared deeply about the issues that the distant, elite, intellectuals in the organization had brought into focus. To the point made earlier that there were never many "radicals" in the nineteenth-century Charleston German community, there were even fewer now that the group had devolved to later generations who had been exposed to the process of acculturation for a longer period. After the turn of the century, the now "genteel" Charleston ethnic community might have found the tactics of the national organization to be rather too aggressive. Collectively, however, it could not remain unaware that there was a chartered organization purportedly working on behalf of the deep-seated interests of the German-American community. If a small number of second-generation German-Americans in Charleston actually identified with the NGAA's mission, they were not inclined to make too much of a fuss about what the national organization suggested were "German interests." In his study of the NGAA, Charles Johnson claims that while "Americans of German descent made up the nation's largest ethnic group, less than 10 percent were dues-paying members of the Alliance."

> Were German-Americans truly concerned about preserving ways of the fatherland? By 1905 Americans of German descent were by far the most "assimilated" of all the non-English speaking ethnic groups. Perhaps the threat to German culture was not external but within the German-American community itself. For this reason the Alliance placed heavy emphasis on membership drives, and in stirring up enthusiasm through celebrations of German-Americana at the local, state, and national levels.[6]

The constitution of the NGAA steered the organization toward anything that emphasized the preservation of German culture, one aspect of which was

---

6. *Culture at Twilight: the National German-American Alliance, 1901-1918* (New York: Peter Lang, 1999), 29.

the maintenance of German language instruction. It advocated the teaching of the German language in the public school system on a widespread basis as both "a means of preserving the language within the German-American community and to expand its usage within the non-German population." In terms that would be considered boastful by the American public, the NGAA let it be known that its membership considered German "the equal of English as a language of world civilization, trade, commerce and science." It went so far as to argue that a knowledge of both German and English would assist the individual in gaining a clearer understanding of the world as well as promoting closer relations between nations.[7]

In Charleston's case, what was perceived by the NGAA elite as a "threat to German culture"— the disappearance of language facility—had long been in evidence in the local community. As noted previously, the German Friendly Society founded in 1766 on behalf of "German" interests, kept its records in English. Three years later in 1769, the Society's membership was assessed to pay for its rules to be translated from English into German and printed in Philadelphia.[8] Over the course of the following century-and-a-quarter, the immigrants' German had been giving way to the host society's English. In the *Zeitung* in June of 1898, it was announced to the ethnic community that the *German* St. Matthew's Church would begin regularly offering the sermon in English: the Church Council had taken this step in recognition of the fact that the younger German-Americans did not know enough German to understand a sermon in German and were leaving the fold to join other congregations.[9] An "English Edition" was the practice of the *Zeitung* by early 1915: its German subscriber base had undoubtedly grown smaller as fewer of the second- and third-generation carried forward an interest or facility in reading the newspaper in German. It was more and more evident that later-generation Germans had little interest in preserving the language spoken by their parents or grandparents.

As for the NGAA's ideal of teaching the German language in the public schools, such a proposal had little chance of being widely adopted in

---

7. Johnson, 12.

8. A. G. Roeber, *Palatines, Liberty, and Property: German Lutherans in colonial British America* (Baltimore: Johns Hopkins University Press, 1993), 237.

9. *Deutsche Zeitung*, June 6, 1898.

Charleston. Already in 1802 the German Friendly Society had appointed a committee to engage a school master and establish a school for the children of members. In keeping with the Society's apparent preference for English in its public activities, the school committee was charged to hire a school master to "regularly and carefully instruct in the English grammar, in writing and in arithmetic, also. If he is capable and if requested by the school committee, in the Latin language such children and descendants of members of the German Friendly Society and all such children qualified for admission into the Society under the second rule of the constitution. If he understands the German language, or hath a partner or obtains an assistant in the same, those children whose parents are guardians may wish it, *if not less than six*, shall be instructed therein, and in six hours in every week shall they be employed in teaching such children that language."[10] That early on, members of the Society clearly felt it their civic duty to facilitate the acculturation process by instructing their children in the language that would enable them to more easily fit into the English-speaking majority population. It also clearly signaled that the German community was not intent on remaining separate from the city's native-born English-speaking residents. The German Friendly Society's efforts to educate its members' progeny lasted for the first half of the century. The school was discontinued in 1857 when the Society's school rooms were sold to Charleston's Commissioners of Free Schools. Before the end of Reconstruction, in 1874, a German School Association had been organized "by leading German citizens … for the purpose of establishing and maintaining a school for the instruction of children of German parents."[11] Establishing such a German School at that time, however, had nothing to do with maintaining the German language: "At the time of its organization the public schools of Charleston were threatened with an invasion of negro children and the founders of the German school sought to provide an institution which would safeguard the German children against such undesirable co-education."[12]

---

10. *The History of the German Friendly Society of Charleston, South Carolina 1766 – 1916.* Compiled from original sources by George J. Gongaware (The German Friendly Society, Charleston, South Carolina: Garrett & Massie, Richmond 1935), 47.

11. *News and Courier,* July 4, 1904

12. The July 4, 1904, *News and Courier* column was reporting on the dissolution of the German School Association earlier that year: "The excellence of the public schools

In some ways, Charlestonians were fortunate to have a public school system at all. It was only in 1895 that the state's constitution called for establishing a system of public education. In the following decades up to WWI, state and school authorities were primarily concerned with the education of *white* children. It is doubtful that the Charleston populace as a whole would have agreed with the German "defender," George von Skal, who in a 1915 address argued:

> [I]t would be indeed a great boon for the American people and this country if instruction in foreign languages in the public schools could be extended. There can be only one opinion as to the value of such instruction. No man or woman can claim to be in possession of an education sufficient to give a right to judge others unless he or she is conversant with at least one language in addition to the mother tongue. The advantages are clear, and I have always believed that the reason why Americans have such a defective command of their own language is to be found in their ignorance of foreign languages. I do not believe that there is any other country in the world where it is so rare to find men or women who speak and write their language correctly.[13]

Such a "German" attitude would never play well in the city whose English traditions dominated, whose citizens were more than content to speak the "King's English," and who were loath to suffer anyone intimating that their command of English was defective.

Possibly the most publicized aspect of the NGAA's efforts to "preserve" German culture was its campaign against prohibition, an effort that moved it into the political arena and brought German-Americans considerable attention. It had become the organization's top priority already in 1903, and its activity in defense of German beer-drinking traditions afforded plenty of ammunition

---

has rendered superfluous the maintenance of the German School, and a few months ago the Association decided to dispose of the property and terminate the existence of the Association."

13. *The German-Americans and the European War. A Reply to M. Oswald Garrison Villard and Others* (New York: n.p., 1915), 22.

to the Anti-Saloon League. Before long, the NGAA enjoyed the support of the brewing industry, noticeably garnering the endorsement of the United States Brewers' Association. "From this point on, the fight against laws prohibiting the manufacture, sale, and consumption of alcoholic beverages remained a key issue. By late 1908 it was the main topic of concern until the onset of World War One in 1914 forced the Alliance to concentrate on international events."[14] With respect to the agenda of the NGAA, the prohibition issue was interpreted as an attack on German-Americans' social customs and ethnic, age-old, traditions and, not insignificantly, a violation of individual rights.

Charleston—its natives and its immigrants—had been fighting against the forces of temperance for a century or more. The determined exponents of temperance in up-state South Carolina made every effort to wage war on the city's intemperate good-time drinkers. South Carolinians had passed a non-binding referendum in 1892 calling for prohibition. Subsequently, the famous/infamous governor, "Pitchfork Ben Tillman," managed to subvert the teetotalers by having his Dispensary Law enacted, enabling the state to regulate the manufacturing, distribution, and sale of liquor. Effective July 1, 1893, the law prevented the private sale of liquor and required that it be sold between sunrise and sunset in sealed packages which could not be opened on the Dispensary premises. After resistance to the law led to rioting in the city of Darlington in 1894, the state Supreme Court declared the law unconstitutional. Within a year, Tillman managed to replace one of the Supreme Court judges, and the court subsequently declared the 1893 law constitutional.

Ever since their arrival earlier in the nineteenth century, the city's German immigrants had, it might be said, "institutionalized" the consumption of beer. Nowhere did it flow more freely than at the Schützenplatz. Understandably, Charleston Germans had little tolerance for any effort to curtail their right to drink. Within weeks of the Dispensary law's initial passage, the *News and Courier*[15] furnished a list of those "freehold voters" who had signed a petition for Henry A. Meyer (a German-American) to be appointed Dispenser for Charleston County. It was questionable how conscientiously the law would have to be followed, and it was assumed that with a fellow German as the Dispenser, there would be some wiggle room. Among the individuals met

14. Johnson, *Culture at Twilight,* 24.
15. *News and Courier,* July 18, 1893.

in previous chapters, the twice-king of the Schützenfest, Bernhard Bequest, was one of the signatories to the petition for Meyer to be put in charge of the Dispensary, and it mattered to no one in the ethnic community that twice in 1896, B. H. Bequest was subjected to "police raids," one of which found him harboring "a demijohn of whisky and 15 bottles of palmetto beer."[16] His brother August, proprietor of Bequest's Restaurant, railed against the ordinances prohibiting the sale of anything intoxicating. From the beginning, the restaurant owner had trouble with the "Sunday Law," the "blue laws," and the "Sunday cocktail" issue. The *News and Courier* quoted him extensively on the matter in December 1887, when he vowed to fight aggressively if the campaign to have barrooms and restaurants close on Sundays became law.[17] In April 1892 he was one of four "saloon keepers" arraigned before the Recorder in the Police Court, charged with selling liquor on Sunday.

When the NGAA entered the prohibition fray, it both united German-Americans in the battle over their traditions and rights, as well as drew hardnosed opposition from those who viewed the consolidated hyphenated group as a threat to American values. The battle was not so much with "established authority as such (for who has more respect for authority, law, and public discipline than the German?), but conflict with the older, often consciously anti-alien element in American life."[18] The constant argument between *Americans* for temperance and *Germans* against prohibition only increased the undercurrent of doubt about the ethnic community's divided loyalties.

After the onset of the war in 1914, and with the prohibition issue unresolved, the NGAA concluded that there were other matters that needed its attention The reluctance of the United States to get involved in the European conflict created the opportunity for the NGAA to turn its attention—once again in the interest of its German-American constituency—to ensuring that the nation remained neutral. It focused its effort on avoiding a direct confrontation between the United States and Germany, while continually venting its frustration with what was clearly the government's pro-British bias.

---

16. *Charleston Evening Post*, February 6, 1896. The police also raided C. H. Hutmacher, P. J. Hilson, and C. F. Klencke, all of whom were guilty of hiding a few bottles of beer.

17. *News and Courier*, December 17, 1887.

18. Clifton James Child, *The German-Americans in Politics* (New York: Arno Press, 1970), 21.

In defense of its German heritage, the larger ethnic community's voice got louder and louder, warding off anti-German sentiment by shouting assertions of Germany's superiority. On the day after the *Lusitania* was sunk, when word of the disaster had not yet reached Charleston, the *Zeitung* ran in its English edition two lengthy articles. In one article, headlined "The world's prize article ... written by Francis Muench, Ph.D., formerly of Charleston, S.C., who is well remembered here by hundreds of friends," Muench described the terms of peace that could be expected if Germany lost and the consequences thereof, in contrast to terms that would likely be formulated if Germany won and the results that would follow. He continued in his "prize" essay with a wide-ranging assessment of Germany's superiority in religion, in education, in science, in literature and art, in commerce, and in social and political conditions, concluding that "perhaps more than one generation will pass ere the feeling of animosity engendered by the war will yield to kindlier sentiments and man will reap the full fruit of universal peace." The second of the two articles excoriated the British press under the headline "Once and Now / England's Press before the War and Now. A Comparison Between Sanity and Insanity," claiming that "[t]he English press show symptoms of disorganization, disruption and editorial brain storms that are nauseating. The English press is already diseased. The German Emperor is pictured as a cruel monster, as a man of unbalanced mind and God knows what else." The article suggested that it was "refreshing to compare these ravings of a crazed press with the dignity of its former expression." [19] The *Zeitung* was not really out of line in its tone, nor was its position on these topics peculiar to the city in which it operated. In his *Bonds of Loyalty*, Frederick Luebke argues that "a detailed examination of the German-language press during World War I shows remarkable uniformity of thought. Almost without exception, the German-American editors accepted uncritically the official German explanation for the outbreak of war, and many predicted a quick and decisive victory for German arms."[20]

One did not have to read many issues of the *Deutsche Zeitung* to realize that Charleston's "German" press was at one with its sister organs in other cities. Was it not, after all, the organ of the NGAA's South Atlantic League of German Societies, Lodges and Singers? In October, the paper featured

19. *Deutsche Zeitung*, May 8, 1915.
20. Luebke, *Bonds of loyalty*, 89.

(in English) an article entitled "The German Day and its significance," in which Paul Wierse, the *Zeitung*'s editorial writer and himself the editor of the pro-German *American*, preached from his pulpit:

> The annual celebration of German Day has fostered American patriotism among the descendants of the German immigrants as well as among later arrivals to a degree of enthusiasm that is characteristic of the Teutonic race, and this enthusiastic patriotism imbued sages and historians with the desire to search the records of all the larger cities and all the states for data pertaining to the achievements for the benefit of this country by Americans of Teutonic progenitors. The vast material collected by historians became a revelation of the prominent part German immigrants played in the commercial, industrial, economic, agricultural and religious development of this country ... The record of the Teutonic elements of this nation is spotless. That element has ever performed all the duties of its citizenship without ever making any concerted demands for its citizen rights. Conscious of its loyalty to the Union, German Day becomes a Day of Resentment against the un-American propaganda by other elements of this nation, a day of refuting the slander indulged in by a hired press and bought politicians posing as "statesmen." ... Throughout the length and breadth of this country, the much slandered and most loyal element of this nation begins to unite in demanding its right, in demanding a voice in the council of this independent nation, which it has helped to create and to bring to the pinnacle of its success.[21]

If the remnants of Charleston's nineteenth-century German community were sympathetic to the stridency on display in newspaper editorials like Wierse's, they, like their compatriots elsewhere, seemed unaware that such attitudes would before too long turn the world against them. Charleston's *Zeitung*, nonetheless, seems to have appreciated the fact that aggressive pro-German

---

21. *Deutsche Zeitung*, American Edition, October 2, 1915.

statements might negatively impact the "German-Friendliness" of its advertisers. The newspaper in 1915 was carrying a "notice" on its front page that seemed intent on smoothing over any ruffled feathers: "TO THE PUBLIC. The Zeitung is the organ of the German-Americans and as such widely read in every German-American family. The readers appreciate the German-Friendliness of our Merchants, and take the patronage of their organ (as expressed by the Ads of our merchants) as the visible sign of German-Friendliness. An ad in our paper means the good will of all German-Americans toward the firm that advertises. And the German trade is worth having! There is hardly ever any trouble in getting payment for the goods. The Germans, as a rule, are good payers. They are also appreciative citizens and patronize the patrons of their organ."

The matter of keeping the United States out of a war with Germany became something akin to the NGAA's *raison d'etre* from the very beginning of the conflict in 1914. The Alliance almost immediately assumed responsibility to speak for all German-Americans and anyone else advocating the neutrality of the United States vis à vis the Europeans at war. Charles Johnson argues that "[as] American neutrality policy evolved and the American press took on an increasingly pro-British attitude, the Alliance increasingly voiced strong objections to the actions by the American government and press."[22] Johnson further contends that when the Alliance worked to influence the election of 1916, the organization overextended itself in trying to direct U.S. policy regarding the war: "By taking part in foreign and domestic politics it had entered into a realm that was beyond the scope of its purpose." Instead of keeping to its original purpose of promoting the nation's German cultural heritage, "it sailed into unchartered waters with little preparation, obliged ... to take positions on issues that were contrary to popular opinion ... In the eyes of many Americans the shroud had vanished and what one could see emerging from Alliance headquarters at 419 Walnut Street, Philadelphia, was an iron cross."[23]

As the national organization presumed to speak for the collective German-American community with its drumbeat for neutrality in order to avoid having to take sides, the *Deutsche Zeitung* could assure its Charleston constituency that the war was going well for belligerent Germany. The English *Zeitung* of October 2, 1915, reported that Mr. Mendel, "from Wiesbaden but now residing

22. Johnson, *Culture at Twilight*, 99.
23. Johnson, *Culture at Twilight*, 125.

in Savannah," had returned from his trip to Germany and could report that conditions in the homeland were good: plenty of young men available for the army; a plentiful supply of foodstuffs; more submarines than reported; prisoners treated well; a great number of subscriptions to the war loans "desired by the government." "The worst of the campaign ... was passed when the Teutons and their allies threw the Russians out of the Carpathians. One hundred and fifty thousand square miles of Russian territory is now in the hands of the Germans; they hold with an iron hand nineteen-twentieths of Belgium, have in their possession one-eighth of France, comprising the richest coal and iron mining regions, and generally are on the enemy territory." The European conflict, he added, was "due entirely ... to the jealousy of England."

The same issue carried a large advertisement for German Day at the Schützenplatz "for the benefit of widow and orphans of German soldiers." The "American" edition of November 6, 1915, was not beyond sarcasm:

> About 1500 of the Americans to whom the United States advanced money for the purpose of returning from war torn Europe have refused to repay Uncle Sam. One of them was a Belgian and he simply swindled Uncle Sam out of the money; another American took the money and then enlisted in the French army. All of the 1500 dead beats are true and loyal Americans without the hyphen.

A piece by the Germanophile, George Sylvester Viereck,[24] in the *Zeitung*'s "American" edition in August 5, 1916 was meant to assure the German public that "after two years of war against overwhelming odds, Germany is the victor."

> Germany has not only won all the substantial prizes of the war, but her soldiers and sailors, over and under the sea, on earth and under the clouds, have wrought deeds of deering-do that will not be forgotten, while the world goes on. In fact, all the great romantic exploits of the war must be credited to her score. The spiritual impetus of her achievement will enable her

---

24. During the war, Viereck published the journal *The Fatherland*.

to win from peace victories even greater than those which she has wrested from war.

In his 1915 tract, *The German-Americans and the European War. A Reply to M. Oswald Garrison Villard and Others (New* York: n.p.), George von Skal, the advocate for teaching German in the schools mentioned earlier, declared where German-America stood some two years before the United States entered the war in words that reveal the chip on his German-American shoulder. He defied any effort to cast German-Americans in a negative light and affirmed their unquestionable loyalty to the U.S.:

> We do not harbor the faintest trace of enmity against the United States of America, American institutions or the American people as a whole, though we feel bitter against those who have wantonly attacked and abused us. Although our love for the Fatherland can never die, we remain loyal citizens of this great Republic that has become our own country, ready to defend it against all enemies, eager to do our part in securing for it all the blessings the most enthusiastic mind can imagine, and we deplore deeply the dissentions caused by the unreasoning attitude of a considerable part of the population, so detrimental to that harmony which is essential to progress and contentment. But we serve fair notice upon all who may think that they can frighten or cajole us into submission, that our minds are made up, that no matter what happens to us, we shall continue to fight for truth, for justice, for right and for the independence of the United States of America until we have conquered or are no more. As German-Americans have been loyal to this Republic ever since it was created, so will we remain devoted to the country we have sworn allegiance to, to our ideals and to our just case, even unto death.[25]

Charleston's *Evening Post* was, of course, attuned to the negative sentiment that had developed after the *Lusitania* incident, as well as the increasing efforts

---

25. Von Skal, 29.

of prominent individuals to argue for an unbiased evaluation of the military struggle between the powers at war. It ran a lengthy column about a letter that Kuno Francke, head of the Germanic Museum of Harvard University and "one of the most distinguished German-Americans in the United States," had sent to U.S. Representative Richard Bartholdt, who was urging the U.S. government to establish an embargo on war munitions to the allies. Francke wrote:

> I fully believe in the righteousness of the German cause in the present world conflict, and I shall avail myself of every opportunity, as I have done before, to express publicly, my fervent hope that Germany will remain victorious in a struggle forced upon them by the aggression of a most unnatural coalition of powers held together by nothing but irrational fear of German ascendancy... What I do wish to emphasize is that the establishment of such an embargo would inevitably bring our government into conflict with England and might drive us into war with England. As a man of German blood I might welcome the help which would accrue to Germany by such a conflict between the United States and England. But as an American citizen I cannot possibly support a policy which would bring the terrors of war to our own country. What I feel bound to support, as an American citizen is a policy which holds itself strictly within the now accepted rules of neutrality, although to my regret, this policy through circumstances over which the United States has no control, practically turns out to the advantage of England, and to the detriment of Germany.[26]

Representative Bartholdt of Missouri was another prominent German-American voice defending the patriotism of his fellow German-Americans. The *Evening Post* of February 19, 1915, reported on his farewell speech in the U.S. House of Representatives, in which he denounced "the newspaper war against Germany" and declared that Americans of German descent "are with all other true Americans for America first, last and always." Further, he declared:

---

26. *Evening Post*, February 12, 1915.

If, unfortunately, the United States ever again should be embroiled in war, which Heaven forbid, the Germans of this country would again loyally rally around the Stars and Stripes. The Germans of this country are for America against England, for America against Germany, for America against the world. They will never waiver for one second in their allegiance to their adopted land... The war was started with a monstrous lie, and to support it a thousand other lies had to be told. The Germans were denounced as ravishers and plunderers and worse. The struggle is a warfare of falsehood against truth.

If Charleston's *Evening Post* was attempting to offer the opportunity for both sides of the argument to be heard, its readership, a substantial number of whom were Charlestonians of German heritage, may not have taken comfort in Professor Franke's arguments, nor, for that matter, in the Missouri Representative's strong defense of German-American loyalty before the U.S. Congress. Both very public declarations were bringing national—and local—attention to the loyalty issue, whereas for many, silence would have been preferable. What the outspoken defenders accomplished was to give the issue traction on the national stage as well as in Charleston.

In early 1916, the *New York Times* published a letter it had received from Dr. James A. B. Scherer, the former pastor of Charleston's St. Andrew's Lutheran Church.[27] In his letter—which he undoubtedly wrote with the expectation that it would be published for the newspaper's reading public—Scherer lamented the transformation of the Germany he knew into the worrisome European power it had become:

Bearing a German name, ordained at the age of 21 to the Lutheran ministry, and president before I came here, of a college established by German-Americans and maintained by their descendants, I have many dear friends and close kinfolk whom I would not lightly grieve by an open attack on positions which are presumably as vital to them as mine are to

---

27. Scherer was pastor at St. Andrew's from 1898-1904. He subsequently served as president of South Carolina's Lutheran Newberry College from 1904 to 1908.

me… The Germany I had been taught to believe in seemed, in a word, to have undergone a complete metamorphosis: the Germany of Luther and Goethe and Beethoven, big and warm and tender and free, has been shaped by the iron hand of the Hohenzollern into a marvelous but soulless machine, tended by a comfortable people going blind… With a cynicism that strikes the heart cold, this Prussic Germania tears the sacred law of contract, on which all civilization is founded, into scraps of paper, massacres Belgium, stealthily murders American women and children on the high seas, and flirts with an effeminate administration at Washington with small effort to hide her contempt.[28]

Scherer's letter expressed what many in the ethnic community probably felt as the awkward tension between the German cultural past and the present Prussian militarism. Scherer was writing not only as a Lutheran minister to a national audience, but also to his own South Carolina congregation of Lutherans. It is doubtful that he anticipated the reaction to his *New York Times* letter that came two days later in a letter published in the local *Evening Post*. Paul Wierse—now editor of the *Deutsche Zeitung* under its publisher, Albert Orth, and also, as mentioned earlier, editor of the pro-German *American*— submitted to the *Evening Post*'s editor an unabashedly vituperative essay about the Scherer letter in the *Times*:

Editor Evening Post,

Sir: If ever this community has been shocked, it was by the letter of Dr. James A. B. Scherer, published in the New York Times and republished in the Charleston Evening Post… His narrow-minded views of Germany and his somewhat hazy ideas concerning the cause of the European conflict would not have shocked anyone, especially not that large part of this polyglot nation that is being called the "German-American element." These hyphenated Americans have learned forbearance

28. *Evening Post*, April 24, 1916.

with the artificial growth of anti-German sentiments and they remain unmoved by all that foolish criticism that is the off-spring of ignorance: they even refuse to be shocked anymore by utterances that clearly show the poison tooth of malicious falsehood … Dr. James A. B. Scherer has apparently a superficial one-sided knowledge of some Lutheran and war literature and if he chooses to mix them up and to rush with incoherent appeals before the public, that is his business. What makes his attempt at helping The New York Times and England extraordinarily and especially offensive is the fact that he boasts of his German ancestry only to turn on the land of his fathers and sink his fangs in her throat … Equally grave is the doctor's offense in selecting the crucial moment for the attack on the people of his blood. His excuse that the President wished us to indulge in no unneutral utterances is absolutely silly. Members of the Congress have aired their war views, the President himself had uttered many words that cannot be termed neutral by a long stretch of imagination, all the newspapers have long ago taken sides. But he, the obedient doctor, refused to utter a single unneutral word until things have taken such course that a feather added to the strain may easily precipitate this country into a war which would be the greatest calamity this country has ever seen … To sum up: Dr … Scherer's letter is not only anti-German, but it is just as much anti-American, very unpatriotic to either cause and deplorable … It is further anti-Lutheran and in general anti-Christian. He has been honored and fed by the Germany money that under much sacrifice supports the Newberry College of which he was president, and he now has given the disgusting performance of the bird that befouls his own nest and expects applause for such inhuman performance.[29]

Wierse's response to Scherer would have reverberated especially strongly among the host of Lutheran German-Americans in Charleston. What the one

---

29. *Evening Post*, April 26, 1

denounced as the transformation of the old Lutheranism in which he had been raised into a new creed to be feared, the other denounced as a narrow-minded "anti-Lutheran" stab in Germany's back and all that the Fatherland stood for.

To be sure, Charleston's Lutherans—a body primarily of German-American immigrant descendants—were treading especially difficult waters amidst the rising tide of anti-German sentiment. In her 1995 dissertation, S. W. McArver writes that southern German-American Lutherans—some now fifth-generation descendants of nineteenth-century immigrants—were "puzzled, to find themselves the target of anti-German sentiment because of their church's historic roots." How were they to react to the rumor that the Lutheran seminary in Columbia was reported to be harboring German sympathizers planning to fire artillery shells on the capitol? What should they do about the Lutheran minister in Chapin, South Carolina, who was arrested twice, suspected to be a German spy? McArver reports that the Secret Service had investigated the author of several articles published in the *American Lutheran Survey*, urging the United States to stay out of the war. The tense situation led the South Carolina synod to "defend itself against challenges in the press, voting to 'reaffirm our loyal adherence … of patriotic devotion to the flag of the country [and] of respect for civil authority.'"[30]

In January 1916, Charleston's Lutheran attorney, John Cappelmann, called the officers of the South Carolina branch of the National German-American Alliance to a meeting at the Brüderliche Bund Headquarters, German Artillery Hall, "to decide whether to continue or abandon the organization and if to continue then to reorganize. In any event the writer begs to state that he will not be able to serve longer as President." In what appeared to be a moment of doubt for the local chapter, Cappelmann claimed to be relinquishing the presidency because of other obligations, although he may have wanted to cede his leadership because he was beginning to feel uncomfortable as he read the handwriting on the wall. In any case, the local chapter did not disband. A. W. Wieters was unanimously elected president, and it was decided to combine the branch of the Alliance with the German Day Association and "conduct both by the same board." In June, the *News and Courier* reported that plans were being made for participation by Alliance members in the Flag Day

30. S. W. McArver, "'A spiritual wayside inn': Lutherans, the New South and Cultural Change in South Carolina, 1886-1918." PhD diss., Duke University, 1995, 404.

parade: "All German organizations and lodges are urged to meet Wednesday at Artillery Hall, where all participants will receive their flags. "When it is a question of patriotism," A. W. Wieters said, "the 'hyphenates' are always there with the goods, as every student of American history knows or ought to know." Wieters was still on the offensive, touting the patriotism of his fellow German-Americans and apparently unaware that, here again, his comments smacked of an attitude of superiority. At the end of November, what must have been considered the gall of the Charleston German community was on display when Wieters was on the stage (the Alliance sponsoring the event) for a presentation by a visiting German, Frau von Hanfstaengl. According to the *News and Courier* of the 27th, "Frau von Hanfstaengl, of Munich, delivered an exhaustive and illuminating address on conditions in Germany and East Prussia before an immense audience in Freundschaftsbund Hall last night, receiving at the conclusion of the address an ovation of applause."[31]

If the *News and Courier*'s reporting is taken at face value, Frau von Hanfstaengl's warm reception by "an immense audience" and the enthusiastic applause she received, suggests that a number of Charleston's German-Americans were genuinely blinded by their own sense of worth and not hesitant to embrace this measure of political activism. In the wider view, it is evident that a minority of "activists" could be found working to influence the rest of the ethnic community. Those leading figures were apparently immune to the sensitivities of the majority in the community, who had an innate reluctance to be preached to by their own, much less by those whom they had long indulged.

---

31. *News and Courier*, November 27, 1916.

# CHAPTER 8:

# 1917 AND AFTER

There is no need to furnish additional evidence of the extensive efforts of the NGAA and/or individuals to defend the right of German-America to promote and defend itself, nor to elaborate further the organization's reasoned opposition to the involvement of the United States in the European war. It is clear that the manifest anti-German sentiment had, over a period of years, pushed German immigrants and their descendants into an uncomfortable corner. The collective ethnic community was painfully aware that if the U.S. policy of neutrality turned into a declaration of war against Germany it would exacerbate what was already the individual German-American's personal dilemma: how to deal with his purported dual loyalty, that is, his inherent affinity to the country that defined him and his ancestors vs. his obligation, duty, and desire to be a loyal citizen of the United States. By the time the United States entered the war in 1917, German-Americans were, as suggested earlier, damned if they defended their Germanic heritage and suspect if they declared their loyalty to the United States. All the while, the United States had taken its complex course to move agonizingly slowly in determining its response to the hostilities in Europe. The process was fraught with political maneuvers, a perceptible bias in support of one of the belligerents, international crises, vacillating presidential leadership, economic calculations, an angry public, and pacifist leanings. The predicament of German-America would worsen to become life-threatening as the war against Germany ran its course.

Two months before the fateful day in April 1917 when the U.S. declared itself at war with Germany, the February 1, 1917, edition of Charleston's *Evening Post* reported that it had been "an exciting day in Charleston":

> The new turn in German-American relations apparently came directly home to Charleston today when the German steamer Liebenfels sank in the harbor. Whether or not the Liebenfels was scuttled, that was the interpretation many placed upon the vessel's sinking.
>
> There was much excitement on the streets throughout the day. It was not the same kind of excitement, however, as that which followed receipt of news of the sinking of the Lusitania ... It was rather a keen interest colored considerably by bewilderment and puzzlement as to the meaning of local events which seemed to have direct bearing on the great international issue of the moment ... Throughout the day people were telephoning to The Evening Post to ask about the Liebenfels and about German-American relations, but chiefly to state wild rumors which they had heard and to ask whether or not they were true. In about nine cases out of ten, the rumors inquired about were without foundation. [1]

The "exciting" event in Charleston was reported in newspapers everywhere: in German-language newspapers, for example, the Omaha *Tägliche Tribune* and *Detroiter Abend-Post*, and in English-language media from Juneau to Brattleboro, to Albuquerque, to Chicago, to El Paso, and most places in-between. What transpired that *exciting* day in Charleston can be read in the following concise summary[2] of the *Liebenfels* "affair":

---

1. *Evening Post*, February 1, 1917.

2. By Tinsley E. Yarbrough in his *A Passion for Justice: J. Waties Waring and Civil Rights* (New York: Oxford University Press, 1987), 8-9.

On August 4, 1914, the freight steamer *Liebenfels* arrived in Charleston harbor with a cargo of fertilizer. Germany and Britain had recently broken relations, and the ship's captain was fearful of venturing back to sea after unloading his cargo on the Charleston docks. Instead, the *Liebenfels* dropped anchor in the Cooper River. The ship's East Indian crew was eventually taken off the ship and returned to their homeland, but the German officers and crew remained aboard ship, living in Charleston harbor. Charleston had a large German population, and the ship's crew mixed extensively with the city's citizenry.

As German-American relations deteriorated, however, the situation changed. In the early morning of February 1, 1917, the day fixed by the German government for the resumption of unrestricted submarine warfare, the *Liebenfels* was spotted partially sunk in the harbor. Two tug captains offered assistance, but the ship's captain refused aid. It was quickly determined that the *Liebenfels* posed no obstacle to entry at the Charleston Navy Yard but was a hazard to other navigation. On February 2, the port collector took possession of the ship and placed guards on board. Eventually, the *Liebenfels* was raised, equipped, renamed the U. S. S. *Houston*, and put into the service of American forces.

Soon after its sinking, [Assistant U.S. Attorney] Waring, U.S. Attorney Weston, and the port collector boarded the *Liebenfels* for an inspection. Their investigation revealed that much of the ship's equipment had been intentionally damaged, and they suspected that the captain and crew had sabotaged the vessel to prevent its falling into American hands. In mid-February, Waring secured an arrest warrant against the captain, J. R. Klattenhoff, and eight crewmen.

The summary includes additional details about the individuals involved and what happened subsequently:

In March, the crewmen were convicted in Florence, South Carolina, of sinking the *Liebenfels* but acquitted of conspiracy. In June, Klattenhoff, who had been ill when the crewmen were tried, pleaded guilty to sinking the *Liebenfels* but not guilty of conspiracy. In October, he was tried in Aiken, South Carolina on the conspiracy account.

Tried along with Klattenhoff was Paul Wierse, an editorial writer and state news editor for the pro-German Charleston *American*. The government contended that Wierse had served as a go-between in the conspiracy for Klattenhoff and the German consul in Atlanta, who was believed to have fled the United States for Equador. The consul had received instructions regarding the *Liebenfels* from the German government, and Wierse allegedly had delivered messages from the consul to the captain.

The Aiken trial reflected the current divisions in Charleston politics almost as much as the legal issues the case had raised. Chief counsel for Wierse, as he had been for the *Liebenfels* crewmen, was John P. Grace, owner of the Charleston *American* and perhaps the most colorful and controversial of the city's politicians of that period. Grace had served as Charleston's mayor from 1911 to 1915 and would be elected for another term in 1919. Though at times a demagogue and not above occasional race-baiting, Grace was something of a progressive for his time—campaigning against "special privilege," monopoly, and the city's "bluebloods"; inaugurating numerous improvements in city services; even blasting that most venerable of Charleston social institution, the St. Cecilia Society.

Frank Weston made a closing argument, but Waties Waring had developed the government's case and had examined all witnesses. Squaring off in the courtroom, Waring and Grace seemed to personify the Charleston aristocracy and the challenge that Grace posed for much of that tradition. In fact, although repeatedly overruled by the presiding judge, Grace attempted to depict the case as a persecution of the *American* by the aristocratic owners of the leading Charleston papers, the *News and Courier* and *Evening Post*. The effort failed. Waring produced an incriminating letter and telegrams. Two of the convicted crewmen also testified for the government. … After less than an hour's deliberation, the jury returned guilty verdicts against both Wierse and Klattenhoff.

There is much to unpack in this summary, many dots to connect, if we want to understand the ramifications of the purposeful scuttling of a German ship that for two years had been sitting at a dock on Charleston's Cooper River— this occurring on the very day that Germany was to undertake its declared program of unrestricted submarine warfare. The statement that "Charleston had a large German population, and the ship's crew mixed extensively with the city's citizenry" is but a hint to what this all meant. Charleston's German-American population found itself all of a sudden under the microscope for everyone in the country to examine and then draw the same conclusions that were already in nationwide circulation. What was in the background were "German-American relations," and that context had now been brought to bear on the local situation. The magnifying glass of national attention would focus on several local actors in a drama similar to the one that was playing out on the national stage. The cast of characters included an Assistant U.S. Attorney, the captain of a scuttled German vessel, the local pro-German editor of a widely known German-language newspaper, and a local attorney who was himself the owner of a pro-German publication and who had previously served as Charleston's mayor. On stage in the background, somewhat like the chorus in an opera or a Greek play, was the city's German-American community itself. The drama would focus on the following: —the significance of the German crew having "mixed" with the Charleston population during their two years of residency in Charleston; —the purported direct connection between the German ship in Charleston and the German government in Berlin, and the apparent military purpose of Berlin's "order" to destroy its own property; —the significance of the fact that Germans were found guilty of their actions and sentenced by U.S. federal authorities; —the question of whether Charleston Germans were capable of conspiring against the United States, even though the German crew was not convicted of conspiring to harm the United States or the local population of fellow Germany-sympathizers; —the underlying implications of a courtroom drama between an Assistant U.S. Attorney representing the government and a well-known local politician and former mayor defending the accused Germans; —the import of the conviction and sentencing of the well-known activist-editor of the German newspaper, along with the ship's captain, an association that suggested that the pro-German editor might be considered a criminal, along with the entire ethnic community for whom he spoke.

It was likely Paul Wierse who cornered the most attention by the local populace. The individual in court with Captain Klattenhoff was indeed the editor of Alfred Orth's[3] *Deutsche Zeitung* and the publisher/editor of the pro-German *American,* the latter an organ owned by the courtroom advocate for the defense, John P. Grace, former mayor of Charleston. It was a tangled web that most likely made the city's German-Americans uncomfortable. Here they were, in the spotlight, in nativist cross hairs, associated with indicted criminals, accused of conspiracy, and with one of their own—a well-known voice in their community, who for some time had positioned himself as a spokesman for local German-Americans—accused of disloyalty to the United States.

It was also likely that Wierse was a lightning rod to channel the attention of those in the community who were thinking that the Germans in their midst were guilty of *something.* The local community would struggle with the inherent tension brought to the surface between the sinking of the *Liebenfels* and the several roles in the drama played by Paul Wierse. The *Evening Post* 's diligent reporting on Wierse's indictment would bring to the public's attention the following: 1) Wierse had been involved in establishing the Charleston chapter of the NGAA as early as 1907; 2) As editor of the *Deutsche Zeitung,* he had debuted a new weekly called *Common Sense* in 1908 as "an organ of opinion rather than a news publication"; 3) Wierse's partner in that endeavor had been Attorney John P. Grace, known in public to take "the German point of view" on the war in Europe; 4) Wierse and Grace had had a falling out over the editorial policy of *Common Sense,* which resulted in the publication's early end the following year.

In his account of the *Liebenfels* affair, J. Waties Waring's biographer Yarbrough writes that the two opposing attorneys Waring and Grace personified the antagonism between the traditional Charleston aristocracy and the

---

3.   Albert Orth was editor/publisher from 1905 to 1917.

city's other citizens, inasmuch as "Grace attempted to depict the case as persecution of the *American* by the aristocratic owners of the leading Charleston papers, the *News and Courier* and *Evening Post.*" The allegation by Grace that the "leading" Charleston newspapers were prejudiced against the smaller *American* edited by a German-American may indeed have had some merit: while it might have been generally known in Charleston circles, it was not divulged in the courtroom at the time that the Assistant U.S. Attorney leading the prosecution was a brother to the editor of the *Evening Post.* Against this background, it might be argued that the courtroom tension between the "aristocratic" government prosecutor and the former mayor representing the accused mirrored what had become a somewhat tense relationship between native "old" Charlestonians and the less affluent German-American subscribers to the city's less-influential German newspaper.

The case against Wierse for his role in the *Liebenfels* affair was closely followed by the local public through all the legal proceedings it generated: from his Federal District Court trial in Aiken, South Carolina, to the Fourth Federal District's Appeals Court (which upheld the lower Court's ruling), to the U.S. Supreme Court (which declined to hear the appeal). At the end of December 1918, Paul Wierse was taken into custody and forced to pay a fine of $1,000 and serve two years in the Atlanta penitentiary.[4]

John P. Grace, mayor of Charleston from 1911 to 1915, and who would be elected again in 1919, was often criticized for his relationship with Charleston's German-Americans, most vociferously during the run-up to his re-election. His ownership of the pro-German *American* and his numerous public statements in defense of Germany before and after the United States entered the war linked him permanently to Charleston's German-American "block" involved in the local political scene. The *Evening Post's* issue of August 8, 1919, had nothing good to say about the candidate for mayor and everything negative to say about his "German" sympathies. It quoted a "letter" written by "a citizen" to the editor of another paper:

> [I]t occurred to me that in one sense it was immaterial whether or not the American was debarred from the mails, whether or not John P. Grace violated the espionage act. The thing

---

4. *Evening Post*, December 21, 1918.

that does concern the people of Charleston is that John P. Grace's heart was full of Pro-Germanism. Grace has written that "justice is on the side of Germany" and "The Lusitania was one of the things over which we could not for a moment grow hysterical." ... [T]he fact is that the public had already classed John P. Grace as one tainted forever with malignant Prussianism ... Grace can't drive from the hearts of the people THE SETTLED CONVICTION OF HIS DISLOYALTY.[5]

The following week, the *Post* put Grace on its spit for roasting in its "Hard-nut" column under the headline: "Today's 'Hard-Nut' for Candidate John P. Grace to crack (if he is able to do so)." The newspaper insisted that two months after the US had been at war with Germany, Grace had published in his paper the statement: "Suppose the American people do NOT know why they are at war, and can never find out, does that alter the fact? The two hundred thousand coffins that were bought the other day can hold boys who did not know why they were forced to die in France as readily as those who did know." The *Post* urged its readers to "clip this and the preceding 'Hard-Nuts' from this paper (as published below in this column), carry them to one of the Grace meetings and demand from Mr. Grace the answer, 'Yes' or 'No' to each of these gems ... If he did not say these things, HE is entitled to have you know it; and if he did say them, YOU are entitled to know that he did." The newspaper's previously published "hard nuts," that is, statements made by Grace, were listed—some with commentary—as follows:

—"The whole fake Belgian tragedy has become a huge comedy."

—"Every man jack on a submarine is a hero per se."

—"Why the U-boat warfare has not been carried into our waters long ago is something hard to explain."

---

5. The Postal Service had threatened to refuse mailing privileges to Grace's *American* if he did not refrain from his biased editorials.

—"We want to point out that justice is on the side of Germany, and whoever draws the sword against justice is flying in the face of heaven."

—"The Lusitania was one of the things over which we could not for a moment grow hysterical. Let the war go on, and let the U-boat do its worst."

—"We have from time to time exploded the various and vagarious reasons for war against Germany."

—"Of course we know why the United States is at war. We have not hesitated, SINCE THE DECLARATION of war, to say it. * * * We have called it Woodrow Wilson's War, and so it is, and so history will declare it." ('Loyal' utterance of Editor John P. Grace after we were at war.)

—"We are opposed to sending Americans to France. We cannot follow the logic of the little editors who clamor for the sending of our boys to France, but who are 'conscientious objectors' themselves." (Published after we were at war.)

—"Wilson has at last achieved the power for which his icy heart has yearned for three years." ('Charleston American,' February 27, 1917, three weeks after we had severed relations with Germany.)

—"We have great respect for the power of Germany, and we believe that God has blessed her cause in Europe, where she fights righteously for her salvation." (John P. Grace in his paper, The Charleston American, more than one month after we were actually at war with Germany.)[6]

---

6. *Evening Post*, August 15, 1919.

It did not matter whether Grace's words were quoted by the *Evening Post* accurately, in or out of context, out of ignorance, or politically motivated: such statements by a prominent politician did nothing but add to the social discomfort of the German-American community—on the one hand, grateful for Grace's anti-British stance, and on the other, embarrassed by words that were an affront to the sensibilities of Charleston's citizens of un-hyphenated heritage.

This journalistic umbrage taken at statements made by Grace as the owner of an acknowledged pro-German publication—someone who would subsequently serve a second four-year term as the city's Democratic mayor—was superimposed on the newspaper's intrinsic animus against Grace, who, a year earlier, had defended Paul Wierse, in this instance, against the government's attempt to relieve him of his citizenship. In November 1918, Waties Waring represented the government in a hearing before Judge H. A. M. Smith to have Wierse's citizenship annulled "on the grounds that Wierse had not become a citizen of the United States in good faith:

> Wierse has been convicted of conspiracy along with others to sink the S.S. Liebenfels in Charleston harbor, and the prosecution contends that this act, committed at the time that America was on the verge of severing relations with Germany, proved that the defendant was more loyal to Germany than to America: that when the opportunity came to show whether he was with America or Germany, he stood with the latter. The defendant was represented by John P. Grace, Esq., who asserted that loyalty was not an issue in the Liebenfels case: that the law under which the proceedings were instituted was intended for cases where citizenship was fraudulently obtained. He claimed that the defendant was loyal to America, and took issue with the prosecution which had cited similar cases in support of the proceedings. [7]

In late December 1918, it was reported that "Judge Smith has as yet made no decision in the matter of Wierse's citizenship. The government has entered proceedings to have his citizenship annulled, on the grounds that his acts have

---

7. *Evening Post*, November 15, 1918.

shown that he was not a loyal American citizen, and a hearing in the matter was held a few weeks ago before judge Smith, at which J. Waites Waring represented the government J. P. Grace the defendant."[8] It would later be disclosed that the effort in late 1918 to annul Wierse's naturalized citizenship was not pursued further.

All of Charleston would know that Paul Wierse, a strong defender of pro-German interests, was a link between the owners of the city's two pro-German newspapers, the *American*, owned by John P. Grace, and the *Deutsche Zeitung* owned by Albert Orth, since Wierse wrote for both publications. It was as if the three men, Grace, Wierse, and Orth, had become a new triumvirate assuming to speak for Charleston's German-American community, each apparently willing to expose himself to judgment and ridicule in promulgating pro-Germany arguments and expressing opposition to President Wilson's war-time program.[9]

In May 1917, Albert Orth was arrested by United States authorities and charged with "giving aid and assistance to a deserter from a British vessel." The deserter was Gustav Drewes, a German reservist, "who with six other German subjects escaped from the British steamship Wingate in August, 1914, while she lay at a dock on the Ashley River." When the charges against Orth were brought three years after the deserters' escape, the newspaper reported that Gustav Drewes was living on a nearby island, married to a local woman. The newspaper account concluded with the statement that "the authorities … intimated that they have for some time suspected various persons alleged to be instrumental in assisting such men to enter the United States without formally presenting themselves before the immigration authorities for examination, as required by law."[10] There is no evidence, however, that Albert Orth was ever tried on this charge. Having escaped punishment in this instance, it would later be inferred that Orth had felt free to continue his suspect activities on behalf

---

8. *Evening Post*, December 21, 1918.

9. The publicists Grace and Orth were not alone in this regard: A fellow editor from up-state Abbeville, W. P. Beard, was convicted in federal court in November 1917 of violating the espionage act and sentenced to a $500 fine and a year in the federal prison in Atlanta. His offense was making "disloyal utterances" in an article entitled the "Great Fizzle" published in his weekly, *The Scimitar*.

10. *Evening Post*, May 8, 1917.

of his native Germany. In late 1917, he was again in federal court, charged that "he did willfully aid, abet, and assist a certain person, to wit, Robert Fay, to escape from the custody of an officer of the United States," and that he "harbored and concealed Robert Fay, 'so as to prevent his arrest'."[11] Lieutenant Fay and another German convict, William Knobloch, had escaped together from the Atlanta prison and both had come—or had been sent—to Orth for help to get back to Germany. Orth was convicted on charges growing out of his assistance to Fay and Knobloch. U.S. District Judge Henry A. M. Smith (the same judge who heard the Wierse case) imposed accumulative sentences on Orth of fourteen months in the federal penitentiary and a fine of $1,200. The *Post* reported on November 15, 1917:

> Albert Orth, convicted in the U.S. district court now in session at Columbia on two indictments, charging him with assisting Robert Fay and William Knobloch to escape from the federal prison and harboring them in Charleston, returned to Charleston in the custody of the U.S. marshal and gave bond for $6,000 before U.S. Commissioner Huger for his appearance at the U.S. Circuit Court of Appeals to which the defendant has appealed. C.F. Hottinger and A.W. Wieters went on his bond.[12]

Orth appealed, but was not successful. He was finally sentenced in August of 1918 after differences between the Circuit Court and the Appeals Court were resolved. The *Evening Post* of August 10, 1918, provided the details:

> Orth was found guilty at the November term of court of having aided in the escape of federal prisoners from the Atlanta penitentiary and of aiding them afterwards, and sentences

---

11. *Evening Post*, November 13, 1917.

12. C. F. Hottinger was a Charleston merchant, and August W. Wieters was president of the Consumers' Ice Company. Wieters, after taking over the presidency of the Charleston chapter of the NGAA, had arranged for the event at the Freundschaftsbund Hall in November, 1916, where Orth had introduced Frau von Hanfstaengl for her presentation on "conditions in the Fatherland."

were imposed as follows: For aiding Robert Fay to escape, $1,000 fine, costs, and one year in the Atlanta penitentiary, and for the same offenses regarding one William Knobloch, $200 and costs and two months in the Atlanta penitentiary. The cases were appealed and the Circuit Court of Appeals ruled that Judge Smith should have given the jury direction to find the defendant not guilty on the first count of both case, that of aiding in the escape, as it appeared the prisoners had already escaped when given aid by the defendant. Consequently, the heavier of the two sentences was ordered changed, as it was more than the maximum for one count, while the other, which was below the maximum for one count, was permitted to remain. As the law provides, however, that the minimum time any prisoner can spend in the Atlanta penitentiary is a year, the imprisonment in the second case has been changed to the Florence county jail, to be served after the six months sentence in the Fay case.

After sentencing, Orth was given a few days to arrange his affairs: "It was brought out that the condition of the printing house owned by Mr. Orth was very precarious, as the two men in his employ, on whom he was largely dependent, had just been drafted."[13]

In the 1940s, when America was in a second war with Germany, the South Carolina Federal District Court again heard a case against Albert Orth, *United States v. Orth*, "an action … to revoke the citizenship of the defendant Albert Orth and to cancel his certificate of naturalization." A host of individuals who knew, or had known, Orth gave testimony on his behalf, and a number spoke against him. There were lengthy citations of his words as they appeared in numerous issues of the *Deutsche Zeitung*, all of which were intended to verify his pro-German stance before and during the war. In the end, Judge Timmermann declared that "upon the facts and the law judgment must go against the defendants." The judge found that "the aforesaid representations of the defendant

13. The last issue of the *Deutsche Zeitung* was December 22, 1917, its end brought about by "Zwang der Zeit" (forces of the times). After the newspaper folded, Orth was reduced to running a "printing house."

Albert Orth, concerning his behavior, feelings and intent, were false, fraudulent and illegal; and his said certificate of citizenship was fraudulently and illegally obtained, and should be delivered up, set aside and cancelled of record." He ruled further that "the citizenship of Anna Orth, being derivative, falls with that of her husband Albert Orth."

Orth appealed to the Fourth Circuit's Court of Appeals and the judgment was reversed on May 24, 1944. The Court explained the reasoning behind its decision:

> [Citizenship] can be taken only upon evidence clearly and positively establishing definite fraud. It cannot be taken under suspicion or surmise of fraud or upon mere proof that since his naturalization this citizen has given expression to views or allied himself with organizations which in the then state of public opinion seemed dangerous or inimical to the public welfare. If these expressions or acts of the naturalized citizen are criminal, he is subject like every other citizen to prosecution for them; if they are not, they subject him to no other legal consequences than a native born citizen doing and seeing the same thing would be subject to.

The prosecution's allegations based on Orth's statements in his *Deutsche Zeitung* were dismissed as invalid:

> It is strenuously urged by counsel for the Government that certain editorials appearing in the Deutsche Zeitung, the editorial policies of which were allegedly dictated by Orth, in the year 1916, while not alone sufficient to convict him, are indicative of his real allegiance and show that he held a mental reservation of attachment for Germany when he took his oath of allegiance to the United States in 1900. A careful reading of these editorials, however, convinces us that they do not tend to establish any such mental reservation. They were written prior to the entry of this country into the First World War; and, while they show an interest in the cause of Germany as against England and a desire that this country stay out of

the war, they cannot be said to show a lack of loyalty to this country, much less a lack of loyalty and good faith as of the time the naturalization oath was taken, sixteen years before.

The Government had also argued that Mrs. Orth should be relieved of her "derivative" citizenship. The Court was unconvinced:

> Even if we were in accord with the decadent common-law fiction of marital unity (this we emphatically deny), we have no room in our imaginative processes whereby it can be shown that these statements made by Mrs Orth in 1942 are clearly and convincingly indicative of the state of Orth's mind in 1900.

In summary, the Court stated:

> Orth has resided in the United States for many years. With the exception of the allegations of his aide to Drewes, Knobloch and Fay, no concrete act of Orth has been proven to be subversive. There are no allegations, not a scintilla of evidence, in regard to his conduct prior to his naturalization, or within a period of 14 years thereafter. [14]

The question might be raised as to why Orth was again in court some twenty-five years after his earlier conviction. Granted, he was there in 1943 for a different matter, but it was an indication that the U.S. government had apparently had him under surveillance during the interwar period and suggests that the anti-German sentiment palpable during the first World War had endured in the minds of some and continued to resonate during the second. The carry-over of that xenophobia during the interwar years will be explored in the following chapter. Here, we can note how the two widely-separated efforts of the government to condemn Albert Orth for privately and publicly expressing—and acting on—a pro-German stance were connected: the link was then Assistant U.S. Attorney Waring, who had been instrumental in prosecuting the earlier case. In the intervening years Waring had become a U.S.

---

14. 142 F.2d 969 (4th Cir. 1944) as cited by *Casetext: Smarter Legal Research.*

District Judge, and was now called to testify in the second attempt to revoke Orth's naturalization. This was revealed in the *Evening Post*'s account of the trial's conclusion,[15].

> The testimony of Judge J. Waties Waring in reply to a statement by witness L. A. R. Nelson quoting the judge as saying Orth was a good American citizen, came as a surprise during the afternoon session .
>
> The judge, who as assistant district attorney, had helped to present the case against Orth in 1916, when the latter was convicted of harboring escaped convicts, said that in fairness to all parties concerned, and especially himself, he felt that he should make a brief statement. He had disqualified himself as judge in this case.
>
> Judge Waring said that he had no independent recollection of furnishing Nelson with a suit of clothing or of advising him about taking employment with Orth, although he may have done so, but "it is fantastic for Nelson to say that he had said Albert Orth was a loyal American citizen."
>
> Asked by Thomas P Stoney, member of defense counsel, if he had not finished with the Orth case after the defendant was convicted in 1916, Judge Waring said "not exactly." He had recommended to the Department of Justice that proceedings be instituted against Orth and his former editor Paul Wierse, seeking to revoke their citizenship, but that the Department had dropped the matter when the armistice was declared. [16]

When in November 1918 Assistant U.S. Attorney Waties Waring sparred with the counsel for the defense, John P. Grace, during Paul Wierse's citizenship trial, it was clear that J. Waties Waring was patently Charleston's Germans' antagonist. It seems that in Charleston he was considered something of an

---

15. *Evening Post*, April 23, 1943.

16. The two references to a 1916 date in the *Evening Post* report are somewhat misleading: Orth's "offenses" in regard to Fay and Knobloch were committed in 1916. His indictment and conviction occurred in 1917, and he was sentenced in 1918.

expert on German matters. Earlier in 1918, he had been the featured speaker at the "People's Forum":

> J Waties Waring Will Discuss German Spy System/ Someone has tersely said that wherever there is a German sympathizer there is the German front. That there are many German fronts in America no one can deny. There are strong indications that the public is growing restless under the seeming lack of adequate repression of German propaganda in this country. But in order to make repressive measures effective the public should be made better acquainted with the methods of the Kaiser's agents. At the People's Forum tomorrow night Assistant District Attorney J. Waties Waring will speak on "Some Phases of the German Spy System." Mr. Waring is in a position to know how the Prussian game is played and how it can be effectively checkmated.[17]

It is not without irony that the Assistant District Attorney who began his career with a prejudice against Charleston's German-Americans should later become the much-admired, much-maligned, advocate of the civil rights of the nation's African-Americans—another group of hyphenated citizens. Accounts of Waring's complicated relationship with the Charleston community are usually silent on this early evidence of his animus toward the hyphenated group that was of concern to Charlestonians before, during, and after WWI.[18]

---

17. *Evening Post*, April 13, 1918.

18. After he divorced his "old Charleston" wife in 1945, Waring married a twice-divorced woman from New York. The Charlestonian with a long southern heritage and his second wife were shunned by Charleston, initially because of the divorce, then more and more because of their work with, and on behalf of, African-Americans. Despite being pariahs in Charleston, the couple worked for racial justice throughout Waring's career. They turned their backs on Charleston and made their home in New York until he died in 1968, she in 1969. Yarbrough's 1987 study, *A Passion for Justice,* provides fascinating detail on Waring's rise to prominence as an advocate for racial justice for the nation's African-Americans while challenging "the most fundamental racial values of his native community."

The government prosecutions of Paul Wierse and Albert Orth were not the only instances to demonstrate that the anti-German sentiment that prevailed in Charleston after the United States entered the war found solid footing in the courts. The afternoon session of the August 1918 District Court that sentenced Orth to eight months in prison was devoted to the case of a Dr. Turnbull, who was accused of violating the espionage act: "The defendant is charged with having claimed that Germany was justified in violating Belgium as a military necessity, that since Germany had warned Americans to keep off the sea, the United States had no right to make a protest when her citizens were drowned on the Lusitania, and that England had three million soldiers ready to invade the United States when the time came."[19] Four months earlier, John Weinacht, an "enemy alien," was arrested at, of all places, Capt. Frederick Wagener's Pine Forest Inn, for what were regarded as dangerous utterances: "A Presidential warrant was issued for his arrest, which was accomplished by Federal officials … and at present he is awaiting the disposition that the authorities see fit to make of him."[20] In Weinacht's case, it appears that the government was not altogether clear on what constituted a "dangerous utterance," nor was it sure about the exact nature of the charge to be brought against the enemy alien.

The year before, only three months after the United States entered the war, another well-known Charleston German-American had been arrested:

> H. L. Koester, merchant at Three Mile, who was arrested by order of the district attorney's office under the President's war proclamation relative to actions of aliens in this country, was released this morning from jail where he has been confined. Mister Koester was released on parole by the President. All of these matters are handled through the district attorney's office and no hearing was granted the prisoner. A bond of $10,000 was furnished by Mister Koester for his liberty. As to the nature of the cause of the arrest little has been given out. No charges have to be made in any case of this nature. This parole is revocable at the pleasure of the District Attorney should

19. *Evening Post*, August 10, 1918.

20. *Evening Post*, April 13, 1918, the same issue that reported on Waring's address at the People's Forum.

he think that the actions of Mister Koester hereafter justify further steps. At certain intervals he will have to report to a supervisor and also to the district attorney's office.[21]

The "alien" H. L. Koester was a well-known local German-American who had twice been named King of the Schützenfest (1910 and 1915).[22] Koester, undoubtedly a target of the Dispensary laws and despite—or perhaps because of—wearing his King's crown, was sentenced to three months in prison and a fine of $50 for "storing liquor." With his reputation called into question, he resigned from his position on the Charleston County Board of Assessors in 1918. Although he was awarded the Logan[23] Trophy at the 1921 Schützenfest, he advertised the following year to sell his Three Mile grocery: "Reason for selling want to leave town." Whether or not he managed to sell his grocery store, four years later he advertised acreage he owned as a hunting preserve: "3,000 acres. Plenty of deer, wild turkey, partridge and other game. Apply H. L. Koester, 3-Mile House, or address Myers, S. C."[24] Although his "Three-Mile" address was just beyond the city's northern boundary, Koester had obviously not left the Charleston that had earlier accused him of indeterminate suspicious behavior.

Each of these stories of harassment, incarceration, fines, legal prosecution, and judicial judgment, some of them presenting specific charges, some with hardly more than a suspicion of "guilt," is indicative of how treacherous it was at the time for any German-American to suggest restraint in U.S. foreign policy, argue for an unbiased assessment of the European belligerents, or express an opinion or sentiment that carried the least hint of any allegiance or loyalty to Germany. What had been latent in the lead-up to the war became

---

21. *Evening Post*, July 27, 1917.

22. Worth noting is the fact that on the occasion of Koester's coronation at the Schützenfest in 1915, "the address of Mayor Grace was heard with much interest and applause. The Mayor confined his remarks to the aims of the German Rifle Club and his views of the European war, declaring that since the first tocsin of the titanic struggle had sounded, he had been German to the core." [*Evening Post*, May 7, 1915.]

23. W. Turner Logan, a close associate of John P. Grace, was corporation counsel of Charleston 1914-1918.

24. *Evening Post*, August 7, 1925.

demonstrably evident after the United States entered the fray on the side of its cousin Britain. By this point in time, except for the few outspoken, the majority of Charlestonians of German descent were loath to declare any affiliation—membership, heritage, relationships, or anything else—that marked them as German. They went silent.

# CHAPTER 9:

# TOWARD THE END

The internalized silence did nothing to avert the looks, the eyes, the ears, of those in Charleston who were not of German "extraction": the neighbor, the friend, the acquaintance, the co-worker, the supervisor, or the employer, among whom the second- or third-generation German-American had comfortably moved all these years. Since the beginning of the war in 1914, German-American life was haunted by suspicion, misunderstanding, conflicted emotions, and bewilderment as to what to do. There was blame hinted at on every front, no escape from association with pan-Germanism, Prussianism, militarism, imperialism. The patriotism of the "100 Percent America" campaign fostered a pervasive animus toward the "Hun" and "Teutonism." There were xenophobic attacks on the German language, German literature, German music, German newspapers, German street and family names, and anything else that could be ascribed to a German origin. According to Frederick Luebke, "anti-Germanism was more subtle than simple harassment. German-Americans sensed it in whispers and rumors, in glances charged with suspicions, in offhand remarks and in the heated eloquence of impersonal editorials, speeches, and sermons. A vague, generalized feeling, it was the more insidious because it lacked specificity."[1] The *unity* of the German "element" that had gradually become pronounced after the founding of the National German-American Alliance in 1901 brought most German-Americans only a modicum of comfort and a great deal of exposure. The tension between the inclination of some to openly defend their German-ness and the desire of others to escape notice by lying low signaled the division between those vocal spokespersons who kept roiling the waters and the quiet citizens who resented having to demonstrate a loyalty that had heretofore been unquestioned.

There is little evidence to indicate that Charleston persecuted its German-American citizens in anything like a wholesale manner. The city's culture was too uniquely well-mannered to carry out an overt anti-German campaign. Other than the instances described earlier, the surface remained calm. It is safe to say that the acculturated later generations of German-American Charlestonians were safe from being considered en masse as "enemy-aliens" to be run out of town. There was undoubtedly a subconscious civic awareness that the forebears of Charleston's German-Americans had indeed played an important role in the city's history and development. Likely, as well, was a local acknowledgment that the majority of those of recognizable German ancestry were not currently behaving as threatening agitators or activists. Charleston's German-Americans thus endured the prejudices that were more pronounced elsewhere relatively unscathed. As late as a few months before the United States entered the war, for example, there was little overt antipathy to Charleston's German-Americans openly contributing to the German Red Cross Aid Association: since the outbreak of the war, the local branch had sent $22,000 in voluntary contributions to Germany.[2]

Even after the United States was officially at war with Germany, there was little public evidence that Charleston's German-Americans were suffering from an aggressive campaign of anti-German nativism. Most of the associations, such as the Brüderliche Bund, the Schützen, or the fraternal Sons of Herman continued their activities, seemingly invincible, until closer to the end of the war. Anyone reading the *Deutsche Zeitung* in July 1917, could think that ethnic life went on as normal. In the issue of July 14th, there was mention

1. Luebke, *Bonds of loyalty*, 151.
2. *Evening Post*, January 5, 1917.

228

of last week's thunderstorm; several obituaries of well-regarded friends; an account of the wedding of a couple—both descendants of immigrant families—known to the German-American community; a report that the five German prisoners-of-war held in the County jail were being transferred to Columbia on their way to the Richland County jail; a small announcement of the upcoming Schützen ball (now only for members); a notice that a new serialized novel would begin soon; information about the upcoming meeting of the St. Matthew's Church Ladies' Circle; the usual column listing the weekly church services: St. Matthew's 11 a.m. English service, St. Johannes's 11 a.m. German service.

While the *Zeitung* was making an effort to convey normalcy, the federal government was moving to rein in German-language newspapers. A bill that Congress passed in October 1917 required that "all foreign language publications ... provide an exact translation of any articles dealing with the United States or with the war effort to the local postmaster." Newspapers could be released of the requirement, but only after they had thereby demonstrated their patriotism for a period of several months.[3] The *Deutsche Zeitung,* although it had published issues as both "English" and "American" editions for some time, followed suit for the remainder of its time, but the requirement undoubtedly affected its production costs. The requirement to publish all war-related matter in English may have contributed to the paper's demise by the end of the year and forced Orth into the "very precarious" position he acknowledged at his sentencing in early 1918. In response to pressure from all directions, Orth advertised in mid-October 1917 that the newspaper was offering its services for "Job Printing": "Let us prove to you that we are able to produce a class of General Job Printing as well as any concern in the South, and at reasonable prices ... Having recently purchased new type faces, we intend making a specialty of general job work, etc ... No job too small." It was a sign of the times: if nationally the German-language press comprised 750 publications in 1904, it was diminished to only 225 in 1924.[4]

However precarious its financial condition, the *Zeitung* nonetheless continued to position itself as an objective reporter of local affairs and "news"

3. Erik Kirschbaum, *The Eradication of German Culture*, 82.

4. Phyllis Keller, *States of Belonging: German-American Intellectuals and the First World War* (Cambridge: Harvard University Press, 1979), 175.

from elsewhere up to the end of 1917. A column in the issue of October 6, 1917, quoted an article from the Cincinnati paper lamenting the overwhelming evidence of strong anti-German sentiment in that city. The article argued for vigilance in reporting to the authorities any anti-German slurs or actions, acknowledged the negative effect of pro-German agitation, and proposed that a declaration of one's loyalty to the United States was of utmost importance. The same issue of the *Zeitung* printed a large blocked "ad" featuring the three-stanza patriotic poem "Run Up Old Glory!" The paper did not avoid acknowledging the predicament that members of the local German-American community found themselves in and continued to offer its paternalistic advice. One month before its demise, the *Zeitung* editorialized on the definition of "Enemy Alien." No matter what the individual German might think, it argued, U.S. authorities viewed the issue in binary terms: if you were born in Germany and not naturalized as a citizen of the United States, you were an *enemy* alien. The editor urged that no one risk an attempt to elude the government's either/or definition. In the same issue, the paper ran a lengthy article under the headline "High Army Official tells of Fidelity of Citizens of Teutonic Extraction": its readership might have found some consolation in the Army officer's urging that

> [t]he best thing we can do in this country is to get away from the idea that every citizen of German blood is a spy. The German American is primarily a man who respects the law. I venture to say that the percentage of citizens of German blood who are disloyal to the United States is very small. It would be the better plan for us to recognize our fellow citizens of German blood as Americans. Of course, the call of the Fatherland is felt. We cannot expect a man of German ancestry to forget his forefathers or entirely subjugate his natural feelings. What we want from our citizens of German blood is cooperation. We can't get it by abusing them. If we keep on as we are going we are certain to build up a disturbance within our borders which will interfere with the operation of our armies across the Atlantic. Internal differences will be as disastrous to us as reverses in France or wherever our armies are sent.

Citing a host of statistics and accounting for the numerous individuals with German names in the service of the United States, the officer concluded, "Our German citizens are on the job in so far as the army is concerned."[5]

When the *Zeitung* printed its last issue at the end of December 1917, the United States had been at war with Germany for eight months, during which time anti-German sentiment had become more pronounced, whether overt in nature or lurking just beneath the surface. In November 1917, columns in the *Evening Post* reflected the growing tension in the country between "foreigners" and nativists: the Metropolitan Opera was dropping the season's German operas at the same time Dr. Muck, the conductor of the Boston Symphony, was refusing to have the orchestra play "The Star Spangled Banner." In its "Music and Musicians" column under the sub-headline "Discord and Jangles," the *Post* reported that

> In Washington the orchestra is warmly greeted but is warned from Baltimore by a mass meeting of indignant citizens. Kreisler, Austrian violinist, is barred from playing in Pittsburgh … The directors of the Metropolitan reached the conclusion that to continue to produce German opera might enable Germany by garbling and patching to print news dispatches for home consumption which would tend to put heart in the German people and to convince the German people that this nation was not heart and soul in the war.

It went on to report that Dr. Muck, born in Darmstadt, had refused to play the national anthem at a concert in Providence, Rhode Island, then offered to resign in the face of all the turmoil that ensued. The esteemed Dr. Muck explained that is was "very embarrassing for a man of his artistic status, and that an insistence on a rendition of our national anthem was almost an insult for it was not high-class and would spoil the program." In defending his position, the conductor had said:

> Why will people be so silly? Art is a thing by itself and not related to any particular nation of group. Therefore it would

---

5. *Deutsche Zeitung*, December 1, 1917.

be a gross mistake—a violation of the artistic taste and principles—for such an organization as ours to play patriotic airs. Does the public think that the Symphony Orchestra is a military band or a ballroom orchestra? Art is international. I have representatives from … different nationalities in my orchestra. All the nations at war are represented. For months I have tried to keep peace among them. So far I have succeeded. And I do not want to introduce anything that would destroy the esprit de corps which it has taken so many years to bring to its present state of perfection. We want no consciousness of national differences in the orchestra.

Charleston's *Evening Post* commented that the *New York Evening Post* (carrying the original report) was "a dissenter against the almost universal approval of the anti-German music move." The New York paper had stated its regret that performances of German operas were being dropped—"if only because it shows less breath [*sic*] of tolerance than is to be found in London, where they are giving German opera right along, or in Vienna, where Shakespeare's plays are frequently produced. These great works of art surely rise above international rivalries and warfare." The *New York World,* on the other hand, wondered whether there was not too much of an "ado" about the Muck affair:

> There is no public clamor against German symphony music, which is wholly different from German opera, and there is no desire anywhere to have the famous Boston orchestra disband. The whole question is as concerns its alien conductor's position with regard to playing the national anthem, a position he made needlessly offensive by his failure to use ordinary tact in the matter. His artistic usefulness in this country may be done for, but that fact in no way impairs the orchestra's usefulness. It was a great musical organization before Muck and should continue to exemplify its high ideals without him.[6]

6. *Evening Post*, November 16, 1917.

The twain, it seemed, could never meet: the patriotic American wanted to hear his national anthem, regardless whether it was played by a symphony orchestra or a military band, and the high-minded German would not condescend to violate his artistic principles. In any case, the Metropolitan Opera and the Boston Symphony lent the dissention a national dimension and made it clear that American interests would prevail.

Closer to home, in 1917 South Carolina's Governor Richard Manning created a "State Council of Defense" to serve the state's public relations and propaganda efforts during the war. It published a *South Carolina Handbook on the War* that "reflected the zeal with which Americans went to war to overthrow 'the barbarous rule of brutal Prussia.'" The preface of the State Council of Defense's *Handbook*, dated "Columbia, September 29, 1917," quoted the National Security League's *Handbook*:

> The task to which this book is meant to contribute is a task more fundamental than any other, when a democracy prepares for war—that of informing the understanding, of awakening the moral vision and the moral passion, of the entire people, concerning the cause for which they fight. It is essential to bring to the mind of every honest and loyal citizen the momentousness of the present crisis; to make him or her understand what deep concerns of humanity are at stake; to bring all to feel that America has never entered upon a more just or more necessary war.

Despite such apparent objectivity in its mission, the *South Carolina Handbook*'s Table of Contents listed fifty-eight titled essays or commentaries, twenty-two of which either specifically or by innuendo addressed Germany or Germans in the United States: —"The Submarine Aggressions"; —"America's Case Against Germany–National Security League's Handbook"; —"Why We Are Fighting Germany"; —"The German Tragedy"; —"The Issue: Autocracy against Democracy"; —"Why Germany Is Not a Democracy–National Security League's Handbook"; —"Germany's Theory of War: 'Out of Their Own Mouths'"; —"Terrorism in Action Three German Military Proclamations"; —"The Prussian Preparation for World Conquest"; —"German Frightfulness"; —"Prussianism's Perfect Work"; —"No Room for Treachery"; —"Rules for

Disloyalists"; —"What 'America' Means"; —"The German Intrigue for Peace"; —"Two World Peace Programs–National Security League's Handbook"; —"Fight Germany on The Other Side"; —"One Hundred Per Cent Loyalty"; —"Loyalty and Service"; —"Help The Red Cross–National Security League's Handbook"; —"Unselfish Patriotism"; finally, "The Germ as Deadly as The German."

The referenced National Security League, founded in 1915, had an agenda that was ostensibly devoted to America's military "preparedness," and the agenda of South Carolina's State Council of Defense, founded two years later, was remarkably similar: both were nationalistic and patriotic organizations that, whatever their broad purpose, had Germany and German-Americans as targets of their concern. William Brewster, "field secretary" of the National Security League, was in Charleston in December 1915 to organize a local branch. In April 1916, Charleston hosted a "Southwide" conference of the League, the purpose of which was "to arouse greater interest in military pre-paredness, especially in this section of the country."[7] The conference, some-what ironically, was held at the German Artillery Hall. After the conference was over, a large blocked notice appeared in the *Evening Post* of April 29th, that read:

LEADING MEN AND WOMEN IN THE SOUTH ARE JOINING? / THE NATIONAL SECURITY LEAGUE / WHY? / BECAUSE they know that the League is telling the American people the facts about unpreparedness. BECAUSE the League is doing this work as a patriotic duty. BECAUSE if this country does not get adequate National Defense it will not be secure against attack. HELP US IN THIS WORK BY JOINING THE CHARLESTON BRANCH OF THE LEAGUE.

How many Charlestonians joined is not known, but it would have been obvious to all that even before the United States officially became a belligerent, Germany was indisputably the enemy likely to "attack," the enemy necessitat-ing a greater preparedness on the part of the nation's military forces. There were

---

7. *Evening Post,* April 27, 1916.

doubtless a number of Charleston's German-Americans in attendance at the "mass meeting" of the conference, in all likelihood because they felt the need to demonstrate their loyalty, or because their absence would draw the attention of the League's membership and expose them as advocates of the enemy.

The *Committee on Public Information* that President Woodrow Wilson established by executive order shortly after the United States entered the war was another blatant attempt to stir the public to support the Allies' cause, an effort that would inevitably call forth opposition to anything associated with the Axis powers. Under the direction of George Creel, the Committee was the first official propaganda agency of the United States, created, as Creel had insisted, to coordinate "not propaganda as the Germans defined it, but propaganda in the true sense of the word, meaning the 'propagation of faith.'" In organizing a sophisticated approach to aggressively propagandize for citizen support of the war, one of Creel's accomplishments was to recruit some 75,000 "Four Minute Men" to act as spokespersons for the Allied cause—specifically, to celebrate the President's war program and to denigrate the enemy. The Four Minute Men were available to speak briefly in every imaginable venue on behalf of a patriotism that had little tolerance for anything less than "One Hundred Percent American." Charleston was as susceptible to the Creel program as countless other cities were. Under the headline "Hun propaganda is being fought," the *Evening Post* announced that the Four Minute Men of Charleston were speaking out against "insidious plots":

> The four-minute men of Charleston are conducting a vigorous campaign against the insidious and dangerous pro-German propaganda which seeks to arouse suspicions and undermine confidence in America's war purposes … In the bulletin of information issued for the use of four-minute speakers by the committee on public information it is stated … that nine-tenths of all the German plotting against the country has taken the form of printed and spoken propaganda. In this work full advantage has been taken of statements made by German sympathizers of American birth, the propagandist realizing that greater consideration might be anticipated for such works than for material originating from more obviously prejudiced quarters. The Department of Justice is thoroughly

organized to catch the propagandist, and, if the people will combine to put a stop to his propaganda, this phase of the German offensive will also meet defeat … To accomplish this, it is recognized that it will not be possible for the public to memorize all the facts upon the war and so be in a position to give official denial to each and any rumor. The volume of such rumors is too great, and, in addition, new subjects for propaganda are being uncovered daily.[8]

Nationally, Creel's Committee was never very popular, and there was considerable opposition to his censorship of the press with regard to military information. The Charleston press (*Evening Post*) was of the opinion that "the committee on public information is performing the functions of its office very poorly, in that it supplies relatively little information of public value or interest, but it is attempting to usurp functions which have not been conferred upon it in assuming to censor information given out by the responsible officials. The committee is hardly more than a public irritant. It ought to be censored."[9] Once the armistice was signed in November 1918, the Committee's activities stopped, and President Wilson formally abolished it in August 1919. There is little doubt that the entire U.S. German-American community had interpreted the Creel Committee on Public Information's control of pro-America information to be inherently anti-German.

In the months between April 1917, and the armistice in November 1918, the individual German-American would sense that there was little he could do to relieve the ever-increasing negativity coming from all directions. The options were either to maintain a decidedly low profile—virtually disappear—or to find some demonstrably inoffensive way to proclaim allegiance and loyalty to *only* the United States. If ever there had been anything like a national consensus among German-Americans that they were being unduly maligned, the opportunity for effective defensive arguments was obviated in 1917 when the National German-American Alliance was forced by circumstances to take a different tack. It gave up on its pleas for objectivity, on voicing its resentment of anti-German slurs and provocations, on further arguments about the

---

8. *Evening Post*, August 27, 1918.
9. *Evening Post*, August 2, 1917.

involvement of the United States in the war, on its battle against prohibition, on its campaign to raise funds for the German Red Cross. In early February 1917, at a meeting in Philadelphia, the Alliance passed resolutions endorsing the President's severing diplomatic relations with Germany and pledged its loyalty to the United States. It also resolved to turn over to the American Red Cross the funds it had been collecting for German war zone relief.[10] Charles Hexamer, the Alliance's founder and President, declared (it would seem, with some reluctance): "Our delegates feel that we have been greatly misunderstood and unjustly criticized during the war, but if it comes to war with Germany our actions will not be susceptible to any further misunderstanding, for we will back up our American government with our lives and our means."[11]

Yet despite its apparent change of heart and the curtailment of its efforts to respond to criticism, the Alliance was still suspect. Less than a year later, in January 1918, a bill to repeal the charter of the NGAA was introduced in Congress by Senator Henry King of Utah. With little recourse at that point, the directors of the NGAA, at a meeting in Philadelphia on April 11th, agreed to dissolve the organization and turn over all remaining funds to the American Red Cross. On July 2, 1918, Charleston's *Evening Post* reported that "without a word of discussion or a record vote, the Senate … adopted the resolution of Senator King of Utah annulling the Federal charter of the National German American Alliance."[12] The House of Representatives concurred. According to the *Evening Post*, the annulment was "of interest" in Charleston: "The disbanding of the German-American Alliance yesterday at Philadelphia causes considerable interest here by reason of the fact that Charleston was headquarters for the South Carolina branch of the organization. It is not known whether a meeting of the S. C. branch will be necessary, but it is thought that the disbanding of the parent organization will automatically disband the state body."[13] Indeed, it did.

---

10. As discussed earlier, the Alliance had promoted raising money for humanitarian aid to German and Austrian war victims soon after the war had begun in 1914. By early 1917, it had raised close to $900,000. Once the United States entered the war in April, the state branches stopped soliciting contributions.

11. *Evening Post*, February 9, 1917.

12. *Evening Post*, July 2, 1918.

13. *Evening Post*, April 13, 1918.

Already in the fall of 1917, strong anti-German sentiment had manifested itself in the campaign to discontinue German-language instruction in schools throughout the country. The German-American Societies of Greater New York were unsuccessful in their efforts urging resistance to any attempt to banish instruction in German in the city's public schools. By the following fall, Charleston's *Evening Post* would report that "fourteen states have abolished the teaching of the German language in schools, and the campaign to abolish German is under good headway in sixteen other states, according to a report made public by the American Defense Society."[14] It listed Alabama, California, Connecticut, Delaware, Louisiana, Maine, Mississippi, Montana, North Dakota, Oklahoma, South Dakota, Tennessee, Utah, and West Virginia as the "honor roll" of states that had abolished the teaching of German entirely. Twenty-four named cities had "thrown German out of the schools."[15] In Milwaukee, for example, "in 1916, 200 teachers were employed to give instruction in the German language to 30,000 pupils and at the end of 1918, only one teacher was employed to instruct 400 pupils in the German language."[16] German had been taught at the High School of Charleston since 1881, but it was phased out in 1917 along with French, purportedly because the war made it impossible to find instructors.

Concurrent with the movement to eliminate the teaching of German, a campaign to "Americanize" all the foreign-born was underway. Speaking to "an assembly of State governors, chairmen of State defense councils, heads of civic organizations, industrial leaders and businessmen" invited to a "Conference on Americanization" in Washington in April 1918, the Secretary of the Interior declared that "America can become a composite and purposeful nation and impose no authority other than the compelling influence of affection, sympathy, understanding, and education" through its plan to make Americans of "many millions of foreign born." The Americanization effort was considered a war measure "to counteract the anti-American propaganda among aliens."[17]

The Americanization drive persisted for a number of years. In 1920, the presidential nominee who would succeed Woodrow Wilson, Senator Warren

---

14. Splinter group of the National Security League.

15. *Evening Post*, September 12, 1918.

16. *Evening Post*, January 24, 1919.

17. *Evening Post*, April 3, 1918.

Harding, warned against the dangers of a hyphenated citizenship. Addressing a gathering of foreign-born Americans in Marion, Ohio, Harding declared that he did not "blame" the foreign-born for having conflicted sympathies during the World War." He asserted, rather, that it was the fault "of the nation itself" which had neglected its obligation to thoroughly Americanize "those of foreign extraction. The work of Americanization had to be renewed "with new determination."

> Let us all pray that America shall never become divided into classes and shall never feel the menace of hyphenated sympathies . . . I speak for the fullest American devotion, not in putting aside all that tenderer and dearer attributes of the human heart, but in the consecrations of citizenship. We are unalterably against any present or future hyphenated Americanism. We have put an end to pretexts. The way to unite and blend foreign blood in the life stream of America is to put an end to groups, an end to classes, an end to spiritual appeal to any of them, and an end to particular favor for any of them."[18]

Such statements might have been taken by some as little more than political rhetoric. Even if only rhetorical, however, the senator's warning apparently had little effect on the purported "conflicted sympathies" of some individuals among the hyphenated. There was, for example, very little *conflict* in evidence in the words of the (previously-mentioned) hyphenated American, George Sylvester Viereck, who had assumed the role of spokesperson for German-Americans—at least for some of them. The German-born son of a German father and an American mother was a graduate of the College of the City of New York. A nationally acclaimed poet and an outspoken Germanophile, he was the editor of a weekly, *The Fatherland,* and, with the support of the German government, was a radically driven propagandist of the pro-German cause during the First War and a Nazi sympathizer during the Second. At the same time Warren Harding was issuing warnings about hyphenated Americans, Viereck was proposing that German-Americans attend a national conference in Chicago in early 1921 "to become active and to insist that the promises

18. *Evening Post*, September 18, 1920.

which were given to us by the party now in power should be fulfilled." Viereck explained to *The New York World*:

> The first meeting of the German-American National Conference took place in 1916, when we prevented the nomination of Roosevelt by serving notice that the German-Americans would not support him. We met again before the nomination of Harding and laid down certain principles, and later we drew a set of resolutions which pledged support to Harding. We crystallized German-American sentiment and we were responsible for 6,000,000 German-American votes which, I believe, were cast solidly for Mr. Harding. The object of this conference is to bring all of German-American descent to insist on our civic rights.[19]

Viereck advocated that a committee be formed that would be charged with influencing the new president to appoint a German-American to his cabinet. Such pro-German advocacy echoed the stance and arguments of the pre-war National German American Alliance. It was an indication that long after the war with Germany had been brought to an end, the duality of hyphenism with regard to those of German "extraction" continued to be a matter of opposing positions.

It is questionable how many later-generation descendants were anxious to belong in Viereck's camp. After the war, most would have wanted to let sleeping dogs lie. The awkwardness that Viereck and his kind were causing is suggested in a column in the *Evening Post* in October of 1921 under the headline "Hyphenating Again":

> Certain German-American elements in this country, emboldened by the reaction from war hatred which has taken place quite rapidly since the armistice, are resuming their old-time attitude toward American relations a little too soon for the best interests of those relations and themselves. Led by the irrepressible George Sylvester Viereck, who seems to know the

---

19. *Evening Post*, December 31, 1920.

art of taking high jumps and landing on his feet, they have been after President Harding ever since his election to appoint a man they like to be ambassador to Germany. Recently they have sent the president an "ultimatum" in double form, one portion containing the names of men to be eliminated from consideration for the post and the other the names of men who are "unobjectionable." ... As for Mr. Viereck, it is difficult to see how he can have any more interest in Germany since his friend and idol was driven over into Holland by "Kaiser-baiters" of German blood who must be even more objection-able to Mr. Viereck than the "German-baiters" he proscribes to Mr. Harding.[20]

Viereck was still in the news in February 1922, when he testified that the former German ambassador, Count Von Bernsdorff, had sought his (Viereck's) support for Woodrow Wilson in the election of 1916. In addition, "Mr. Viereck dramatically declared that former President Wilson 'had plotted the war from the very beginning,' and held that he should be brought to trial under the terms of the peace treaty providing for trial of those responsible for the World War."[21]

There is no evidence that this kind of political background noise made the atmosphere in Charleston any more or less negative for those citizens who were identifiably German-American. Even the "heat" of the pre-armistice anti-German mood had not risen in Charleston to anywhere near the temperature that it did in other locations, e.g. in Midwest cities with significant assimilated German populations. The most severe incident of anti-German hatred had occurred in early April of 1918 when Robert Prager, an "enemy alien" coal miner, was lynched in Collinsville, Illinois, by a mob of fellow miners for making "disloyal utterances," remarks that were "derogatory to [the] President of [the] United States." Purportedly, Prager had prayed on his knees in German for three minutes before he was hanged by the angry mob. The Associated Press reported from Washington:

20. *Evening Post*, October 15, 1921.
21. *Evening Post*, February 7, 1922.

All other business was laid aside by the Senate today for denunciation of disloyalty, sedition, German spies and I. W. W.
and discussion of how the Espionage Act should be extended
so as to curb these evils and avoid mob law, without abridging
the fundamental liberties of American citizens. While the
Senate debated the pending sedition bill carrying severe pen-
alties for disloyal utterances and attempts to obstruct the draft
or Liberty loan, President Wilson and the cabinet gave attention to reports of the lynching of Robert Prager, a German,
at Collinsville, Ill., last night. Members of the cabinet said
afterward the deplorable incident emphasized the necessity
for immediate legislation that would enable the government
to deal with disloyalty and enemy agitation so that the people
would not be tempted to take the law into their own hands.[22]

With Washington apprised of the Collinsville lynching, an autopsy was
held, and while the authorities publicly condemned the lynching, heels were
dragged during an investigation by the local sheriff before eleven men were ultimately indicted and finally brought to trial. It came out in the reporting by several Illinois newspapers that the mob had intended only to tar and feather the
enemy alien, but the necessary supplies were not on hand. The rope was. It was
not until June 1st that the eleven men were acquitted by a jury that had delib-
erated for only forty-five minutes. The not-guilty verdict was "greeted by a wild
demonstration in the courtroom in which the accused men were overwhelmed
with congratulations by relatives and friends who throughout the long vigil of
taking testimony crowded the room. Judge Bernreuter, the presiding official,
made only perfunctory effort to stop the cheers and handshaking."[23]

The Collinsville lynching was only one incident in which citizens took
the law into their own hands. As reported a few days after the lynching, the
Rockford, Illinois, *Morning Star,* under the headline "How Anti-German
Feeling Has Spread," apprised its readers as follows:

---

22. *Morning Star* (Rockford, IL), April 6, 1918.

23. *Morning Star,* June 2, 1918.

These scattered flag-kissing episodes, tarrings and beatings show how the rounding up of suspected pro-Germans by loyalty crowds, has spread over the nation:

OHIO—At Delfos hundreds joined in loyalty bands which toured the town for several nights making suspected pro-Germans kiss the flag. At Coshocton 300 citizens in autos made 30 suspects kneel, kiss the flag and say "to hell with the Kaiser." One woman who brandished a revolver at the crowd was carried to the courthouse steps and put through a long loyalty ceremony. At Wellington one man was compelled to kiss the flag and fly it on his home.

MICHIGAN—At Jackson and Lansing crowds tarred a man charged with disloyalty.

NEVADA—A Reno mob bound a suspected disloyalist to a stake whipped him, tarred and feathered him, and ran him out of town.

OKLAHOMA—"Knights of Liberty" at Altus forced a man and a boy to kiss the flag after tarring and whipping them. They were ordered to leave town.

CALIFORNIA—Ten men were roughly handled after it was charged they drank a toast to the Kaiser. They were later convicted and jailed.

KANSAS—A Kansas City carpenter was badly beaten when he was found with a German flag in his possession.

WISCONSIN—Ashland teacher tarred and feathered.

WASHINGTON—One man in Yakima tarred and feathered and ordered out of town.

VERMONT—Windsor preacher roughly handled and arrested. Convicted of disloyalty and sentenced to 15 years in prison.

NEW JERSEY—Hoboken man who called soldiers passing "bums" was beaten, rescued by police and sentenced. Two men, pro-German suspects, beaten at Passaic. [24]

---

24. *Morning Star*, April 11, 1918.

In another column in the same issue, the newspaper explained how it was that anti-German sentiment had reached the boiling point in Collinsville (excerpted):

— There are more outward evidences of patriotism in the hotbed of anti-German feeling—the mining towns across the river from here—than in any other place in the country.

— As a rumor factory, southern Illinois leads the world.

— Walk down Collinsville's Main Street and look at the names on the store and office windows—Wurzbacher, Keifer, Schossed, Schoebel, Armsburger, Koffman, Goebel, and so on—German name after German name.

— It's the same in most of the towns of the district. A great percentage of the business and professional people are of German stock. But they are loyal Americans, second, third, fourth generations in this country most of them. In Collinsville, a town of 10,000, only 38 aliens registered.

— The constant sight of German names, one after another, everywhere, has its psychological effect. It adds to the "nerves"— the suspicion of the district—which explains the repeated flag-kissing episodes, tar-and-featherings, rail-ridings, and the lynching of Robert Prager, suspected as pro-German—first lynching of the war.

— The business people understand how the miners feel about it and they go out of their way to proclaim their patriotism ... Passive loyalty isn't enough—you must work at it out here.

— There's ground for some of the miners' suspicions and their dread of Huns who'd blow in a shaft.

— Explosives have been found stored away by suspects. Strikes in the coal fields last summer are laid to German agitation. A German sympathizer blew up a bridge over which many miners went to and from work. Other such cases are history.

— Where there's one story with a foundation there are 50 without. This district turns out the wildest rumors imaginable, one a minute! [25]

Responding to the Prager lynching, Germany demanded on June 12, 1918, that safeguards be taken to avoid such excesses occurring in the United States. The federal government responded that it could not interfere with the proceedings being carried out under Illinois state law. Only in late July did Wilson denounce "mob rule" and plead for every American to "make an end of this disgraceful evil." Wilson declared

that any man who even so much as countenanced mob violence is a betrayer of American democracy and adopts the "standards of the enemies of his country, whom he affects to despise."

The president's statement addressed to "my fellow countrymen" was inspired by the numerous lynchings of which suspected pro- Germans were the victims. It is understood, however, that the lynching of Robert P. Prager at Collinsville, Ill., last April was responsible, more than any other, for the president's appeal today. Every lynching, the president points out, is a blow at the heart of law and justice and directly opposes to the principle for which America, as a democracy, stands.[26]

Miles away from the Midwest, there were no miners in Charleston. Nonetheless, there was certainly no shortage of German names on storefronts and businesses, and plenty of business and professional people of German stock—all second-, third-, and fourth-generation German-Americans—who

---

25. *Morning Star*, April 11, 1918.
26. *Rockford Republic*, July 26, 1918.

undoubtedly felt the same pressure to prove their loyalty and who were the subject of whatever rumor mill the city had running at the time. As might have been expected, Charleston's civility prevented it from ever experiencing an anti-German "mob," ready to attack the city's citizens with an ethnic heritage. In the context of what had transpired in the rest of the country, the incidents in Charleston in 1917 and 1918 involving the arrests of Paul Wierse, Albert Orth, H. L. Koester, Dr. Turnbull, and John Weinacht had been relatively low-key events.

Indirectly, a column in the *Evening Post* of July 1, 1918, reveals what perhaps set Charleston's Lutherans "of German extraction" apart from other German-American communities such as those in the Midwest. The Rev. Dr. Scherer's sermon to the congregation of Charleston's St. Andrew's Lutheran Church entitled "If the Kaiser is not a Lutheran, what is he? On the Church in Germany" was reported on by the local newspaper as being of particular interest since it contained "information not generally known." Dr. Scherer proposed that:

> There appears to be a dearth of information and a deluge of confusion in regard to the relations of church and state in Germany. Recently the statement was made in the Press of the city by perfectly competent authority that the German Emperor, more commonly called the Kaiser, is not a Lutheran. The statement elicited much comment at the time and no little surprise was expressed thereat. Conversations which were started by the statement referred to have disclosed the fact that many otherwise well-informed people know very little about Church affairs in Germany: and this fact has suggested that a discourse treating of these matters would have at least a certain educational value. It is not surprising that there should be such a lack of knowledge about church matters in Germany, since knowledge of such things even in regard to our own country is acquired chiefly nowadays not by reading but by contact with church life. In the case of foreign countries it must be by reading and where the literature of a country is in a language which very few of our people read they could hardly be expected to be informed as to such matters. Here in the South

more than 90 per cent of our own Lutheran church membership do neither read, write, nor speak the German language;
nay, there are more than 90 per cent of them who do not even
understand it when it is spoken. At the present time there is
not one of our churches in the South in which the German
is used in the services and with the exception of one or two
churches the substitution of the English for German had taken
place long before the war began; in fact, at no time within the
last 76 years has the German language been in use in more
than a half dozen of our churches. We have not taught the
people German but English; and as fully 90 per cent of those
of German extraction are from one to six generations removed
from German soil and environment, even our own Lutheran
people are about as ill-informed as others with regard to affairs
of religion and the church in Germany. We have not thought it
important that they should be instructed in reference to these
matters; much less have we deemed it a part of our work to
instruct the public concerning them.[27]

In Scherer's view, Charleston's homogeneous community of later-generation
German Lutherans, through no fault of their own, were at this point almost
completely innocent of "things German." With regard to the nature of the
German Church, for example, they and their Charleston neighbors were operating with frames of reference both knew very little about.

The rest of Dr. Scherer's sermon was a history lesson on the evolution
of the German church that likely fell on the deaf ears of the congregation's
members. The latter, as Scherer pointed out, were at this point far removed
from the German church of their ancestors and the language in which sermons
formerly had been preached. Before launching his history lesson, however,
Dr. Scherer assured his congregation that the Lutherans who had come to the
United States had, from the very beginning, been nothing, if not loyal citizens
and brave soldiers:

---

27. *Evening Post*, July 1, 1918. The Rev. Dr. Scherer had been lambasted by Paul
Wierse two years earlier.

As rapidly, perhaps, as has been possible consistently with the maintenance of their religious life and worship they have adopted the language of the country. The process has only been retarded by the continuous stream of immigration which is kept up until within recent years. They have never cherished the thought of allegiance to any other country than this, the proof of which is that so few of them, if we except the later adult immigration, know very little about the church in Germany or any of the institutions of that land. Whatever the Imperial German government may have wished and devised concerning those who have left Germany for the United States of America, the Lutherans of this country are Americans and Americans they will be in spite of the Kaiser; and like other Americans, as a rule, they know about as much about Germany as they do about the Chinese Republic. [28]

The avowal of allegiance, as so frequently documented in these pages, needed to be reiterated yet again.

By the time the war came to an end in November of 1918, Charleston's German-Americans had weathered the worst of whatever prejudicial anti-German sentiment had risen to the surface. The arrest and/or incarceration of a few outspoken individuals had been the only price the by-now-well-assimilated German-American community had had to pay. In September, there was already something seemingly more dangerous to worry about than the final days of the war against Germany. The 1918 influenza pandemic was at hand and soon took its toll: 18,500 Charlestonians were stricken and 450 of them died, including any number of the city's German-Americans. There would have been very few among the later, fully-acculturated, English-speaking, individuals of "German extraction" paying close attention to what was happening in Germany during those first post-war days when the Weimar Republic was being founded. For most, it was indisputably appropriate that the Allies had defeated the country that was no longer anyone's "Fatherland."

---

28. *Rockford Republic*, July 26,1918.

# CHAPTER 10:

# POSTLUDE

P ost-war 1919 would have found few Charlestonians of German heritage obsessing about Germany's defeat, nor any longer noticeably paranoid about their ethnic background. Third-generation German-American children were in their teens or twenties, the younger ones sheltered from what had been going on, the older ones still occupied in finding their place in a city that would have a decade to address its social, economic, and political problems before the Great Depression would re-order its priorities. In general, those children had little, if any, awareness of the family's immigrant beginnings, since their parents had been the generation to mature as fully-acculturated, English-speaking citizens within the community's native-born of various heritages. The parents themselves were the sons and daughters of a first generation that itself had begun to forget its origins as it lost the facility to speak and read the language of its birth. It was primarily the second generation that experienced the prejudices of a xenophobic culture that had developed during the previous decade—prejudices it had sought to shield its progeny from experiencing. The third generation of German-Americans was thus distanced from its ancestral heritage both by time and the circumstances under which the cultural markers of the ancestors had been questioned and suppressed. Almost innocent of the anti-German provocations that had called their parents' existence into question, this younger generation was now native-born of native-born and mostly free of cultural baggage.

The second generation, however, was never to be fully in the clear. As the war neared its end, anti-German suspicions still prevailed. National and local efforts to prove German-Americans' loyalty were still in evidence in mid-1918: a group calling itself "Friends of German Democracy" arranged for German-American organizations nationwide to participate in the celebration of July Fourth in New York:

> Preliminary arrangements for the participation of American citizens of German extraction in the Fourth of July celebration in honor of the nation's unity in the war have already been completed by the Friends of German Democracy, it is announced at national headquarters, 32 Union Square, New York City. Singing societies, socio-literary, and athletic clubs composed of Americans of German origin are formally signifying their intention to cooperate. Branch societies of the Friends of German Democracy representing every section of the country are expressing their willingness to aid in making the coming celebration one that will disillusion the people in Germany and Austria from the belief, the product of the Kaiser's propaganda, that their brothers who have become Americans and millions of fellow citizens of other races are not united in their defense of the United States ... The mammoth exhibition of union and loyalty to be staged July 4 promises to make that day a momentous one in the history of the country. American citizens of many foreign origins will be bound together by the indissoluble ties of patriotism. Native-born Americans will be convinced that an overwhelming majority of those who came here to enjoy the rights and privileges of a country founded upon free institutions are ready to defend that country with all the resources at their command.[1]

---

1. *Evening Post*, June 15, 1918.

The community in Charleston responded to the call a few weeks later by forming a local branch of the Friends of German Democracy. It was made clear that the national organization had the full support of the President, "as it supports enthusiastically the war purposes which President Wilson has stated as America's aims. Its purpose is to help make Germany democratic by crushing the German military autocracy which dominates the Central Powers and which seeks to subjugate the rest of the world and loyal Americans of any descent are eligible to membership."[2]

The following year, at the annual meeting of the Charleston Rifle Club—the re-named German Rifle Club[3]—the Club's president, A. J. W. Gorse, reported on the previous year (1918) as having been marked by the continuing "good and brotherly feeling between the members." Looking forward, he told the members:

> The non-holding of our Schuetzenfests in recent years, for causes known to all of you, has to a certain extent, been the cause of some of our members relaxing interest in the organization's affairs. But I am pleased to say that with the prospect of peace being declared in the near future, I see no reason why we should not in the early spring of 1920 again hold our usual annual festival, which I believe will stir the enthusiasm of those that are now somewhat lukewarm to continue as members of this organization. The festival of 1920 should, to my mind, be of such magnitude that whatever ill feeling or thought that may exist against the German Americans of the city, and especially against those of our members [to] be forever banished from the minds of those of our fellow citizens who were led to believe that the German-American is not true to our country and flag. We must make a determined effort to convince those against us that the organization you as

---

2. *Evening Post*, June 26, 1918.

3. The three-step transformation of the *Schützengesellschaft*, founded 1855, by which it subsequently became known as the *German* Rifle Club, then finally re-named in late 1917 as the *Charleston* Rifle Club, succinctly capsulizes the process whereby the German immigrant transitioned to become a German-American, then a Charlestonian.

members represent has and always will be for the upbuilding of the laws and people of our adopted home and country. Our entire actions during the unfortunate world's great calamities has been above reproach, and our record of loyalty stands as a great monument to our benefit and credit.[4]

The 1919 election of John Grace for a second term as mayor again brought attention to the sector of Charleston's population that had supported him and which he had defended in his brash manner. The antagonism between the Grace "machine" and those who condemned the politician's "unpatriotic" statements was often transferred to the ethnic group that was part of his constituency. The following "quips" were to be found in the *Evening Post* of June 30, 1919:

> — When enemy aliens eat their last meal in Charleston before boarding a transport for "The Fatherland," they all say "Grace."

> — If all the enemy aliens in Charleston at the present time could be listed on our club rolls, for whom would they vote for Mayor in the coming primary?

> — For whom will the lawless element vote solidly on August 19th for Mayor?

> — For whom will the few persons in Charleston who are disloyal to the country vote solidly in the August primary for Mayor?

> — "The man who proves a traitor to the country that has given him shelter from old world oppression will hand a legacy of infamy down to his descendants." —From speech of John L. McLaurin reported in "The Charleston American" on April 22, 1917.

---

4. *Evening Post*, June 10, 1919.

— Editor, the Patriot: I noticed in your paper that on several occasions you refer to candidate John P. Grace. What do you mean by the term "Candidate?" CURIOUS

— By Candidate is meant that Mr. Grace was "candid" in boosting the Germans on more than one "date." ED PATRIOT.

Before the August primary, the *Post* carried a full page of "political advertisement" assembled by the campaign committee of incumbent Mayor Hyde that included a letter by Mr. H. Rudloff, "for many years a resident of Charleston," who "expresses himself as to the civic duty of naturalized citizens like himself." Not that very many of Charleston's citizens were at that point naturalized Germans, but many of them were descendants of ancestors who belonged in that category, and Rudloff 's arguments pointedly targeted the city's German faction that was now, and had been earlier, an ethnic group that supported John P. Grace:

[W]hen becoming a citizen, the alien took an oath to defend and protect the United States and its Constitution, and foreswore allegiance to any foreign prince or potentate, especially the one to whom he was born a subject. Mr. Grace has repeatedly declared himself unfavorably to the United States government and favorably to the enemy of the United States. Therefore, every naturalized citizen by voting for Mr. Grace, would repudiate his solemn oath of allegiance to the United States; and by this act, would make himself a liar and a perjurer. These are hard names, but, Mr. Naturalized Voter, by no amount of sophistry or reasoning can you get away from the stubborn fact that you have sworn to do one thing, and then deliberately do the very thing you have sworn not to do. You may believe that Mr. Grace's policy of a wide-open town is good for business (I don't), but even if it were, would that fact be sufficient inducement for you to break your solemn oath? If your word is worth anything, and you regard the sanctity of your oath, you must repudiate Mr. Grace and all he stands for or be a self-convicted perjurer.[5]

Statements such as Rudloff's "advertised" that anyone who identified in any way as *German* was still on the defensive in 1920. The Charleston Rifle Club felt obliged to respond to what was apparently a charge of disloyalty by the local American Legion, Post 10: "The Charleston Rifle Club feels that for the sake of the good opinion of the people of Charleston its position should be clearly defined. The local post of the American Legion was in many respects in error." The published statement by the Club explained that its uniforms were actually copies of a Swiss design and, in fact, were closely akin to the uniform of the Confederacy, "which we revere." The statement acknowledged that the Charleston Rifle Club was of German origin, but argued that "it was formed sixty-five years ago—long before there was any thought of war between this country and Germany." Lest there be any lingering doubt, the statement declared:

> We are strictly an American organization. Throughout the war we went as far as our means would permit in buying Liberty bonds and war savings stamps, and in all the Liberty bond parades, when it was necessary to express the unity of the community, we turned out almost to a man. In the first parade we had the largest representation of any organization, or equally as large...We do not like to be put in a defensive position in this matter. It is unfair...Our sixty-five years have been devoted exclusively to the welfare of this community. Our membership while, of course, primarily men of German origin of birth, nevertheless includes men of all classes, races and creeds, who will parade with us in the "contemplated parade." It is an insult to them, especially to the men whose blood is not German, to suppose that they would put themselves under the German flag, but in a way it is more of an insult to the man of German blood, for it contains the suggestion that because

---

5. *Evening Post*, August 15, 1919.

they are of German blood they harbor in their hearts loyalty for their Fatherland as against our land.[6]

By the following year, a "healing" was purportedly taking place. At the 1921 Schützenfest of the Charleston Rifle Club, Congressman Turner Logan (as noted, an associate of Mayor Grace) spoke on "German-American Citizenship." In his speech, he paid tribute to the city's Americans of German descent, and referred to the spirit of tolerance that currently prevailed. At the 1922 Fest, both Mayor Grace and the Rev. S. L. Blomgren of St. Matthew's gave addresses. In his address, Mayor Grace stressed the fact that "the country was now at peace with Germany, and that there should be cooperation between the German and American peoples. He recalled the peaceful relations that had long existed between the two countries before the recent era of war. Rev. Mr. Blomgren spoke along similar lines."[7] By this point, almost five years after the end of the war, Charleston's German-American descendants were doubtless aware of their heritage, but, as suggested earlier, somewhat insulated from it through years of denial and general suppression. The crowds at the "Platz" were certainly fewer, and possibly the revelers felt forced to be jovial in the manner of their ancestors.

Yet if in this year Charleston's families of German origin were feeling less guilty for being who they were, they would soon find themselves subjected to additional years of negative opinion about the country of their forefathers and its emerging dominance in Europe. Such opinions, however, would impact them less than had earlier been the case, since they were at this point hardly recognizable as members of an identifiable ethnic group. As full-fledged Charlestonians, they wore very few remnants of the past on their sleeves. But on the broader national stage, there was still agitation by some—as in the case of George Viereck—to assert the right to be politically active and to identify with the new Germany that had become a Republic. There were still ways for some German-Americans to be troubled by activists interested in pushing ethnic identity and purpose, still opportunity to be pro-German or pro-American, but hardly both. In 1924, Hans Hackel, the "prominent German language editor and president of the corporation publishing the

---

6. *Evening Post*, April 16, 1920.
7. *Evening Post*, May 5, 1922.

Westliche Post," committed suicide because of the criticism he had incurred
for his opposition to the Steuben Society, leaving a note saying "I cannot stand
the strain any longer."[8] In May 1919 the Steuben Society had been founded
"by patriotic Americans of German descent to foster good citizenship in the
German-American community, to educate the public as to the positive role our
ethnic group has always played in American society, and to preserve a sense
of ethnic pride amongst German-Americans.[9] One of its stated goals was "to
bring about a complete rehabilitation of the Germanic element in the United
States, politically, socially and economically, and its universal recognition as an
integral part of our citizenry on the basis of absolute equality in all things."[10]

There was, of course, a continued interest and awareness of the political situation in Germany as the United States observed from a distance the
Republic that had arisen out of defeat. But German-American descendants
in the United States could now read local reports on German matters with a
certain equanimity: by this point they had been mostly cleared of suspicion
and somewhat rehabilitated after their collective experiences in purgatory. They
were now, by virtue of their demonstrated Americanism, barely in an identifiable relationship with Germany. Opinions about how Hindenburg would
perform as President of Germany, for example, were editorialized in numerous
U.S. newspapers, as the United States "settled back calmly to watch the course
and give General Hindenburg a chance to prove he can hold to the Republican
highway."[11] There was doubtless little sympathy in Charleston for the former
Kaiser and his financial troubles: *all* the readers of the city's *News and Courier*
could take satisfaction in learning from a news story in *Time* magazine that
Wilhelm Hohenzollern, reported to be "the richest of all Germans," had a
cash-flow problem.[12]

---

8. *Evening Post*, November 3, 1924. The *Westliche Post* was a well-known German-
language paper in St. Louis.

9. https://www.germaniapok.com/2016/01/04/dr-charles-gilbert-spross-unit-
steuben-society-of-america/.

10. http://depts.washington.edu/heritage/Immigration/steuben.htm. For many Americans, the Society's program, like that of its predecessor, would come across again as too
much of a good thing.

11. *Evening Post*, June 5, 1925.

12. *News and Courier*, August 8, 1929.

A decade after the war, in the somewhat provincial environs of the Lowcountry, Charleston's formerly-identifiable residents of German heritage had faded into the background. Anyone reading the obituary of Paul Wierse in the *Evening Post* of July 9, 1928, would have thought that the life of the deceased was of no more consequence than that of any other Lutheran citizen:

> Funeral services for Mr. Paul Wierse, former newspaper editor of this city … will be held at the residence Tuesday morning at 10:30 o'clock with the Rev. W. C. Davis, pastor of Saint Matthew's Lutheran Church officiating. Mr. Wierse will be laid to rest in the family plot at Bethany Cemetery where Mrs. Wierse is buried. Mr. Wierse was 67 years old, a native of Germany, but he had resided in this country since a young man, most of which time he had lived in Charleston. For a number of years he was employed on a German language weekly printed here and later was a member of the staff of a local newspaper, serving as one of its editors for a time. Many years ago he was an accountant with the Atlantic Coast Line at Wilmington, but more recently was an accountant for the Plenge Chemical Company. Several days ago Mr. Wierse suffered a stroke from which he never rallied and during the last few hours of his life was unconscious. He is survived by four sons and a daughter.

As I initially suggested, the social, economic, and political framework of Charleston had determined what Charlestonians of German extraction experienced in the past: the same would hold for what they would yet experience in the coming years. For them, as for their fellow citizens, what was happening on the "'local" scene was what mattered most. There were positives, as well as negatives. Tourism was on the rise, as "outsiders" came in increasing numbers to bask in the "mellowing old city." The influx of tourists coincided with the resident population's increasing interest in preserving its antebellum and colonial treasures, so that tourism and preservation would become the city's main industry. In 1929, the mayor and the Preservation Society pushed for ordinances that would protect a large section of the downtown city as "Old and Historic Charleston." The economic prosperity that had been evident in the years after the war was in decline, employment curtailed by severe cuts in jobs, coupled with rising costs and tax increases: of the city's approximately 65,000 men, women, and children, some 6,500 of them were unemployed. The city and county health departments were combined, and the change in administration in 1926 led to a number of improvements: the sewer and water mains were extended, advances were made to the city's mosquito-control operations, health education programs were instituted, and milk had to be pasteurized. With the stock market crash of 1929, northern capital "essential to Charleston's tourist trade and the truck farming industry" disappeared. "Tonnage through the Port of Charleston dropped 16 percent from 1931 to 1941 and the harbor traffic consisted mainly of tramp steamers and sailing ships." Prohibition was repealed in 1933. The sale of beer was legalized by the state in 1934 and a state-licensed dispensary established for the sale of liquor, while "blind tigers" enjoyed "a flourishing business outside the law in Charleston and with the consent of the city's administration." The popularity of alcohol, in whatever form, might have been credited to the previous century's anti-prohibitionist German beer-drinkers. On the other hand, many of Charleston's blind-tiger customers may have been driven to drink because of their miserable living conditions: A 1934 federal survey "described Charleston's housing as he worst of any city under study. Of 22,369 housing units, 21.7 percent had no running water, 48.9 percent had no indoor toilets, and 25.8 percent were without electricity." [13]

While Charleston's later-generation German-American descendants, like the rest of the city's residents, were occupied with the complexities of the local scene iterated above, they could hardly have avoided reading the local newspaper reports on an organization called the "German American Bund." At the least, the accounts would have been "interesting," at the most, they again would have been disconcerting. Everything related to the Bund was reported in the *Evening Post* and *News and Courier* from 1937 through 1943, none of it positive. Charleston's informed readers would learn that the organization was established in 1936, its membership to comprise only American citizens of German descent, its goal to promote Nazi Germany. They would know the following salient facts about the organization: —the Bund's elected leader was Fritz Julius Kuhn, naturalized in 1934; —the administrative structure of the

---

13. Summarized from Fraser's *Charleston! Charleston!*, 368-385, a section he labels "'America's most historic city' and the New Deal."

Bund mimicked the organizational structure of the Nazi Party; —the Bund received no financial or verbal support from the Nazi Party: embarrassed by the Bund's rhetoric and actions, the Nazi government in 1938 forbade German nationals from belonging to the U S. organization; —the zenith of the Bund's activities was a rally it organized at Madison Square Garden on February 20, 1939 that attracted 20,000 Nazi supporters; —in December 1939, Kuhn was sentenced to two and half years in prison for tax evasion and embezzlement; —the most well-known of Kuhn's successors was Gerhard Kunze: Kunze fled to Mexico in 1941; —as a Nazi-sympathetic organization, the Bund was denied the ability to operate freely during World War II through the efforts of U.S. Congressman Martin Dies (D-Texas) and his House Committee on Un-American Activities; —Kuhn's citizenship was canceled in June 1943, and he was deported to Germany in 1945.[14]

While the Bund itself was marginalized as a far-right, antisemitic, white supremacist "Nazi" organization, its existence during the period focused attention on all manner of other "un-American," pro-Germany, activity in the United States. The existence and work of "spy rings," for example, would have been disavowed by the majority of the nation's Americans of German extraction, and most definitely by those in Charleston. Having effectively suppressed their cultural heritage and faded into the city's general population, no one in Charleston would have admitted any sympathy with the Germany that was increasingly viewed in the United States as a threat to Europe and to humanity itself.

If Charleston had earlier been viewed as a kind of "police state" with everyone on guard against imminent insurrection, the years leading up to, and during, WWII lent the city a similar "military" atmosphere. The Navy Yard played a major role in the country's defense program, and its expansion was an engine of local industrial activity. Life, nonetheless, was lived somewhat on the edge: Charleston's homicide rate was four times that of New York City. Danger on the streets was matched by danger in the off-shore waters:

> Early in the war German submarines waited off Charleston where no enemy vessels had been since 1865. These U-boats laid mines in the harbor approaches on three occasions and

<hr>

14. https://en.wikipedia.org/wiki/German_American_Bund

beach patrols were organized to prevent them from landing saboteurs on the nearby barrier islands. In June 1942 antisubmarine nets were laid in the harbor and aircraft patrolled the coast to help protect the transports and freighters carrying men and supplies out of Charleston for Europe. By mid-1943 the U boat threat had been neutralized.[15]

An abbreviated account of the unique situation of Charleston's "Germans" during the interwar years could be derived from the following salient observations:

—When their German Artillery Hall was demolished in 1930 it was not because the Germans had been so ostracized or condemned after WWI by other, non-Lutheran, not-of German descent, citizens who viewed the Hall as representative of the lately discredited German presence in the city and wanted it torn down. It had remained a popular venue for all sorts of events, as had the Freundschaftbund's hall. Rather, the German-styled Artillery Hall was razed because it was located in the section of Charleston that the Mayor and the Preservation Society wanted at the time to constitute an "old and historic district." Over the preceding decade, the local government and the general population had gotten over fretting about Germans in their midst. In any case, the Hall had always belonged to German and non-German alike, and its removal was never perceived as an ethnic slur. It was just that the German community's Artillery Hall was not sufficiently old enough to exist in the newly defined "historic" district. In 1930, some might have asked "Who were the Germans anyway?" They had become woven into the fabric of the city, no longer distinguishable as a particular demographic in the local community. Even those bearing distinctly German names had forgotten their by-now diluted genealogy.

---

15. Fraser, 389.

*Constructed in 1845, the crenelated structure stood on Wentworth Street,*
*between King and Meeting Streets, until 1930. The Hall served as a venue for*
*numerous events that brought the ethnic and native community together.*

— Suspicions about German disloyalty and sabotage efforts manifest before, during, and after WWI were redirected after Pearl Harbor toward the Japanese living in the United States. Mayor Lockwood's order in late 1941 for the police to apprehend for questioning any Japanese individual as a possible saboteur of the Navy Yard or any of the city's other defense points represented a radically more extreme reaction by the local populace to the "threat" than what had lain behind the agitated whispers, sideways glances, and rumors about German-American sympathies for the fatherland or the Kaiser. It bears repeating here that the anti-German sentiment that had earlier riled the waters across the United States was never so aggressive that German-Americans as a group were rounded up and relocated to internment camps, as was the case for the much smaller population of foreign-born (Issei) and second-generation (Nisei) Japanese. During WWII, the "Jap" absorbed a lot of the antipathy toward those who were the declared "enemies" of the United States. There were German prisoners-of-war incarcerated near Charleston, but they were distinctly not Charleston "Germans."

— The mine and net defenses against German submarine activity off Charleston's beaches was the response of a city unified in civil-defense efforts against a national enemy that had just recently been defeated, only to return a second time as an even greater threat. This time, however, there were no sympathizers with the Nazi dictatorship in Europe, no evidence that the German American Bund had found an audience, nor any Nazi-sympathetic fellow-travelers in Charleston. There was no question about whether it was desirable or necessary for the United States to be at war with Germany. The city's former German-Americans had no inclination to stand against their neighbor Americans. By this time, they were one and the same.

— When E. Edward Wehman was named mayor after the death of Mayor Henry Lockwood in 1944, he was the fourth "German" Charlestonian to hold that leadership position. Only some in the Charleston populace would have known that the Lutheran Wehman had deep German roots, had been admitted to the German Friendly Society in 1927, had served as its president in 1924 and 1925, and was listed as an active member as of 1935. His heritage was no longer a factor in his rise to prominence, and his election to the mayoralty was a clear signal—should anyone have doubts—that by 1944, when Germany was the nation's enemy, Charleston's residents of "German extraction" had been fully rehabilitated into the citizenry of the Lowcountry city that had welcomed their forefathers.

While an almost completely modified attitude prevailed during the years of WWII, in contrast to what had been in evidence during the previous war, the 1943 judicial decisions in a case against Albert Orth, whose German-ness was once again put in the spotlight, nonetheless brought the past once more into focus. For all the indications that there was no longer any anti-German "sentiment" extant in Charleston, the second attempt by the government to revoke Orth's and his wife's naturalization suggested that the past was not completely buried. In the 1943 trial of Orth—one of the founders of the Charleston chapter of the National German-American Alliance, the editor/publisher of the *Deutsche Zeitung*, the compatriot of Paul Wierse, the ally of the Germanophile Mayor Grace, the man sentenced in 1917 to fourteen months in Federal prison for his pro-Germany utterances—the memory of anti-German sentiment came back to haunt. When in 1943 Federal Judge Waties Waring took the stand, it was revealed that he—a Charleston native of southern aristocratic background with a personal and public notoriety that lent weight to his testimony—had been suspicious of Germans ever since the *Liebenfels* affair in 1917, and would again be happy to see Orth's naturalization annulled. In 1943, however, the court was leery of accusations of dubious validity and ruled that an individual's citizenship could not be taken "under suspicion or surmise of fraud or upon mere proof that … [the] citizen has given expression to views or allied himself with organizations which in the then state of public opinion seemed dangerous or inimical to the public welfare." At this later point in Charleston's history, some comfort could thus be taken in the fact that public and judicial opinion seemed distinctly less inimical to naturalized citizens—famous, infamous, or neither—or to their descendants.

# AFTERWORD

In the early chapters of this study, I described the lives of several immigrant families and proposed that their stories were representative of what was experienced by the majority of the North German immigrants who came to Charleston in the nineteenth century. Further, that as these Neudeutsche settled into the unique post-colonial culture of South Carolina's Lowcountry, their and their descendants' lives evolved in parallel with the city, as antebellum Charleston transitioned through the Civil War and Reconstruction into the twentieth century, then to experience the two World Wars by mid-twentieth century. The immigrant stories present a composite picture of the nineteenth-century German ethnic community that developed between the 1830s and the early years of the twentieth century and which then, somewhat precipitously, faded into the background of Charleston's less-appreciated history.

It was predictable that the number and percentage of later-generation descendants of the nineteenth-century immigrants would decrease relative to the rest of the city's population. As Charleston's rapidly-assimilating second-generation German-Americans changed the face of the ethnic community when the foreign-born parents died, later-generation descendants successively joined the population of native-born of native-born, with the result that what had once existed as an "ethnic" community slowly disappeared as a distinct demographic within the general population. By 1920, Charleston had only 527 foreign-born whites born in Germany, some seven hundred fewer than ten years earlier, and a very small fraction of what had once been a community of over three thousand.

But while it was inevitable that the German immigrant community's ethnicity would be diluted in successive generations through the progression of acculturation and assimilation, we have seen that the slow merger of the *ethnic* and the *host* community did not occur in a historical vacuum. By the end of WWII, the firmly-established nineteenth-century German ethnic community had been *forced* by external factors to retreat into the shadows. The catalyst that effected the disappearance of the acculturating community of immigrant descendants was the xenophobic anti-German animus that had been latent in antebellum America and which emerged with vigor prior to WWI, then morphed further during the interwar years in response to local, national, and international developments. By the end of WWII, the city's acculturated German-Americans had suffered sufficient anti-German sentiment—often of their or their ethnic organizations' own making—that they resorted to suppressing completely the cultural markers inherited from their predecessors. All semblance of their German origin had been denied in the course of their ultimately gaining acceptance as loyal, native, American citizens. In reflecting on what transpired in Charleston—a minority ethnic community suppressed by the majority's endemic nativism fearful of the "other"—it is not a far reach to find parallels between what happened in the past and the present tensions between immigrants and natives, majorities and minorities, the willingness of some to accept and the readiness of others to reject, the widening divide between those in power and those who strive to have more of it. In the present, as in the past, the "other" continues to be suspect, loyalty is questioned, rights and privileges are disputed, conspiracies abound.

It bears repeating that Charleston's nineteenth-century community of predominantly North German immigrants was always a minority population. The community never constituted more than a small fraction of the white population, much less of the total population inclusive of what, in many years, was a black majority. In Charleston, once the acculturation process was underway, the increasing minority status of the city's later-generation German-American descendants made it well-nigh impossible to overcome the prejudice that developed prior to WWI and which continued into mid-century. Although in Charleston anti-German sentiment did not rise to the level of persecution evident elsewhere in the country, in the years after 1915 Charleston's citizens of

German heritage nevertheless suffered an intolerance that belied the city's acclaimed gentility, and which, in the end, effected the almost complete elimination of any evidence that Germans had played a significant role in Charleston's past. Given the small ratio of the ethnic vis à vis the host community, the erasure of the German ethnic community in Charleston because of anti-German prejudice was more complete than was the case, say, in Cincinnati, St. Louis, or Milwaukee. The ethnic populations in these larger cities experienced the same xenophobic animus, but with larger percentages of immigrants of a less homogeneous nature, the ethnic heritage continued to be visible long after the threat to its existence had passed. Nevertheless, and in spite of the paucity of its numbers, Charleston's German ethnic community had an outsized effect on the character of its nineteenth- and twentieth-century host society.

In Charleston, the city that has preserved so much of its past to build its future, markers of the legacy left by Charleston's nineteenth-century German immigrants are indeed less visible than in cities elsewhere. Today's tourists in Charleston—usually interested in the city's colonial or Civil War past—are unlikely to learn much about the city's ethnic history. The South Carolina Historical Society's pictorial publication, *Charleston Alone Among the Cities*[1] may represent the lone acknowledgment of the earlier German community in its caption (p. 54) for the Deutsche Freundschaftsbund Hall: "Located at the corner of Meeting and George Streets, this structure serves as a reminder of the powerful influence of Charleston's German community. From the 1730s onward, significant numbers of Germans lived in the city, and their involvement in civic activities was manifested in their founding of a number of organizations including the German Friendly Society, the Arion Society, the German Artillery (among other military units), and four Lutheran churches on the peninsula. A German-language newspaper was in print from 1853 until 1917, and at least one Lutheran church continued to worship in German until 1924. The Deutsche Freundschafts Bund was a literary and social fellowship society of German immigrants in the nineteenth century. This building later housed other German societies, and during World War II, the U.S.O. It is now the home of the Washington Light Infantry."

---

1. Charleston: Arcadia Publishing, 2000.

*The c. 1870 German Freundschafts-Bund Hall, located at the corner of Meeting and George Streets (287-289 Meeting Street). The subsequent re-purposing of the building has obscured awareness of the important role it originally played as a venue for many of the social activities of Charleston's German community.*

In spite of such rare or infrequent mention, other shadows—however muted—of the city's German heritage nonetheless remain. The largest shadow is that cast by the towering steeple of St. Matthew's Lutheran Church. Guidebooks might mention that it was once the tallest structure in South Carolina, a kind of beacon on the local cityscape. That interesting bit of information, however, glosses over the fact that the edifice was constructed for a vibrant nineteenth-century German immigrant community. Although the small brass plaque to the left of the church's main entrance is visible to tourists from the sidewalk, the fact that it specifies St. Matthew's as the *German* Lutheran Church usually goes unnoticed and, these days, does not encourage further inquiry. The guidebook, or the tour guide, or the driver of the horse-drawn carriage, will more than likely draw attention to Marion Square directly across from the church, where, until very recently, the imposing statue of John C. Calhoun gazed down on the lower city, and where, on the Square's northern edge, the crenellated remnant of the "old" Citadel, the former home of the city's guardian cadets, remains. While the current congregation is duly proud of its status as Charleston's largest Lutheran church, the treasure of history contained in its archive is not widely publicized. Even during the 2017 Sunday service celebrating the sesquicentennial of the church's founding, very little was made of the congregation's origin in the earlier German immigrant community.

A few blocks away, the cornerstone of St Johannes Lutheran Church marks the sanctuary of the original St. Matthew's congregation as *German* and, in this instance, in German. Engraved in the large stone are the words: "Deutsch-Evangelisch-Lutherische Kirche, gebaut den Jahren unsers Herrn 1841 und 1842" along with two lines of verse: "Die gepflanzet sind in dem Hause des Herrn / Werden in den Vorhöfen unsers Gottes kommen."[2] This "historical" marker—a testament to the ethnicity of the church's Lutheran founders—is situated on the side of the structure that is barely visible to passers-by on the street. It is doubtful whether Charleston residents, or tourists, or, for that matter, the church's current congregants, are conscious of the significance of the cornerstone engraved in German or able to read it. It is already more than a century ago that services at St. Johannes were conducted in German.

*Cornerstone of St. Johannes Lutheran Church on Hasell Street. The German inscription dates the sanctuary of the original St. Matthew's congregation to 1841-1842 and promised the founding immigrants that "those planted in the house of the Lord shall flourish in the courts of our God."*

Many of Charleston's tourists are able to lodge in the city's numerous historic houses that have been transformed into boutique hotels. If they choose

---

2. Psalm 92:13: "Those planted in the house of the Lord shall flourish in the courts of our God."

the Governor's House Inn on Broad Street, they may book accommodation in the Inn's "Wagener Room."[3] The Inn's current website indicates that the "spacious first floor room is named for Captain Wagener, the mansion's wealthy grocery merchant who owned the home in 1995 [*sic*]. No mention in this room description that the "wealthy grocery merchant" was a native German. A more extensive account of "Captain" Wagener elsewhere on the Inn's website, however, does include a statement about Wagener's immigrant beginning: "Captain Frederick W. Wagener was one of Charleston's greatest rags to riches stories. An immigrant who left his German homeland at the age of 16, Wagener became one of Charleston's wealthiest citizens. He built the largest grocery wholesale company, F. W. Wagener & Co."[4] Here, at least, the successful grocer's German heritage is acknowledged, even though the ethnic community that he was part of receives no commentary. The section of Charleston known as "Wagener Terrace"—named in honor of the immigrant German civic leader—lies to the northwest of the historic district, far beyond the latter's walkable streets and alleys, with the result that both the section and its namesake are often overlooked in summary histories of America's "most historic city."

Jonathan Poston's *The Buildings of Charleston: A Guide to the City's Architecture*[5] references numerous buildings that were built for, built by, occupied/used by, the city's German community. To name just a few: —39 Broad St.: Exchange Bank and Trust (Otto Witte, banker and consul); —8 Chalmers St.: German Fire Steam Engine Co.; —161 East Bay: Wagener-Ohlandt Bldg (grocery); —157 Broad St.: Lutjen's (Burbage's) grocery; —159 King St.: George W. Flach Bldg. (watchmaker and silversmith); –243 King St.: Siegling Music House; —36-38 North Market St.: J. C. H. Claussen Range (wholesale business, bakery, et al); —133 Queen St.: John Henry Bullwinkle grocery); —287-89 Meeting St.: Deutsche Freundschaftsbund Hall; —35 Charlotte St.: Schachte house; —33 Pitt St.: John Schnierle Jr. House;—202 King St.: Rugheimer Bldg. (tailor); 171 Church St.: C. D. Francke Warehouse. These, and Poston's additional mentions of the city's Germans in his extensive photographic history of Charleston's architecture, do not suggest that

---

3.   117 Broad Street was owned and occupied by the Wagener family from the early 1880s until 1921, when Frederick Wagener died.

4.   https://www.governorshouse.com/room-history

5.   Columbia: University of South Carolina Press, 1997.

Charleston's Germans were responsible for creating anything like a distinctive German-style of architecture. Poston's identification of German individuals by name indicates only that many from the ethnic community—as full-fledged Charleston citizens—were integrally involved, in one way or another, in building and/or occupying the city's commercial and residential stock that of late is considered to be of historic architectural interest. The large number of German immigrants connected with the city's significant architectural heritage depicted in Poston's survey should not obscure the fact that a majority of the ethnic community lived and worked in less interesting, less historically-notable, venues. It should also be noted that built Charleston was never challenged to adopt any uniquely "German" design elements. The well-known German blacksmiths, Christopher Werner and Frederic Ortmann, and the German architect, Charles F. Reichardt, cannot be said to have practiced a distinctive "German" style in the examples of their work to be found in Charleston. It was an American architect, John Henry Devereux, who gave Charleston its singular Gothic Revival ("German-style") St. Matthew's German Lutheran Church edifice. [6]

St. Matthew's *German* Lutheran Church on King Street remains the most *visible* embodiment of the earlier immigrant community in Charleston. We are reminded of the newspaper report on the German Ladies' Fair (cited in Chapter 5), in which the reporter took pains to describe in detail the structure itself, inside and out, concluding that this singular effort to build a *large* church for the *large* congregation would be a permanent testament to the contribution the Germans had already made, and would continue to make, to the Charleston community: "The Germans of Charleston are never backward in giving their help to any measure which is for the good of the community, and it is due to them that the people at large should assist them in erecting a building which is necessary for the religious accommodation of a large body of our most valuable citizens." The church would be, the reporter said, "an ornament to Charleston." I suggested earlier that the account of the German Ladies' Fair was rife with hyperbole and revealed how the Germans were at that

---

6. Poston (386) writes that "the Gothicism employed by the architect was said to be related to the German versions of Gothic architecture." The statement suggests that it was little more than a vague historical association that ascribed to the edifice something like a *German* style.

time *judged,* kept separate, marginalized, by Charleston's native community. It is clear now that in the years since 1870 the German presence in the city has somehow endured. The St. Matthew's *German* Lutheran Church on King Street has indeed become a permanent "ornament," one that harks back to a period in Charleston's history when German immigrants contributed substantively to the city's unique character.[7]

The current "historic" Charleston has been developing since the 1920s. Having found its purpose in historic preservation and benefitting from sun-belt migration, the city has successfully promoted itself as one of the premier sites of Southern culture. A tourist destination of the first-order, Charleston has welcomed large numbers of residents from other states and countries to share the ever-more-vibrant and diverse Lowcountry area: resident "newcomers" now far outnumber "old-timers" whose families were the Charlestonians of fifty or sixty years ago. Those of the latter demographic who carry the distinction of being of German "extraction" are indeed now few and far between.

The city's relatively distant German past can be found, perhaps, hidden in family bibles or archival records waiting to be consulted. There are no homes of well-heeled nineteenth-century Germans featured on the numerous tours of "historic" homes, nor is there a *German* neighborhood that horse-drawn carriages can meander through or that walking-tour guides can describe. A similarly less visible aspect of the city's German legacy would be acknowledgment that it was the German immigrants who found their place in the middle of a two-class culture, between plantation-owners and their enslaved, that it was the Neudeutsche who navigated a course between the high-ups and the lowly to establish Charleston's middle class of entrepreneurial businessmen, trades-men, artisans, wholesale and retail grocers, and bakers. The immigrant families featured in the early chapters each played their respective role in that regard.

While gentrification and preservation have undoubtedly altered the character of numerous neighborhoods in the upper part of the Charleston peninsula, there was until not so long ago another facet to the legacy left by the Germans, namely the ubiquitous small "corner grocery" or bakery run by a German (or, in the vernacular, a "Dutchman") that anchored the mixed neighborhoods

---

7. Much of that history can be reconstructed from the ledgers held in the St. Matthew's archives that record the births, deaths, confirmations, and marriages of the entire nineteenth-century ethnic community.

of German immigrant descendants and their neighbors of various other heritages. It would not be an overstatement to claim that much of Charleston's populace depended on German bakers such as Marjenhoff, Wolff, Puckhaber, Bullwinkle, and Beckroge to provide their daily bread and other baked "favorites." Testimony to that effect was expressed in a recent[8] article in Charleston's *Post and Courier* reporting that the unoccupied house on upper Meeting Street that was—as late as 1969—the location of Beckroge's Bakery was to be "renovated under a plan to redo [the] block with a major new apartment building." The article noted that the Beckroge family had carried on what they described as the "traditional" method of making bread, because "baking early in the morning rushed the yeast unnecessarily, resulting in loaves with no texture and little taste." That *German* method of mixing the dough in the afternoon was much appreciated by the bakery's "in-the-know" Charlestonian customers who *loyally* thought there was no other bread (or pastry) worth eating. Under the headline "Beckroge's icing on cake for city's German traditions," the article reprinted a recipe for the bakery's famous "VC's" (Vanilla Cakes) and included a photograph of the dilapidated, boarded-up, house that had been the home of the Beckroge family and its bakery since 1890. Relevant to the *enduring* legacy of Charleston's Germans, it is encouraging that in 2018 the newspaper's headline mentioned the "city's German traditions"—wording that intimated that there was still a modicum of civic awareness that Germans figured significantly in the city's cultural past beyond its "hidden culinary history."

Although Beckroge's Bakery at the corner of Meeting and Line Streets is no longer in existence, just a few miles up Meeting Street, baker John Henry Beckroge lies in Bethany Cemetery along with his fellow German Charlestonians. If Charleston residents or visitors from elsewhere with an interest in the city's history should be interested in the city's German heritage, the "gift" that the St. Matthew's German immigrant community bequeathed to the city when it established Bethany Cemetery for its deceased, would be the place to visit. Walking the cemetery's paths among the many headstones with still-decipherable German names, birth and death dates, and places of origin, the observer might contemplate how the German individuals and families memorialized in this Lutheran cemetery experienced life in nineteenth- and early twentieth-century Charleston. Confronted by such assembled evidence of

---

8. May 16, 2018.

the earlier ethnic community, the visitor can only imagine what it has meant to have had North Germans cross the Atlantic to settle in Charleston and become Charlestonians.

# WORKS CITED

*A History of the Lutheran Church in South Carolina*. 1971. The History of Synod Committee, ed. Columbia: The R. L. Bryan Company.

Andrews, Sidney. 1866. *The South Since the War: As shown by Fourteen Weeks of Travel and Observation in Georgia and the Carolinas*. Boston: Ticknor and Fields. Repr., New York: Arno Press and The New York Times, 1969.

Anonymous. 1860. *Declaration of the Immediate Causes which Induce and Justify the Secession of South Carolina from the Federal Union; and the Ordinance of Secession*. Charleston: Evans and Cogswell.

Bell, Michael Everette. 1996. "Hurrah für dies süsse, dies sonnige Leben": The Anomaly of Charleston, South Carolina's Antebellum German-America. PhD diss., Univ. of South Carolina.

———. 1999. Regional Identity in the Antebellum South: How German Immigrants Became 'Good' Charlestonians. *South Carolina Historical Magazine* 100 (1): 9–28.

Bellows, Barbara. 1993. *Benevolence Among Slaveholders: Assisting the Poor in Charleston 1670-1860*. Baton Rouge: Louisiana State University.

Berlin, Ira and Herbert Gutman. 1983. Natives and Immigrants, Free Men and Slaves: Urban Workingmen in the Antebellum South. *American Historical Review* 88:1175-2000.

Bernheim, G. D. 1872. *History of the German Settlements and of the Lutheran Church in North and South Carolina*. Philadelphia: Regional. Repr., Baltimore, 1975.

Berquist, James M. 1984. German Communities in American Cities: An Interpretation of the Nineteenth Century Experience. *Journal of American Ethnic History* 4 (1): 9–30.

Bullerdiek, Jörg and Daniel Tilgner. 2008. *'Was fernen vorkommt werde ich prompt berichten': Der Auswanderer-Kapitän Heinrich Wieting Briefe 1847 bis 1856*. Bremen: Temmen.

Butt, Winnie J. M. 1940. *100 Years of Christian Life and Service, St. Matthew's Lutheran Church, 1840-1940*. Charleston: St. Matthew's Evangelical Lutheran Church.

Capers, Ellison. 1899. *South Carolina*. Vol 5 of Clement A. Evans, ed., *Confederate Military History: a Library of Confederate States History*. Atlanta: Confederate Publishing Co.

Child, Clifton James. 1970. *The German-Americans in Politics*. New York: Arno Press.

Clark, Thomas D. 1946. The Furnishing and Supply System in Southern Agriculture since 1865. *Journal of Southern History* 12 (1): 24-44.

Cohen, Kathleen Ann Francis. 1986. Immigrant Jacksonville: A Profile of Immigrant Groups in Jacksonville, Florida, 1890-1920. PhD diss., Univ. of North Florida.

Cooper, Jr., William J. 1968. *The Conservative Regime: South Carolina, 1877-1890*. Baltimore: Johns Hopkins Univ. Press.

Fraser, Jr., Walter J. , 1991. *Charleston! Charleston! The History of a Southern City*. Columbia: Univ. of South Carolina Press.

Friedrichs, Erika and Klaus, eds. 2003. *Das Familienbuch des Kirchspiels Geestendorf (heute Bremerhaven-Geestemünde)*. Bd.1.

Gongaware, George J. 1935. *The History of the German Friendly Society of Charleston, South Carolina 1766-1916. Compiled from Original Sources by George J. Gongaware, The Pastor, Since 1913 of St. John's Lutheran Church*. Richmond: Garrett & Massie.

Goodheart, Adam. 2011. *1861. The Civil War Awakening*. New York: Alfred A. Knopf.

Hansen, Marcus. 1940. *The Immigrant in American History*. New York: Harper & Row.

Hoole, W. Stanley. 1945. Charleston's Theatricals during the Tragic Decade, 1860-1869. *Journal of Southern History* 11 (4): 538-547.

Johnson, Charles T. 1999. *Culture at Twilight: The National German-American Alliance, 1901-1918*. New York: Peter Lang.

Johnson, Michael P. 1980. Planters and Patriarchy: Charleston, 1800-1860. *Journal of Southern History* 46 (1): 45-72.

Kamphoefner, Walter D., Wolfgang Helbich, and Ulrike Sommer, eds. 1991. *News from the Land of Freedom: German Immigrants Write Home*. Trans. Susan Carter Vogel. Ithaca: Cornell University Press.

Kamphoefner, Walter D. and Wolfgang Helbich, eds. 2006. *Germans in the Civil War: The Letters They Wrote Home*. Trans. Susan Carter Vogel. Chapel Hill: University of North Carolina Press.

Kamphoefner, Walter D. 2009. Immigrant Epistolary and Epistemology: On the Motivators and Mentality of Nineteenth-Century German Immigrants. *Journal of American Ethnic History* 28 (3): 34-54.

Kantrowitz, Stephen. 2000. *Ben Tillman & the Reconstruction of White Supremacy*. Chapel Hill: Univ. of North Carolina Press.

Kazal, Russell A. 2004. *Becoming Old Stock: The Paradox of German-American Identity*. Princeton: Princeton Univ. Press.

Keller, Phyllis. 1979. *States of Belonging: German-American Intellectuals and the First World War*. Cambridge: Harvard Univ. Press.

Kirschbaum, Erik. 1986. *The Eradication of German Culture in the United States, 1917-1918*. Stuttgart: H. D. Heinz.

Kloss, Heinz. 1974. *Atlas of 19th and Early 20th Century German-American Settlements (Atlas der im 19. [i.e. neunzehnten] und frühen 20. Jh. entstandenen deutschen Siedlungen in USA)*. Marburg: Elwert.

Kytle, Ethan J. and Blain Roberts. 2019. *Denmark Vesey's Garden: Slavery and Memory in the Cradle of the Confederacy*. New York: The New Press.

Levine, Bruce. 1998. "Against All Slavery, Whether White or Black": German-Americans and the Irrepressible Conflict. In *Crosscurrents. African Americans, Africa, and Germany in the Modern World*, eds. David McBride, Leroy Hopkins and C. Aisha Blackshire-Belay, 56-64. Columbia: Camden House.

Lonn, Ella. 1899. *Desertion during the Civil War*. New York: The Century Co.

Luebke, Frederick C.. 1974. *Bonds of Loyalty: German-Americans and World War I*. Dekalb: Northern Illinois Univ. Press.

McArver, Susan Wilds. 1995. "A Spiritual Wayside Inn": Lutherans, the New South and Cultural Change in South Carolina, 1886-1918. PhD diss., Duke Univ.

McCandless, Amy, ed. 1993. *The Historic Landscape of Mount Pleasant: Proceedings of the First Forum on the History of Mount Pleasant*. Mount Pleasant: [publisher not specified].

Mehrländer, Andrea. 2010. "With more Freedom and Independence than the Yankees": The Germans of Richmond, Charleston, and New Orleans during the American Civil War. In *Civil War Citizens: Race, Ethnicity, and Identity in America's Bloodiest Conflict*. Suzannah J. Ural, ed., 57-97. New York: New York Univ. Press.

———. 2011. *The Germans of Charleston, Richmond, and New Orleans during the Civil War Period*. Berlin/New York: DeGruyter.

Miles, Suzannah Smith. 2004. *East Cooper Gazetteer*. Charleston: History Press.

Miller, Randall M. 1984. Introduction. In *Germans in America: Retrospect and Prospect. Tricentennial Lectures Delivered at the German Society of Pennsylvania in 1983*, 1–13. Philadelphia: The German Society of Pennsylvania.

Motes, Margaret. 2005. *Migration to South Carolina. 1850 Census: from England, Scotland, Germany, Italy, France, Spain, Russia, Denmark, Sweden, and Switzerland*. Baltimore: Clearfield Press.

Orvin, Maxwell Clayton. 1961. *In South Carolina Waters*. Charleston: Nelsons' Southern Printing & Publishing Co.

Pawlik, Peter-Michael. 1993. *Von der Weser in die Welt; Die Geschichte der Segelschiffe von Weser und Lesum und ihrer Bauwerften 1770 bis 1893*. Schriften des Deutschen Schifffahrtmuseums 33. Hamburg: Kabel.

Phelps, Chris. 2002. *The Bombardment of Charleston 1863-1865*. Gretna, LA: Pelican.

Poston, Jonathan. 1997. *The Buildings of Charleston: A Guide to the City's Architecture*. Columbia: University of South Carolina Press.

Radford, John P. 1976. Race, Residence and Ideology: Charleston, South Carolina in the Mid-Nineteenth Century. *Journal of Historical Geography* 2 (4): 329-346.

Reinert, Gertha, ed. and trans. 1999. A Letter from John A. Wagener. *South Carolina Historical Magazine* 100 (1): 49-69.

Roeber, A. G. 1993. *Palatines, Liberty, and Property: German Lutherans in Colonial British America*. Baltimore: Johns Hopkins Univ. Press.

Rogers, Jr., George C. 1969. *Charleston in the Age of the Pinckneys*. Norman: Univ. of Oklahoma Press.

Rogers, Jr., George C. and C. James Taylor, 1994. *A South Carolina Chronology 1497-1992*. 2nd edition. Columbia: Univ. of South Carolina Press.

Rosen, Robert N. 1994. *Confederate Charleston: An Illustrated History of the City and People during the Civil War*. Columbia: Univ. of South Carolina Press.

Schieber, Clara Eva. 1921. The Transformation of American Sentiment towards Germany, 1870-1914. *Journal of International Relations* 12 (1): 50–74.

Simkins, Francis Butler. 1944. *Pitchfork Ben Tillman, South Carolinian*. Baton Rouge: Louisiana State Univ. Press.

Skal, George von. 1915. *The German-Americans and the European War. A Reply to M. Oswald Garrison Villard and Others*. New York: [publisher not specified].

South Carolina Historical Society. 2000. *Charleston: Alone Among the Cities*. Charleston: Arcadia Publishing.

Strickland, Jeffery. 2008. How the Germans Became White Southerners: German Immigrants and African Americans in Charleston, South Carolina, 1860-1880. *Journal of American Ethnic History* 28 (1): 52–69.

———. "Frederick Wagener." In *Immigrant Entrepreneurship: German-American Business Biographies, 1720 to the Present*, vol. 2, edited by William J. Hausman. German Historical Institute. Last modified September 25, 2014. http://www.immigrantentrepreneurship.org/entry.php?rec=24

[Tew, Henry Slade]. 1965. An Eyewitness Account of the Occupation of Mt. Pleasant: February 1865. *South Carolina Historical Magazine* 66 (1): 8-14.

Tolzmann, Don Heinrich. 2000. *The German-American Experience*. Amherst, NY: Humanity Books.

Trommler, Frank. 2009. The Lusitania Effect: America's Mobilization against Germany in World War I. *German Studies Review* 32 (2): 241–66.

Walker, Mack. 1964. *Germany and the Immigration 1816-1885*. Cambridge: Harvard Univ. Press.

Wiley, Bell Irvin. 1971. *The Life of Johnny Reb: The Common Soldier of the Confederacy*. Garden City, NY: Doubleday.

Williams, George W. 1971. *Jacob Eckhard's Choirmaster Book of 1809*. Columbia: Univ. of South Carolina Press.

Yarbrough, Tinsley E. 1987. *A Passion for Justice: J. Waties Waring and Civil Rights*. New York: Oxford Univ. Press.

Zuczek, Richard. 1996. *State of Rebellion: Reconstruction in South Carolina*. Columbia: Univ. of South Carolina Press.

CPSIA information can be obtained
at www.ICGtesting.com
Printed in the USA
LVHW012103180522
719128LV00010B/811